WOMEN EDUCATION, EMPLOYMENT AND GENDER-DISCRIMINATION

WOMEN EDUCATION, EMPLOYMENT AND GENDER-DISCRIMINATION

TALWAR SABANNA

SERIALS PUBLICATIONS
NEW DELHI (INDIA)

© Talwar Sabanna

First Published - 2007

ISBN: 81-8387-061-9

Published by

SERIALS PUBLICATIONS
4830/24, Prahlad Street, Ansari Road
Darya Ganj, New Delhi-110002 (India)
Phone : 23245225. Fax : 91-11-23272135
E-mail: serials@satyam.net.in

Contents

Acknowledgements

I place on record my profound gratitude to the University Grants Commission, New Delhi for the financial assistance extended to undertake this Major Research Project.

I am extremely grateful to Dr. S.T. Bagalkoti, Reader, Department of Economics, Karnatak University, Dharwad and Dr.G.K. Boodeppa, Reader, Department of Sociology, Karnatak University K.R.C. P.G. Centre, Belgaum for giving me valuable suggestions.

I thank the Chairman, Department of Economics, Karnatak University, Dharwad; the Administrator, Karnatak University, K.R.C. P.G. Centre, Belgaum and the Local Head, Department of Economics, Karnatak University, K.R.C. P.G. Centre, Belgaum for their support.

I am very thankful to Sri Uttam Kamble, Project Fellow, Department of Economics, Karnataka University, K.R.C. P.G. Centre, Belgaum, for extending timely co-operation and help in completing this study.

I am thankful to the Librarians of Karnatak University, Dharwad; Centre for Multi-disciplinary Research, Dharwad; Karnatak University K.R.C.P.G.Centre, Belgaum; Institute for Social and Economic Change, Bangalore; Bureau of Economics and Statistics, Bangalore; International Institute for Population Sciences, Mumbai; National Institute for Rural Development, Hyderabad for having patiently providing me whatever I wanted to consult the documents, books and journals.

I express my thanks to the authorities and staff of Karnatak University, Dharwad and Karnatak University K.R.C. P.G. Centre, Belgaum, University Grants Commission, New Delhi for their help.

viii   *Water Scarcity in Chennai*

My sincere thanks are to 1200 women respondents from Bidar, Gulbarga, Koppal and Raichur districts for their co-operation and information provided me.

My family members has been my strength, I express my heartfelt gratitude to my wife Smt. T. Hanumakka and my beloved children Chi.Prithvi and Chi.Vishwa.

TALWAR SABANNA

1

Introduction

On November 1967 the United Nations adopted the 'Declaration of the Elimination of discrimination against women'. Article 3 stipulates: 'All appropriate measures shall be taken to educate public opinion and to direct national aspirations towards the eradication of prejudice and the abolition of customary and all other practices which are based on the idea of the inferiority of women'. Yet this idea still has currency. Women do not enjoy all the educational opportunities they should have, and often do not have any at all. Nearly everywhere in the world they are given less education than men, and, over vast areas of the globe, the majority of illiterates are women.

The question remains: is the increase in women's labour force participation is a sign of deepening poverty which has forced women into the labour market for family survival or an indicator of new economic opportunities which are inducing households to move against the cultural gain and send women out to work to raise family living standards? In a sense both answers are correct. The dynamics behind the macro-level patterns vary across regions and agro-ecological zones of the country — and between different socio-economic groups within the same region.

Women's role in socio-economic, political and cultural development has been recognized only partially in the recent past. Their activities which contribute equally as that of men to development process are yet to get full economic recognition in all its dimensions. Their activities have also been gender-stereotyped over the centuries and their roles in different fields have been characterized on the basis of their sex status and reproduction function. Gailey (1987) delineates this point very clearly in the following terms: "sex differences are not gender differences. Few people would say that being a female means being womanly or being a male means being manly. Sex differences are physiological features related to procreation to biological reproduction. The sex division of labour reproduction is well understood. Males produce sperm, females produce eggs; female bear young. Sex differences are found in all mammals. However, humans from their very origin have interpreted and reshaped their physical and social environment through symbolizing. Humans are self-reflective, culture-creating animals. Humans have sex differences, but like all other aspects of physical differentiation, they are experienced symbolically. In human societies, sex differences are experienced as gender. While sex differences physical, gender differences are socially constructed. Concepts of gender are cultural interpretations of sex differences. Gender is related to sex differences but not necessarily to physiological differences as we see them in our society. Gender depends on how society views the relationship of male to man and female to woman. Every culture has prevailing images of what men and women are 'supposed' to be like".

The cultural image of sex status of women has not originated and developed on its own. It has emerged out of economic and social needs for perpetuating the status of some groups by weakening them culturally, economically and politically for establishing the basis of an exploitative system in which one is subordinated for conveniences of another. In this process female became the first victim, and systematically and slowly, in the historical process, she has not only been deprived of her status as equal creature materially but she also has been psychologically prepared to accept her relegated status as 'naturally as she has accepted her reproductive function'. Further, the cultural norms that influence women to participate in manual labour outside the home vary according to their position in the social hierarchy. Generally women of higher socio-economic sections of the society (caste, class) do not engage in manual labour outside the home.

Every society, everywhere, has discriminated against women, with a few exceptions. The result of this discrimination is reflected in every country's intense effort to correct the mistakes made against women for centuries and barriers created to wrest them to realize their potentials. At both the international and national levels, many efforts have been made to eradicate all forms of discrimination against women and opening and providing opportunities to realize their potentials in equal terms with men. The opposition to increasing opportunities for women's participation in the economy stem from different views regarding women's 'proper' role in society. For example, the elite classes/ upper classes in most societies limited the activities of women to home only. In the same society the women of the labour class did participate extensively in economic activities outside the home, but their spheres were often clearly defined by a customarily accepted division of labour between the sexes. "The patterns of this division have however varied, not only from society to society but among different sections of people within the same society'(Mead Margaret,1950). This is evident from the participation of women in the village economy from different castes.

Men are favourably placed than women in their respective strata and regions due to the unequal distribution of resources. This systematic differentiation in terms of access to resources and status between men and women leads to the popular view that there ought to be equality of opportunity for both the genders. Thus, the practice of gender equality strives to provide women with the same rights and opportunities that men experience.

This is problematic, for instance, equality is merely understood to mean equating women with men. This perspective in fact negates the biological differences which are real. The sex differences are real and taking them as the basis of gender differentiation and discrimination, results in role stereotyping. It is this type of roles that restricts women's access to resources. In every society roles have to be allocated but the roles must not be typed according to gender definitions.

The exact nature and extend of involvement of women varies widely across different cultures and at different stages of development. In general, as development proceeds from the pre-industrial phases to the industrial, men and women are faced with differing demands for their labour. As production moves from homes to factories the demand for male skilled labour increases but it is not so for the women as they are not able to participate in industry to any appreciable extent. Women face intense competition in a labour surplus market and are forced to take up jobs usually not preferred by men. These jobs are often extensions of domestic work are invariably low paid. Thus, women suffer from two sets of discrimination in the labour market: (i) pre-market discrimination i.e. the lack of access to factors such as education, training, experience, and so on which increase human capital and enhances the marginal product of labour; and (ii) post-market discrimination, namely, differential wages for a similar quantum of human capital.

WOMEN AND EDUCATION

Males and females are provided access to different types of education. In accordance with the male role of earners, they are given education and skills which have remunerative value. Females, on the other hand, attain education and skills relating to child care and house-keeping.

Social attitudes, beliefs and norms reflect on women's poor access to education. Differences in male-female literacy levels, differences in urban and rural female literacy levels and varying literacy levels in different areas do point out that within the available educational infrastructure, female face social discrimination both in access to education and in the quality of education. Thus, restricted access to female education is furthered not only by the family, even religious practices/caste practices demand that a girl must remain chaste and protected.

Further, the popular notion which is used to explain girl's dropping out of school or not sending them to school at all is that girls are biologically and mentally inferior and incapable of being educated. A combination of these factors determine the socio-cultural atmosphere that restricts female access to education in the region.

We may state that gender bias (discrimination against a person on the basis of sex) is not endemic to education but is systematic. It is interesting to note that while sexism and the apartheid of gender pervades all spheres of public and private life in India, in education, gender-disparities are on the decline and female educational participation and female literacy rates are on the rise. Female-male differentials in literacy rates are lower in the younger age groups and therefore it is perhaps reasonable to assume that given the present pro-girl child policies and a proactive state upholding women's equality and empowerment as the central organizing principles of national development, gender bias in education against women, the adverse sex ratio, what kind of education, what curricular and planning strategies are needed to ensure not only gender equality but preservation and upholding of human dignity of all regardless of sex, caste or creed. Sexism, casteism and communalism are eating into the vitals of our nation.

Further, sex inequalities in educational opportunity have had significant repercussions for women's economic roles in developing societies. Various studies have shown that occupational placement and mobility in most societies increasingly depend on the completion of specified levels of formal education. This is particularly the case in most non-industrialised systems, where stratification in the modern sector tends to flow from educational attainment rather than to reflect traditional status criteria. The extend to which this concern with diplomas, degrees, and certificates governs both the educational process and occupational structure has led one analyst to diagnose modern society as suffering from the diploma disease. If individual and group advancement are predicted on access to certain levels and kinds of formal education, the denial of this training has long-terms consequences for the roles and positions in society to which the educationally disadvantages can aspire. However, sex disparities in educational opportunities also tend to be greater in less-developed regions than in developed regions. The magnitude of historical and contemporary sex inequalities in educational opportunity in low-income regions becomes clearer from an examination of statistics and various studies.

In addition to sex differences in the availability of schooling and in enrolment patterns, there are other types of sex inequalities in educational opportunity that have implications for economic roles. Many educational systems are characterized by pervasive sex-linked streaming, with the result that girls are not offered the same curriculum, standards, and programme options as boys. The nature of this streaming rarely derives from traditional sex-role norms or the traditional division of labour between the sexes, but instead reflects trends and practices. Pre-vocational and vocational programmes usually tract females into homemaking or domestic science courses, while males are taught skills which may lead to remunerative employment. When females are offered career training courses, they are usually encouraged to choose terminal vocational programmes that prepare them for a limited range of sex-stereotyped jobs. The typical over-representation of females in humanities and arts at the secondary and tertiary educational levels and their concomitant under-representation in sciences, engineering, and related fields often reflect the distribution of science facilities and teachers and/or the admissions policies of the relevant institutions. Curricula and textbooks also often have a decidedly male orientation. Thus, the cumulative impact of socialization through the schools may be to depress female aspirations and to discourage their participation in the modern sector.

WOMEN AND EMPLOYMENT

For satisfying the basic need of food, shelter and clothing, work both domestic and non-domestic for money is essential. Domestic works such as cooking, washing clothes and utensils, taking care of the children and elders etc., do not bring 'money' into the household and, therefore, it is not perceived as "work". Since ages, these tasks have been performed by women but their work has never given them the status of being 'employed'.

When the time to enter the field of employment comes, the males are better equipped than the females since, by and large, they have been given better skills, training and competence. Every male child is provided with some kind of training or skill which helps him to get into the workforce smoothly. On the contrary, girls are normally not brought up with the same intention. When suddenly the family feels compelled, she is 'pushed' into the workforce. Further, women's earnings remain significantly below those of men in spite of the increase in the female labour force. Differences in rates of pay and conditions of service between men and women persist till today. At almost all occupational levels women do indeed earn substantially less than men.

Culture, tradition and social beliefs combine to influence and generate an unfavourable occupational discrimination among female workers vis-à-vis male workers and to create pay differences between males and females within the same occupation. The result is the chronic earnings gap between male and female labourers.

Women are the last to acquire skills which fall outside the traditional skills allotted to them. Also with the increased composition for unskilled jobs, globalisation is likely to throw unskilled women workers in fierce competition with men. Consequently, women who are the last in the household to enter the workforce, happen to be the first to be thrown out in the event of market contraction. Thus, the biological qualities are often turned into biological handicaps.

It is observed that there are certain issues/changes have occurred in women labour market in the last three decades. Tradition alone does not prevent a change of sex roles in the labour market and there are other factor also. It is 'employer's interest' which brings a sharp demarcation between male and female jobs. In many cases employers reserve jobs for women are paid less than men for equal work. In some other countries, unequal pay can be maintained by classifying certain jobs for women and placing these jobs in a lower wage category than male jobs which require same level of qualification. Another factor for the deterioration of the female role in labour market is the inferior position of women in the education system particularly vocational training system. Even in countries where women require good education and training but still they feel inferior to men in the labour market as they suffer from the feeling of insecurity and insufficiency. They feel secure only when they get jobs which are traditionally regarded as "female" jobs. Moreover, only a few women want to enter into open competition with men in jobs which are considered as "unsuitable" and "unusual for women".

Urbanisation, increased cost of living, western influence on social roles of women etc., call for a redefinition of women's roles in family and society. Education of women, changes in the size of family, in age of marriage and call for a greater participation of women in different fields lead to subtle but major changes in roles and responsibilities of women. Further, among the agricultural classes the pattern of women's participation vary according to regional and cultural norms.

In the initial phase of Industrial development, most industries continued the traditional pattern of family participation and employed a considerable number of women and children. They confined to certain unskilled and semi-skilled types of work at lower rates of wages. In terms of proportion to total labour employed, women constituted an important segment of the labour force in these industries.

Technological changes have affected the employment of women in these industries adversely. In the absence of training opportunities, women, already handicapped by illiteracy/low education level and lack of mobility cannot acquire the new skills demanded by modern industry. This created a gap in the earning power of men and women (Technical training was opened to men only).

Post independent developments has, however, opened some new avenues to women such as women polytechnic colleges, employment opportunities in factories and professional colleges etc. Modernisation and education enabled some women to enter new professions and occupations which were totally closed to them earlier. Women are even preferred to some jobs like nurses, telephone operators, airhostess etc. As a result urban middle class women, due to many factors like equal opportunities of education and employment, increased cost of living, to continue their professional qualification and skills and for some social reasons like changes in the attitude towards the traditional roles of women etc., started taking up such jobs.

Since the beginning in 1976 of the United Nations Decade for Women considerable amount of work has been done in the developing and other developed countries on how to bring women into the mainstream of economic and social development. This work which is extraordinary in both quantity and quality has led to creating an environment wherein the developing countries have begun to admit and recognize that the status of their women is extremely low and subordinate, and that it is a major source of their underdevelopment. This work has also succeeded in projecting an image of women's role which not only contrasts with the one that dominated the developing countries in the 1960's, e.g., the reproductive roles, but which explicitly recognizes women's economic contributions to development. Many countries have accordingly designed new initiatives and programmes to reach women and to involve them in the economic development processes. Suggestions have been made in a few countries that they should subject the entire development process and the supporting development programmes to some form of gender analysis and appraisal, and, where it is found to be necessary, alter the programmes to suit the needs of women. Gender planning has emerged in a few countries as a potential tool for meeting the strategic needs of women.

In societies in which females traditionally played an important role in agricultural production, some post-primary education probably induces women to leave the agricultural sector and enter the wage-labour market, whereas in the societies characterized by restrictive sex-role norms, secondary or university level education provides access to the technical and professional occupations considered suitable for high-status women.

What is striking and extraordinary in this gender debate is that the role of women in the urban areas, particularly their role in poverty alleviation which is one of the most formidable problem currently facing the urban areas of the developing world, has received comparatively minor attention. Much, rather most, of the work has been done in the context of rural areas. Women's roles have been studied in relation to rural development and rural poverty. In the context of the urban areas, some work has been done to highlight the discrimination that women are subjected to particularly in respect of their access to the labour market, but question such as– whether women help in the reduction of poverty in the urban areas; in what way do women help in reducing poverty; what exactly do women do in the urban poor households; what is the impact of women's work on the levels of literacy, health, nutrition etc; are women able to take advantage of the development programmes to the benefit of families they belong to; and in what way are the families where women work different from those where women do not work have not been directly and systematically addressed.

OBJECTIVES

Taking into account the need for study of the problem of women education, employment and gender discrimination the present study attempts for a comprehensive and indepth analysis of the women education, employment and various aspects responsible for gender discrimination in backward region like Hyderabad-Karnataka. However, the specific objectives of the study are as follows:

1. To draw attention towards the differential nature of male-female education patterns and impact of restricted education on access to women.

2. To understand the reasons for the girls dropping out or not sending them to schools.

3. To know about the gender issues in employment and explain how entry into the workforce is restricted by gender status and to identify the areas of work in which women are discriminated.

4. To find out the extent of wage differential existing between men and women doing various jobs and justification for such differential.

5. To evaluate the use of government schemes by women and develop a summary measures for women's development and gender justice.

HYPOTHESIS

With these objectives in view, the following hypothesis have been framed:

1. There are discriminations and restrictions with regard to the pattern of education and accessibility.

2. The socio-economic factors are causing the job-segregation and also responsible for wage differentials between sexes.

Research Design and Methodology

This study was based on the information and statistics obtained from primary and secondary sources.

Secondary data: The secondary data was collected from the District Statistical Offices, Directorate of Economics and Statistics, Human Development Reports, National Sample Surveys, Census of India (1981,1991 and 2001), various reports and journals etc. to analyse the women education and employment in all districts of H-K region selected for the purpose.

Primary data: The primary data relating to women's education, employment, nature of work, reasons for work, wages and discrimination, family life etc., was collected from the selected sample villages and urban areas, (cities-district headquarters are treated as cities) of the study area through personal interview method. The questionnaire was used exclusively for women respondents in rural areas (selected villages) and urban areas (district head quarters).

Structured interview schedule for women workers was designed and utilised for collecting the data from the field. The schedule was very carefully and systematically designed according to the objectives of the study. The questions were in English language but in the course of field visits, these questions were translated in to Kannada (regional language) while asking the questions to the respondents. In order to avoid redundancy of some of the questions in the interview schedule, the schedule was pre-tested well in advance. As a result, certain modifications were introduced in few questions.

The interview with the respondents was based on the structural interview schedule. It gave an opportunity to the researcher to have a face to face interaction with the respondents. At times the interview drifted away from the structured schedule and led to detailed discussions on certain aspects. A few of the respondents were interviewed in the presence of their husbands because they were reluctant to be talked alone. The interviews were carried on from April 2004 to July 2004.

After the fieldwork was over, all the schedules were checked and some of the information written here and there on the schedules were re-written against the appropriate choices of a particular question so as to facilitate subsequent analysis of this data. After that the whole data of each respondent was fed into computer for further tabulation and interpretation. Statistical methods like average, chi-square, T-test and percentages were used at appropriate places for analyzing this data.

Region Selected for the Study: The choice of Hyderabad–Karnataka region for the present study is prompted, firstly, by the fact that so far no comprehensive studies were undertaken on the women's education, employment and work and gender discrimination. Secondly, because, the region such as Hyderabad–Karnataka is most backward area and gender discrimination is major problem for the overall and sustainable development in the region. Therefore, the dominating socio-economic conditions on women and gender discrimination motivated to choose Hyderabad–Karnataka region.

Selection of the Study Areas and Respondents: The study covers four districts of Hyderabad-Karnataka region viz., Bidar, Gulbarga, Raichur and Koppal. Further, to analyse the socio-economic conditions responsible for gender discrimination against women in the Hyderabad-Karnataka region, one city (district headquarter), two villages from each district (of four districts) were selected. This selection was made to compare the discrimination in both rural and urban areas.

In the beginning a 150 women respondents from rural and urban areas from each district was fixed. In each of these areas (rural and urban areas) information about women in the selected occupational groups was collected. For agriculture, self-employees, private business and Government employees random sampling technique was adopted. Due care was taken to select as many numbers of respondents in the sample which may be proportionate to their size in the universe. Even, the caste-wise women respondents were picked up from both the areas. The female respondents who have completed their education above 4th standard were interviewed (those who involved in economic activities). The study covers 600 female respondents from rural areas and 600 female respondents from urban areas of Hyderabad-Karnataka region (150 women respondents from each district of the region viz., Bidar, Gulbarga, Raichur and Koppal districts). Thus, the total 1200 women respondents were selected and interviewed for the present study (Flow chart 1).

Chapterisation: The study is divided into eight chapters. In Chapter 1 the education and employment status of women and research method of the study has been discussed. Chapter 2 deals with the review of literature on status of women, especially their education and employment. In Chapter 3 the women literacy and work participation in Hyderabad-Karnataka region based on secondary data have been dealt with. Chapter 4 present the geographical and economic profile of the study area. Chapter 5 deals with the socio-economic profile of the working women. In this chapter data concerning the educational, occupational status, caste, age structure, family size, marital status, age at marriage and number of children have been analysed. In Chapter 6 the educational career and background, encouragement from family members, mode of travel, drop-out and reasons for drop-out have been discussed. In Chapter 7 data concerning reasons to start work, constraints faced, effect on family, job satisfaction, savings, tax paid, wages and income and membership of organization have been analysed. In Chapter 8 summary and conclusions of the study have been delineated.

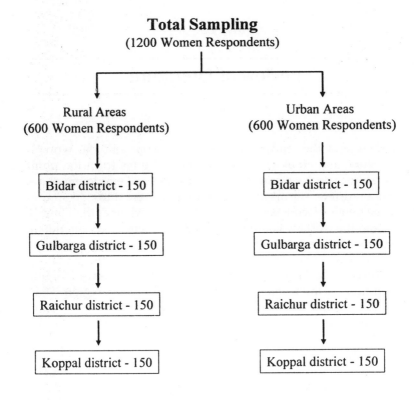

Total Sampling
(1200 Women Respondents)

Rural Areas
(600 Women Respondents)

Urban Areas
(600 Women Respondents)

Bidar district - 150

Gulbarga district - 150

Raichur district - 150

Koppal district - 150

Bidar district - 150

Gulbarga district - 150

Raichur district - 150

Koppal district - 150

2

Review of Literature

A review of the studies of women at large and the women education and employment in particular brings forth the point that studies on the women in the education and employment are only a rare few. The major concentration of these studies is simply on the trends of work participation of women whereas their family life and the working conditions. But the present study intends to explore a wide range of issues ranging from socio-economic conditions, differential education, family life, working relationships and reasons, membership of organizations and living conditions of the women in Hyderabad-Karnataka region. With this background, the following section review the some of literature available on women in general and women education and employment in particular.

Shiryl Samuel (1983) in his study addresses the rate of growth in enrolment in professional higher education with that of general higher education and women participation in professional higher education. The analysis relies on data drawn from the secondary sources with special reference to Karnataka The enrolment trends in higher education for India and Karnataka are taken for five quinquenniams whereas the annual growth rate and percentages are computed for ten years. The study brings to our notice that both in the case of Karnataka and India, the rate of growth in female enrollment was rising at a faster rate than that of male enrolment growth. The annual growth rate in female enrolment was about 90 per cent whereas in males it was about 57 per cent. The sex ratio also shows that the women's participation in general education is much higher than in professional education. By 1975-

76, in India, more than 56 per cent of the enrollment in the faculty of education was constituted by females and 23.49 per cent in medicine. On the other hand, the enrollment in the faculties of engineering/technology, agriculture, veterinary science etc., was negligible. The study concludes that although most women are still enrolled in female intensive fields, there has been some appreciable movements of women into certain male fields such as engineering, law, commerce etc.

Savitri Arputhamurthy (1990) in her study gives an account of factors responsible for the existence of sex discrimination in the Indian situation in general and in Tamil Nadu in particular and to find out the justification for the existence of sex discrimination in agricultural labour market. The author collected primary data from the selected sample villages of Madurai district through personal interview schedule. From 38 villages, 76 female labourers, 76 male labourers and 76 employees (total 228 respondents) were selected at random for collection of primary data. The study accounts that female labourers found in the unorganized sector, nearly 80 per cent belong to agriculture. These agricultural labourers handicapped by poverty, illiteracy and ignorance are affected very badly with regard to wages. The study results reveal that there exists wage discrimination on account of sex and levels of development. The average per centage rates of agricultural operations done by male and female were 80 and 70 respectively and women were discriminated in the matter of sexual division of labour both in the developed and less developed areas. It is evident that prejudice against women is the important cause for deciding the agricultural operation as "female tasks" and "male tasks". The study suggests that the policy measures are to be framed in such a way that it should cause a big jolt to the prevailing socio-economic conditions or rural women in Madurai district and bring about a dramatic improvement in their status.

Seeta Prabhu and Sarkar's (1992) study arrives at an unambiguous classification of the sectoral as well as aggregate levels of development of the districts of Maharashtra for 1985-86. In the final classification, 11 districts were identified as being highly developed, while three districts were considered as belonging to the middle level of development. The remaining 15 districts were classified as underdeveloped. An examination of the regional profile indicates that all the districts of western Maharashtra with the exception of Dhule, were classified as belonging to medium and high levels of development. In sharp contrast, all the districts in Marathwada, except Aurangabad and six out of nine districts in Vidarbha were classified as belonging to the category of underdeveloped districts. The persistence of wide disparities in the development of various regions in Maharashtra despite a quarter century of planned economic development is disconcerting and points to the need for urgent remedial measures.

Kondaveeti Papa (1992) carried out a study to know about the status of women in the rural areas, the impact of the sub-cultural contexts of the people of dis-advantaged sections arising out of poverty conditions and educational interventions in backward district of Andhra Pradesh. As to collect primary data, Chinna Elkicherla village in Mehaboobnagar district was chosen for the study. The analysis of data shows that lack of opportunities for education in rural areas is responsible for the existing gap between urban and rural women, particularly in terms of equal participation is social affairs. Early marriages, much before the attainment of puberty among girls, is a common practice in rural community. The girls likes and dislikes, their hopes and aspirations are never cared for. Wife and husband relationship is marked by absolute dominance of husband and submission of life. The case of women dealt with reveal an increasingly dangerous phenomenon of wife beating, harassment, friction between husband and wife, mother–in–law and daughter-in-law etc. The roots or locus of friction lies in the conditions of objective poverty to which the people are subjected. The condition of depravity and abandonness are evident in the behaviour of most of the women particularly belonging to the weaker sections. The study concludes that girls education is not conscious discrimination perse which is responsible for denial of access but it is condition of poverty which is the major factor preventing them from sending girls to school.

Krishnamurthy's (1993) study observed that the industrial scenario during the last two and half decades (1961-1985) at the regional level does not seem to be very satisfactory. The overall industrial development in Andhra Pradesh, though fairly impressive, has not percolated to the regional levels. Industrial structure of Telangana region, unlike that of the coastal Andhra and Rayalseema, is also diversified but such diversification is found to be based on the development of non-agro-based industries and undergone a process of change during the period concerned. Industries like transport, equipment and parts, metal products, electrical machinery, machinery and machinery tools, chemical products, wood and wood products and non-electrical machinery are the core industries of the region.

An important study by *Kumud Ranjan (1993)* examined the social origin and familial adjustment of women in modern occupations such as teaching, medical engineering, legal, administration, journalism and performing arts. The study covers three major cities of Uttar Pradesh viz., Lucknow, Allahabad and Varnasi. 300 women respondents were chosen for the seven occupational groups in the three cities and simple and cross-tables showing frequency and percentage have been prepared to find out the correlation, chi-square test of significance. The study explores that majority of respondents had been aspiring for the administrative jobs from their early academic career and entered the same when they got the chance for it. Academic qualifications was the second dominant factor governing their selections into the job. Further, the study explores that the reasons for job dissatisfaction were lack of further prospects, insufficient pay, dislike of the work, odd working hours and the transferable nature of job. The study found that working women are still performing the traditional domestic chores of cooking, washing and cleaning in the house. However, the working women wanted that along with education women should enter into the job market, participation in social life and take active interest in politics.

Directorate of Economics and Statistics (1995) studied the trends in employment and unemployment in Karnataka. The analysis is based on data collected by the National Sample Survey Organisation in the quinquennnial surveys on the subject from 1972-73 to 1993-94 (50th round). The results shows that the rate of usually employed (per 1000 population) in case of male was higher than females both in rural and urban areas. Further, the rate of usually employed males and females in rural and urban areas had registered decline between 1972-73 and 1987-88 in case of principal status. During 1983-88, the growth rate of usual status employment in the state was negative (-0.51%). Within the state, the highest growth in employment was in urban areas during 1977-79 to 1983. Further, the highest negative growth was also observed in urban areas during 1983 to 1987-88. During the next quinquennium (1987-

88 to 1993-94) which witnessed negative growth, males had a comparatively lower position. Further, the study shows that the workforce participation in the age groups 5-9 and 10-14, reveals the extend of child labour existing in the State, which was pronounced in rural areas and was to the extend of about 25 per cent. Another important point noticed by the study is that workforce participation among aged (i.e. above 60years) was higher among males compared to females and was more pronounced in the case of rural areas.

Mohammad Iqbal Ali and Ramesh Reddy (1996) in their analysis of the urbanization process in Andhra Pradesh during the last decades, i.e. 1971 to 1991 has revealed that the distribution of urban population is found to be more in Telangana region. The reasons for the highest percentage of urban population in Telangana is due to the concentration of more than half of the urban population in and around Hyderabad city itself. But, if we exclude Hyderabad city, urbanisation process is found to be the lowest in Telangana region compared to that of the other two regions. Thus, the overall distribution of small and medium towns in Telangana region is found to be the lowest and obviously indicates that compared to Andhra and Rayalseema regions, Telangana region lags behind in the process of urbanisation in Andhra Pradesh.

Srilatha Batliwala (1998) in their book studied the impact of major policies and provisions in the areas of law, economic development, health, education, family planning and rural development on women. The study is based on fieldwork carried out in several districts of Karnataka State. The study carried out through questionnaires administered to 1171 women and 1103 men on issues relating to gender relations and problems. The study highlights that in parts of Belgaum district, a form of devadasi institutions exists, while in parts of former Hyderabad state, the preponderance of Dalits and Muslims pose problems of acute poverty and gender segregations. Further, (1) The study has thrown up a rich fund of data, highlighting gender differentials in access to health and health care, and insights on the reproductive health status of the women respondents. The study observed that women report more illness than men and it is clear that women do not have the same access to higher expenditure on their medical care, and must satisfy with low-cost services and other inputs. (2) Women are engaged in not only an equal number of productive activities as men, but even slightly more in terms of mean number of activities per capita; however, only about two-thirds of this work is remunerated. Consequently, although female respondents are engaged in productive work of some kind, only three-fourths earn income from this in their own hands, while virtually all the male respondents do so. (3) The well-established bias against women's schooling and education has been reiterated by the results of the study. Far more women respondents than men did not get an opportunity to go to school in their youth. A disappointingly small proportion had accessed adult literacy classes. (4) While women's awareness of injustice within the family is high, their ability to perceive systematic social deprivation as injustice is much lower than men's. Conversely, men are either intentionally or genuinely oblivious to the violations of women's rights within the home and family.

Ghanashyama Mahanty's (1999) study used 32 indicators and five commonly used methods of indexing for evaluating inter-district disparities in levels of development in Andhra Pradesh. The major conclusions that have emerged out from the study are as follows: Firstly, the potential role of public action (evident from social sector) together with seemingly agricultural activities helped some of the districts from Rayalseema and Telengana to reap the benefits of regional development process. It can also be inferred from the analysis that agricultural development plays a vital role in fostering regional development process. Secondly, though the above results add much to our comfort, what is disheartening is that some of the underdeveloped districts have almost remained untouched by the development process.

Abdul Shaban and Bhole L.M. (1999) in their paper used 62 indicators and an attempt has been made by them to measure the levels of development in various districts and regions in Maharashtra for the benchmark years 1972-73, 1982-83 and 1988-89. The study finds that regions of Vidarbha and Marathwada and the districts of Ratnagiri, Raigad, Dhule and Jalgaon have been the least developed both at sectoral and the aggregate levels of development. The study suggests an urgent need for reviewing the whole gamut of approaches towards development planning in the state and for emphasizing the development of agricultural sector and local resource-based labour-intensive industrialization in the under-developed districts/regions.

Sushmita Chandra's (2001) study addresses the interrelationship between women and development with special reference to human development based on human development index. The study is confined to the experiences of the Uttar Pradesh and other major states constituting India. The secondary data was mainly collected from Census and NSSO. In order to carry out the analysis of the interrelationship between female participation rate and variables like male participation rate, human development index, urbanization were chosen. Further, to assess and analyse the influence of each of the selected independent variables on a selected dependent variables, an application of alternative regression models were developed and applied by the researcher. The empirical results of study presents that the proportion of female workers to the total workers exhibited a significant increase from 17.38 per cent in 1971 to 20.21 per cent during 1981 and 22.48 per cent during 1991 at the national level. Further, an observation of state-wise data available in this regard points out to the fact that almost all the major states of India excepting Himachal Pradesh, Kerala and Uttar Pradesh have also experienced a similar trend in the proportion of female workers to the total workers. The share of rural female workers has demonstrated an indiscriminate increase on all India level from 18.86 per cent in 1971 to 22.45 per cent in 1981 and 25.10 per cent in 1991. Contrary to the rural areas, according to the study, in case of urban areas too, the proportion of the urban female workers has showed a continuous increase from 10.41 per cent in 1971 to 11.65 per cent in 1981 and 13.01 per cent during 1991 on the all India level. Thus, the study concludes that the process of feminisation in the total workforce, which have gained momentum over the period, is a common characteristic applicable to both rural and urban areas.

Jeemol Unni's (2001) study focused on the premia on incomes associated with educational investments and how this varies with ethnic groups. Impact of education on incomes from salaried jobs and self-employment in non-agriculture, consisting of trade, service, business or professional activities, were also discussed in the paper. The results of study presents that the private returns to education among salaried males was equally high, i.e. 8.3 per cent, among scheduled castes, other Hindus and Christian. Men among Scheduled tribes had returns of 7.5 per cent. The most interesting result was that the returns to education for Muslim men with salaried jobs were significant. Further, the most striking result was that salaried males among Muslims and Christians had no significant returns to education at any level. At lower levels of education salary earnings were significantly different from those to illiterate persons. Thus, the study implies that just being literate or with only primary or middle schooling was not enough to obtain better labour markets.

According to *Ajit Kumar (2001)* study, the development and administration of Vidharba, Marathwada continue to be slow and their borders have remained unchanged. Further, the terms regarding allocation of funds for development of different units in proportion to their population with special reference for Marathwada and the requirement that a report in this behalf be placed before the state assembly every year has remained unfulfilled. Irrigation, roads and primary education were the sectors in which both regions lagged behind. In addition Marathwada lagged behind in power development.

Degaonkar Chaya, et al., (2001) observed that as all the districts in the Hyderabad-Karnataka region experienced a higher growth rate of population than at the state level during 1981-91. Although, the decline in crude birth rate and death rate are the testimony for the favourable impact of family welfare programmes in the region, both birth and death rates in the region are still higher than at the State level. Further, they concluded that illiteracy and ignorance backed by religious beliefs and superstitions in the area have prevented large section of the population to be mobile and to develop the scientific temperament in their life. Greater attention is needed for the overall development of some of the talukas in different districts.

Nanjundappa D.M. (2002) examined the regional imbalances existing in the Karnataka state; Regional imbalances in education are assessed by constructing an index of education by using four indicators, viz., literacy rate, pupil-teacher ratio, out of school children and enrolment of students in degree colleges and taking state average as benchmark. Again, the taluks were divided into relatively developed taluks and backward were divided into three categories, viz., backward, more backward and most backward taluks. When we consider the relative share of North Karnataka Region (including Hyderabad-Karnataka region) and South Karnataka region in the three backward categories, the former emerges as the lagging region. Work participation rate is marginally higher in South Karnataka (45.35%) as compared to that in North Karnataka (43.60%). Whereas, Agricultural labour is more predominant in North Karnataka (36.2%) especially in Gulbarga division (40.6%) as compared to South Karnataka (19.4%). Contrary to it, the proportion of industrial workers to total workers is almost double in South Karnataka (13.7%) as compared to North Karnataka (6.9%). Employment in public organized sector shows that South Karnataka region accounts for lion's share (65%) as compared to North Karnataka region (35%).

P.V.L. Raman's (2002) study assessed the relationship between gender, literacy work, the health aspects of slum women including fertility behaviour, family planning practices and the nature of violation of women's human rights. The study specifically address to a slum mainly inhabited by the Muslims in the city of Visakhpatnam. The respondents were the female head of the household and data from 100 households were obtain. The data shows that 48.00 per cent of the respondents were illiterate and 52.00 per cent were literate. There were altogether 46 working women in the sample households and 28.00 per cent of the respondents were working for gainful employment and majority of them were engaged in traditional unskilled occupations like 'coolie' or 'maid servants'. The close observation of the occupations in comparison to literacy levels indicate that (1) illiterate women work mostly in the unskilled occupation (main servants or coolies), (2) literate women (other than primary level educated) work in skilled occupation such as tuitions, (3) those with primary level education were normally dropouts from schools and they also work in unskilled categories of occupations and (4) the income levels of the literates were much lower than that of illiterates because these women were willing to take up low status occupations like coolie which yield more income although physically more strenuous. This shows that there is negative association between literacy and income, but there is positive association between skill levels and literacy levels. The health status of women reveals that the common diseases from which women suffer in the slum are skin diseases, respiratory problems, backache and anemia. The fertility rates of the Muslims was higher than that of the Hindus and the Chistians. Further, the data reveals that a majority (78.7 per cent) of the deliveries took place at home with the help of untrained dais. There are many reported human rights violations on slum women such as violations of right of life, right to equality and right to freedom, right of the girl child and adolescent girls, right to clean environment and health.

Neetha Lodha (2003) while working emphasizes the tribal women involvement in different households activities and their time expenditure pattern, means of travel to work place, reasons for acceptance and leaving the job, awareness and participation in developmental programmes. The results of study highlight that job opportunities of long duration and better remuneration and transportation facilities in advanced region have motivated tribal women towards wage labour, though unpaid family workers were 30 per cent. Whereas, the tendency of tribal women in backward region was towards subsistence farming as unpaid family worker. Further, the study observes that there is a higher concentration of respondents in non-market activities (57 per cent) whereas in the backward region dominance of non-market activities (72 per cent) was found. The study shows that the average time spent for household work by respondents was 236 minutes (240 minutes in advanced region and 232 minutes in backward region). Economically extended activities like fetching of water, collection of fuel, cow-dung and repairing of house consumed 95 minutes in a day (96 minutes in developed region and 93 minutes in backward region. Tribal women's individual income is an important determinant of their status. The researcher observes that the overall mean income of respondents was Rs. 5283.62 with higher mean income in advanced region (Rs. 6360.47) as compared to backward region (Rs. 3104.29). Walking and availing of bus facility was a common practice in both the regions however bicycle facility was utilized by one-tenth of the respondents in advanced region due to proximity to workplace. A majority of women respondents (56 per cent) worked before marriage due to economic necessity and half of married women respondents work because of economic compulsion.

Sivaprakasam P. and Suriakala R. (2003) made an attempt to study the personal profile of the women employees and their positions at home and work. The results of study presents that 20.7 per cent, 1 per cent, 4.1 per cent, 4.1 per cent and 1 per cent women in credit, consumer, marketing, housing and dairy sectors respectively at the district level had completed training before joining the institution, whereas after joining a few had completed the training through correspondence. Further, the results presents that a larger number of women employees lacked the pre-requirement training. The study find that the number of respondents in the lower income group was 11.9 per cent; in the middle income group it was 75 per cent while in the higher income group it was 10.9 per cent. Thus, the majority of the respondents belonged to the middle income group. The author observes that the husbands of 30.2 per cent of the respondents were government employees, 19.8 per cent and 11.2 per cent respondents stated that their husbands were employed in public undertakings, and private sectors, respectively. But, 11.6 per cent stated that their husbands were in business. Thus, it is clear that there were families, which principally depended on the earnings of women and incomes of married women living with their husbands were also important for their families' economic well-being.

The study by *Gidda Reddy P. (2003)* observed the socio-psychological extension related characteristics, the nature of decision making pattern and farming performance of different groups of farm women in rice based farming system. Ranga Reddy district from Andhra Pradesh was chosen for the study. For the primary data a sample size of 180 was selected from the three farm women groups drawn from 12 villages by employing proportionate stratified random sampling procedure. The study found that majority of large farm women were middle aged, however, they can read and write. Most of them belonged to medium category of innovativeness, self-confidence, level of aspiration, scientific orientation and economic orientation. Most of the small farm women were middle aged and illiterate. They lack in innovativeness, self-confidence, risk preference and rationality in decision making. The study findings further revealed that large farm women took decisions by themselves in areas like-use of family labour, selling of milk and milk products, health and management of poultry. However, the decisions like choice of crops/enterprises, selection of seeds, storage and selling of products were the exclusive domains of the husbands of large farm women. Small farm women were sole decision makers in areas such as use of family labour, storage of produce, care and management of animals. These women were also involved in making major decisions on selection of crops, hiring of farm labour, selling surplus far produce and vegetables. The study concludes that the conscious effort should be made to involve women to improve their farming performance related to land based activities to enable them to move from subsistence agriculture to major income source for improved standards.

Dhameja S.K. (2004) has undertaken a study with a view to find out the entrepreneurial performance and problems of women in business in North-Western India. In all 175 women entrepreneurs who had established their entrepreneur during the time frame of 1982 to1996 and were employing 5 or more in their respective enterprises were interviewed personally by the researcher. The results shows that women entrepreneurs generally prefer the so-called soft line servicing or trading, women of today are entering into more challenging area of manufacturing which has hitherto been considered as male bastion. Further, the study found that there was a significant trend of dis-agreement with the statement the 'support agencies are doing a lot for women entrepreneurs. On the contrary, the respondents opined that nothing special is being done to attract the potential women entrepreneurs into starting of their own ventures. The sample respondents complained of harassment in government departments - corruption being major reason behind it. These respondents said that as and when the authorities come to know that the unit is being run by a women, they discourage allotting sales tax number and giving electricity connection.

Chhaya Shukla's (2004) study deals with the position of education among women and various items like literacy level, girls in elementary and secondary education, drop-out rates in schools, female in higher and professional education. The study highlights that education is the key to progress and unless Indian women are educated, they will not be able to enjoy their rights. However, the education of women has been sadly neglected in the past. Though the percentage of literacy among women has increased from what it was 40 years ago, the disparity between boy's education and girl's education is till very high. Further, the study have empirically demonstrated that women tend to work at consistent levels with their husbands and it has also been found that wives who are less educated than their husbands, refrain from employment. Working women not only have greater number of years of schooling but a good number of them have also undergone some kind of professional training. Lastly, the study highlights that women tend to work only in those occupations which would not be considered detrimental from the point of view of their family status.

Indira Kumari Y. and Sambasiva Rao B. (2005) while studying emphasized on the empowerment of the rural women focusing on direct involvement of women in programming and management effective collaboration with community organizations and organizing and strengthening of women's Self Help Groups. 240 groups (120 SHGs and 120 DWCRA groups) were taken for study to find out the social impact which influences group formation, group activity, training taken by the groups and finally the social impact of the groups. Sample groups are drawn from Krishna district in Andhra Pradesh. The study highlights that the Self-Help Groups involved mainly in savings and credit activities to promote thrift among their members. SHGs are emerging as an important activity for the Banks is mobilising deposits from the rural poor people and giving credit to the rural poor women. It is important to note from the study that banks are able to extend credit to the rural poor women without any security and repayment is almost 90 per cent. Lastly, the study suggest that the process of formation of SHG is to be systematically institutionalised, consortium of banks can make lot of contribution for the promotion and growth of SHGs and training is an important aspect for formation and sustainability of SHGs.

Abha Lakshmi Singh et.al (2005) conducted a study about the nature and type of work done by the women in agricultural and non-agricultural fields, environmental conditions at home and work place, women's income and expenditure. The study is based on primary data collected from Aligarh district (selected villages from 12 blocks). In all from the 38 villages 1140 women respondents and from the 37 villages 1098 women respondents were selected (total 2238 women respondents). The findings of study shows that half of women respondents lived in kutchcha houses and 44 per cent were engaged as cultivators and 46 per cent worked as agricultural labourers. Majority of the women respondents reported of being involved in winnowing, weeding, harvesting, transplanting, sowing , threshing and put in 6 to 8 hours of work per day during the peak season. The women respondents further reported that they are working as sweepers, pot makers, in mandies, construction labourers, tailors, petty traders as non-agricultural activities. Further, the study found that the monthly income of the women respondents ranges between Rs. 900 to more than Rs. 1500. Working as agriculture labour 70 per cent were earning between Rs. 901 to 1200 per month. In the non-agricultural sector, they were earning Rs. 900 to 1500 per month. The study suggests that the quality of the rural women will be improved when they are provided with basic services like housing, water and sanitation.

Singh D.P. (2005) in his study underlines the need of intervention by the NGOs and the social activists towards improving the socio-economic status of women working in unorganized sector and require immediate attention towards their poverty, illiteracy, exploitation, deprivation and indebtedness. The study mentioned Hissar division of the Haryana state comprising five districts namely Jind, Bhiwani, Hissar, Sirsa and Fatehabad. A sample of 410 women workers has been drawn from the total 2465 women workers working in the 54 selected brick kiln units. 68 workers were selected from Jind district, 84 from Bhiwani, 113 from Hissar, 92 from Sirsa and 53 from Fatehabad. The socio-economic profile of women workers in brick kilns of the area under study presents that these workers come from the poorer socio-economic backgrounds and most of them are either of scheduled castes or backward classes earning very meager amount that is not always enough to support their families. The life of these women workers is very tough because of the double burden of working at home as well as at the work site. Further, the study after having made an in-depth study establishes that women workers in brick kilns are deprived of good living and working conditions then face occupational health hazards and there are no effective social security provisions for them. The owners do not implement labour welfare legislations very effectively. The study found that the wages of the workers of sampled brick kilns are decided through a group process and these workers don't have any bargaining capacity in determining their wages. However, in recent days, trade unions in these industries have started playing a constructive role. In brick kilns, there are no fixed hours of work and the workers worked according to their own convenience. Since, the wages are given for per thousand bricks, the workers prefer to work more, to earn more. The study suggests to organize awareness programmes regarding their legal rights, health, nutrition and sanitation and make provisions of schools/tutors for the children of these workers.

Nirmal J. and Dhulasi Birundha Varadarajan (2005) study seeks to examine with a women participation in Life Insurance Corporation of Tirunelveli Division and their empowerment through Life Insurance Corporation. The study is based on both primary and secondary data. For the primary data, 75 women staff, 100 women agents and 100 women policy holders have been selected as sample for the study. The study shows that participation of women agents maintaining an increasing trend and it was just 742 in 1994, but increased to 3016 in 2000. The position of women staff in the Tirunelveli Division of Life Insurance Corporation is just 24.6 per cent of its total staff strength. The compound growth rate for women agents is positive throughout the study period and it is maintaining a higher trend than men. Women of the three cadres (staff, agents and policy holders) and their association with Life Insurance Corporation improved their monetary position positively. Salaries earned, loan facilities, incentives, bonus, commissions, maturity values received all these improved their living status in terms of money. Their purchasing power increased leading to a better monetary status. Thus, increased money income empowers women. Majority of women agents in Life Insurance Corporation of Tirunelveli division were self-motivated and nearly others motivate 23 of them. It is also interesting to note from the study that 17 out of 100 respondents were persuaded to be agents in Life Insurance Corporation by other agents. Another 16 of them got inspiration from development officers. Nearly 44 of them were self-motivated. Training of women agents (52 out of 100 attended training programs) improved their skills and sharpens abilities and talents and provides a stimulus to work.

Nilima Srivastava (2005) in her study provides great insight into the change that has taken place in the area of role conflict experienced by women in professionals and establishes that women professionals in India have been continuously marching on the path of progress because of availability of varied kinds of opportunities to them in diverse areas of education, economically gainful work and politics in the Independent India. For the purpose of this study, practicing women professionals from six specialized fields viz. medicine, law, engineering, teaching, nursing and social work, were chosen. The sample size was 272, in the first study in 1990 and the sample size was 120, in the second study, undertaken by the study to assess the decadal shifts, transformation and changes discernible, in any, in 2002. The results of the study describes that period of service is an important determinant in making the working women and majority of the respondents have put in more than 5 years of service (71.69 in 1990 and 56.66 in 2002). Being professionally qualified, the women do bring in a good salary package which leads to better amenities for the whole of the family. The largest percentage (37.50) of professionals in the 2002 study were earning Rs.10000 or more, 28.33 per cent was earning between 5-10 thousand rupees per month. Phenomenal rise in respondents income from 1990 to 2002 was mainly because of massive pay revision in the intermittent period. The majority of respondent were self-motivated in the choice of their profession (50.73% in 1990 and 52.50% in 2002). Fathers were the motivating factors of the respondents in the choice of their profession for 30.15% respondents in 1990 and for 25.00% respondents in 2002; mothers as the motivating factors were 19.85% in 1990 and 9.06% in 2002. A majority of women started practicing the profession as soon as they attained their professional qualification and when they were still unmarried (63.97% and 83.33% in 1990 and 2002, respectively). The main reasons for taking up of professional practice by the working women professionals were to avoid wastage of professional talent and a desire to be free from dependence. Lastly, the study conclude that the women of today are ready to come out of the traditional mould, and pursue their academic, professional, creative and even adventure related career options.

Thota Jyothi Rani (2005) study has examined the impact of DWCRA on the work, income and status of rural woman. The study was based on primary as well as secondary sources of data. Khammam, Warangal and Karimnagar districts of North Telangana region of Andhra Pradesh have been chosen for the study. 300 respondents from Khammam district, 300 respondents from Warangal district and 220 respondents from Karimanagar district (total 820 respondents) were selected and interviewed personally by the researcher. The results shows that the majority of small and marginal farmers have preferred the trades related to agriculture and allied activities in all the selected three districts.

However, the forward caste respondents could get the opportunity to have degree level education and no other caste respondents found in this level. Contrastingly, scheduled tribe respondents could not go beyond secondary level education. Moreover, 42.9 per cent of the scheduled caste respondents, 63.8 per cent of the scheduled tribe respondents were illiterate while it was 37.6 per cent in backward classes and only 24 per cent in forward caste. Thus, illiteracy was more pronounced in scheduled tribes followed by scheduled castes. Further, study observed that 60 per cent of the respondents sell their product only through DWCRA bazars. However, the respondents face problems due to inadequate of demand while transport and lack of attractive package were other problems. Study noticed that the average employment in terms of number of days of employment per month is as high as 25.09 for illiterates and as the level of education increases the average employment has declined upto intermediate level. Further, the difference between pre-post DWCRA employment was highest for the degree holders followed by illiterates. Thus, either no education or higher level education is resulting in the success of the scheme in terms of employment generation. Further, from study it is observed that the additional income earned by the respondents due to DWCRA is in the range of Rs.501-750 for 101 beneficiaries out of 300 selected respondents and it is followed by 96 in the income range of Rs.251-500 and 37 respondents could get an additional income in the highest range of Rs.1001-1500 per month. Lastly, the study recommends for the provision of training in various skills, enlargement of marketing network, encourage interlink between NGOs and DWCRA, encourage DWCRA groups to take up programmes to increase their social awareness and encourage effective participation of women in decision making.

Thus, not much has been studied on the status of women in backward region like Hyderabad-Karnataka. Hence, the present study is special effort to know about the educational and employment status of women and gender-discrimination in the region.

3

Women Literacy and Work Participation in Hyderabad-Karnataka Region

SECTION - I

Literacy is considered as an important determinant of human development. It explains people's capability and thereby their choice. Besides contributing to the ability of the people to read and write, it has significant implications for matters pertaining to life and death like CBR, IMR, TFR, etc (Nanjundappa, 2002).

Total: As presented in Table 3.1 census data indicate that the literacy rate in Hyderabad-Karnataka region has moved from 30.89 per cent in 1981 to 54.97 per cent in 2001. 2001 census figures show that although the male-female differential is narrowing, it is still high-literacy among males is 67.13 per cent while it is only 42.40 per cent among females (gender difference accounts 24.73 per cent).

Table 3.1 further shows the consistent increase of all districts in Hyderabad-Karnataka region in literacy rate of both male and female during the study period. It is pertinent to note that as in the case of male literacy rate, Bidar stood first (73.29 per cent) among all districts of Hyderabad-Karnataka region followed by Raichur/Koppal district (65.58 per cent) and Gulbarga district (62.52 per cent) during 2001. In case of female, again Bidar district stood first (50.01 per cent) followed by Raichur/Koppal district (38.80 per cent) and Gulbarga district (38.40 per cent) during the same period. Gender difference of literacy was high in Raichur/ Koppal district (26.78 per cent) during 2001 which was greater than Hyderabad-Karnataka region and State average. This is

Table 3.1
Literacy rate in Hyderabad-Karnataka Region (Total=Rural + Urban)

District	1981				1991				2001			
	P	M	F	G.D.	P	M	F	G.D.	P	M	F	G.D.
Bidar	32.17	46.85	17.11	29.74	45.11	58.97	30.53	28.44	61.98	73.29	50.01	23.28
Gulbarga	30.38	44.54	15.99	28.55	38.54	52.08	24.49	27.59	50.65	62.52	38.40	24.12
Raichur/Koppal	30.13	43.99	16.14	27.85	35.96	49.53	22.15	27.38	52.28	65.58	38.80	26.78
H-K. Region	30.89	45.13	16.41	28.72	39.87	53.53	25.72	27.81	54.97	67.13	42.40	24.73
Karnataka State	46.21	58.73	33.17	25.56	56.05	67.26	44.34	22.92	67.04	76.29	57.45	18.84

Source: Census of India.
Note: P=Person, M=Male, F=Female and G.D.= Gender Difference.

Table 3.2
Literacy rate in Hyderabad – Karnataka region (Rural Areas).

District	1981				1991				2001			
	P	M	F	G.D.	P	M	F	G.D.	P	M	F	G.D.
Bidar	22.02	33.95	9.85	24.10	39.43	53.85	24.51	29.34	57.72	69.95	44.88	25.07
Gulbarga	19.10	29.86	8.29	21.57	30.36	44.32	16.06	28.26	42.73	55.55	29.67	25.88
Raichur/Koppal	21.16	32.97	10.00	22.97	30.42	44.26	16.48	27.78	43.15	56.87	29.38	27.49
H-K. Region	20.76	32.26	9.38	22.88	33.40	47.48	19.02	28.46	47.87	60.79	34.64	26.15
Karnataka State	31.08	41.88	20.04	21.84	47.69	60.03	34.76	25.27	59.68	70.63	48.50	22.13

Source: Census of India.
Note: P=Person, M=Male, F=Female and G.D.= Gender Difference.

definitely the largest number (percentage) of illiterate women existing in any region of the State. Because, the cultural perception of women here is different from the cultural norms applied to women in other regions of the State. This is affecting the status of women in many ways in the region.

Rural Areas: The literacy rate of Hyderabad-Karnataka region for rural areas has moved from 20.76 per cent in 1981 to 33.40 per cent in 1991 and further to 47.87 per cent in 2001 (Table 3.2). The male literacy in Hyderabad-Karnataka region has moved forward by 15.22 percentage points from 1981-1991 (i.e. from 32.26 per cent to 47.48 per cent) and 13.31 percentage points from 1991-2001 (i.e. from 47.48 per cent to 60.79 per cent). Among females it has gone up by 9.64 percentage points during 1981-1991 (i.e. from 9.38 per cent to 19.02 per cent) and 15.62 percentage points during 1991-2001 (i.e. from 19.02 per cent to 34.64 per cent). Further, Table 3.2 presents the district-wise literacy rates of Hyderabad-Karnataka region. The highest literacy rate of male was reported in Bidar district (69.95 per cent) followed by Raichur/Koppal district (56.87 per cent) and Gulbarga district (55.55 per cent) during 2001. Further, among the females, the highest literacy rate was recorded in Bidar district (44.88 per cent) followed by Gulbarga district (29.67 per cent) and Raichur/Koppal district (29.38 per cent) during the same period. Though literacy rate for female has increased, the gender-difference is substantial in Raichur/Koppal district (27.49 per cent) and Bidar district (25.07 per cent). Lower literacy rates in rural areas are primarily due to the more conservative nature of Hyderabad-Karnataka region. The low female literacy rates here bring down the total literacy rate of the region. Lower male literacy in the villages are primarily due to the physical nature of work of agricultural labour and migration of literate men to towns/cities.

Urban Areas: The increase in Urban literacy rate in Hyderabad-Karnataka region observed during 1981-1991 and 1991-2001 in respect of persons, males, as well as females (Table 3.3). The literacy rate which was recorded 44.82 per cent in 1981 increased to 64.87 per cent in 1991, further to 72.06 per cent in 2001. Literacy rate for males was 56.39 per cent during 1981, which increased to 75.70 per cent during 1991 and to80.88 per cent during 2001. Among females, literacy rate was 32.45 per cent in 1981, which forwarded to 53.14 per cent in 1991 and to 62.65 per cent in

Table 3.3
Literacy rate in Hyderabad – Karnataka region (Urban Areas)

District	1981				1991				2001			
	P	M	F	G.D.	P	M	F	G.D.	P	M	F	G.D.
Bidar	48.52	60.09	35.92	24.17	68.03	78.76	55.91	22.85	76.18	84.23	67.42	16.81
Gulbarga	45.30	57.17	32.63	24.54	70.20	79.82	59.93	19.89	71.28	80.22	61.70	18.52
Raichur/Koppal	40.64	51.92	28.80	23.12	56.38	68.53	43.59	24.94	68.71	79.19	58.84	19.35
H-K. Region	44.82	56.39	56.39	23.94	64.87	75.70	53.14	22.56	72.06	80.88	62.65	18.23
Karnataka State	56.44	64.69	64.69	17.17	74.20	82.04	65.74	16.30	81.05	86.85	74.87	11.98

Source: Census of India.
Note: P=Person, M=Male, F=Female and G.D. = Gender Difference.

2001. The gap in male-female literacy rates of 23.94 per cent in 2001. Bidar district continues to occupy the top both in male literacy with 84.23 per cent and female literacy with 67.42 per cent followed by Gulbarga district (80.22 per cent for male and 61.70 per cent for female) and Raichur/Koppal district (78.19 per cent for male and 58.84 per cent for female) during 2001. Even in urban areas, the highest gap in male-female literacy rates has been observed for Raichur/Koppal district (19.35 per cent), Gulbarga district (18.52 per cent) and Bidar district (16.81 per cent) during 2001.

SECTION - II

In this section, efforts are made to provide a comparative panorama of the working-population in the Hyderabad-Karnataka region and three Census, those of 1981, 1991 and 2001 are used. For portraying the changing profile of occupations, we present the district-wise share of main-workers, marginal workers, cultivators, agricultural labourers, household industry workers and other workers, literacy level of workers, workers in organized sector in Hyderabad-Karnataka region.

According to the census definition, a person is categorized as a worker when he or she has participated in any economically productive activity at any time during one year preceding the date of enumeration. Similarly, a person who has worked for six months or more during the last one years preceding the date of enumeration is termed as a main worker and a person who has worked for less than six months (including even for a single day) is termed as a marginal worker. According to the census definition, all that is necessary is that a person must have done some work and his or her status either as a main worker or as a marginal worker depends upon the total length of time he spent in doing the work or several items of works during the reference period. Koppal district is formed from Raichur district in 1997 and therefore the data for Raichur and Koppal districts merged and used in the analysis.

WORK PARTICIPATION RATE

Total: There has been a decrease in the percentage of male workers in the male population and an increase in the percentage of female workers in the female population in Hyderabad-Karnataka region.

Table 3.4 presents the Work Participation Rates (WPRs) in Hyderabad-Karnataka region and shown decreasing trend from 43.17 per cent in 1981 to 42.56 per cent in 1991 further to 41.90 per cent in 2001. Work participation rates of total workers in Hyderabad-Karnataka region which has shown a slight decrease for male workers from 55.17 per cent to 51.23 per cent between 1981-1991 and further slightly to 50.76 per cent in 2001. Female work participation rates indicates a clear increase in both the decades; i.e., from 30.92 per cent in 1981 to 33.53 per cent in 1991 and to 37.70 per cent in 2001. This region-level trend is manifested at the district-level too. All districts have experienced a decline in the case of male workers in the Hyderabad-Karnataka region between 1981-2001; i.e., from 53.28 per cent in 1981 to 47.60 per cent in 2001 in case of Bidar district, from 55.36 per cent in 1981 to 51.20 per cent in 2001 in case of Gulbarga district and from 56.88 per cent in 1981 to 53.50 per cent in case of Raichur/Koppal district (since Koppal district is formed in 1997, the information is clubbed with Raichur for all censuses). Similarly, all districts have registered an increase in the female workers' percentage between 1981-1991, further increased except Bidar district during 1991 to 2001. During 2001, female work participation rates in Raichur/Koppal district have highest percentage (35.50) followed by Gulbarga district (34.60) and Bidar district (30.50) in Hyderabad-Karnataka region.

Rural Areas: In rural areas of Hyderabad-Karnataka region the work participation rate has declined from 47.14 per cent in 1981 to 46.40 per cent in 1991, further to 45.83 per cent in 2001 (Table 3.5). As per 2001 census, the proportion of workers to total population or work participation rate was marginally lower in Hyderabad-Karnataka region (45.83 per cent) as compared to that in Karnataka state (49.20 per cent) as a whole. Further, the work participation rate in rural areas of Hyderabad-Karnataka region was much higher among male than female. However, male work participation rate has decreased from 56.51 per cent in 1981 to 52.53 per cent in 2001, whereas the female work participation rate has increased from 37.64 per cent in 1981 to 39.03 per cent in 2001. The work participation by districts reveal that Raichur/Koppal district has registered the highest male work participation rate of 54.60 per cent, while Bidar district has the lowest male work participation rate of 49.10 per cent in 2001. In the case of female

Table 3.4
Work Participation Rate in Hyderabad-Karnataka region (Total= Rural+Urban).

(In percent)

Districts	1981				1991				2001			
	Person	Male	Female	Gender Difference	Person	Male	Female	Gender Difference	Person	Male	Female	Gender Difference
Bidar	40.39	53.28	27.06	26.22	39.90	48.80	30.50	18.30	37.20	47.60	26.30	21.30
Gulbarga	45.25	55.36	34.96	20.40	43.10	51.20	34.60	16.60	43.20	51.20	34.90	16.30
Raichur/Koppal	43.89	56.88	30.75	26.13	44.70	53.70	35.50	18.20	45.30	53.50	36.90	16.60
H-K Region	43.17	55.17	30.92	24.25	42.56	51.23	33.53	17.70	41.90	50.76	37.70	13.06
State	40.24	54.59	25.33	29.26	42.00	54.10	29.40	24.70	44.60	56.90	31.90	25.00

Source: Census of India.

Table 3.5
Work Participation Rate in Hyderabad-Karnataka region (Rural Areas)

(In percent)

Districts	1981				1991				2001			
	Person	Male	Female	Gender Difference	Person	Male	Female	Gender Difference	Person	Male	Female	Gender Difference
Bidar	43.43	55.67	39.90	15.77	43.30	50.70	35.60	15.10	40.40	49.10	31.40	17.70
Gulbarga	50.11	58.62	41.57	17.05	47.90	53.80	41.90	11.90	48.40	53.90	42.90	11.00
Raichur/Koppal	47.89	55.25	40.44	14.81	48.00	55.20	40.60	14.60	48.70	54.60	42.80	11.80
H-K Region	47.14	56.51	37.64	18.87	46.40	53.23	39.37	13.86	45.83	52.53	39.03	13.50
State	46.24	55.91	36.33	19.58	46.40	56.00	36.60	19.40	49.20	58.30	39.90	18.40

Source: Census of India.

work participation rate, Gulbarga occupies the first place with 42.90 per cent, while Bidar district the last place with 31.40 per cent in 2001.

Urban Areas: Table 3.6 which gives the district-wise work participation rate in urban areas of Hyderabad-Karnataka region for 1981, 1991 and 2001 censuses, one may observe considerable changes in the trend of work participation rates among districts.

As can be seen from Table 3.6 the work participation rate in urban areas of Hyderabad-Karnataka region has declined from 34.02 per cent in 1981 to 28.27 per cent in 1991, however, increased marginally to 29.40 per cent in 2001. Raichur/Koppal district with 32.50 per cent work participation rate in 2001 census tops the region followed by Gulbarga district (29.20 per cent) and Bidar district (26.50 per cent).

The male work participation rate in Hyderabad-Karnataka region as a whole has come down from 49.13 per cent in 1981 to 44.20 per cent in 1991, however increased marginally to 45.63 per cent in 2001. Raichur/Koppal district has registered the highest in the Hyderabad-Karnataka region i.e. 49.90 per cent followed by Gulbarga district (44.40 per cent) and Bidar district (42.60 per cent) during 2001.

Further, the Table 3.6 reveals that the female work participation rate in the urban areas of Hyderabad-Karnataka region has decreased from 18.10 per cent in 1981 to 11.13 per cent in 1991, further increased to 12.13 per cent in 2001. However, a wide variations in the female work participation rate is seen among the districts in Hyderabad-Karnataka region. Raichur/Koppala with a work participation rate of 14.40 per cent tops the list followed by Gulbarga (13.00 per cent) and Bidar (9.00 per cent) in 2001.

MAIN WORKERS

Total: The proportion of total main workers of Hyderabad-Karnataka region to the population was 39.53 per cent in 1981 which declined to 31.57 per cent in 2001 (Table 3.7). As per the census 2001, the proportion of main workers was highest in Raichur/Koppal (34.10 per cent) and Gulbarga (32.40 per cent), whereas it is the lowest in Bidar district (28.20 per cent).

The proportion of main workers among males and females was 44.37 per cent and 18.300 per cent in 2001 respectively in the

Table 3.6
Work Participation Rate in Hyderabad-Karnataka region (Urban Areas)

(In percent)

Districts	1981				1991				2001			
	Person	Male	Female	Gender Difference	Person	Male	Female	Gender Difference	Person	Male	Female	Gender Difference
Bidar	40.39	53.28	27.06	26.22	25.70	41.30	8.50	32.80	26.50	42.60	9.00	33.60
Gulbarga	28.86	44.71	11.91	32.80	27.30	43.00	10.40	32.60	29.20	44.40	13.00	31.40
Raichur/Koppal	32.80	49.41	15.34	34.07	31.80	48.30	14.50	33.80	32.50	49.90	14.40	35.55
H-K Region	34.02	49.13	18.10	31.03	28.27	44.20	11.13	33.07	29.40	45.63	12.13	33.50
State	30.81	48.40	11.83	36.57	32.00	49.80	12.90	36.90	35.70	54.10	16.10	38.00

Source: Census of India.

Table 3.7
Main Workers in Hyderabad-Karnataka region (Total= Rural+Urban).

(In percent)

Districts	1981				1991				2001			
	Person	Male	Female	Gender Difference	Person	Male	Female	Gender Difference	Person	Male	Female	Gender Difference
Bidar	37.15	52.65	21.15	31.50	37.21	48.47	25.40	23.07	28.20	41.10	14.70	26.40
Gulbarga	40.34	54.49	25.94	28.55	40.24	50.87	29.20	21.67	32.40	45.00	19.30	25.70
Raichur/Koppal	41.09	56.27	25.72	30.55	42.01	53.37	30.41	22.96	34.10	47.00	20.90	26.10
H-K Region	39.53	54.47	24.27	30.20	39.82	50.90	28.34	22.56	31.57	44.37	18.30	26.06
State	36.82	53.75	19.23	34.52	38.48	53.34	23.03	30.31	36.70	51.90	20.90	31.00

Source: Census of India.

Hyderabad-Karnataka region showing wide gap in employment among males and females (gender-gap was 26.07 per cent). However, the number of women joining the labour force as main workers has declined during 1981-2001.

The proportion of males as the main workers in Hyderabad-Karnataka region has declined from 54.47 per cent in 1981 to 44.37 per cent in 2001, and also proportion of female main workers has decreased from 24.27 per cent to 18.30 per cent during the same period. The proportion of main workers among males was higher in Raichur district (47.00 per cent) and lower in Bidar district (41.10 per cent) in 2001. Similarly, the proportion of main workers among females was higher in Raichur/Koppal district (20.90 per cent) and lower in Bidar district (14.70 per cent) during the same period. The gender difference was the highest in Bidar/Koppal district (26.40 per cent) followed by Raichur/Koppal district (26.10 per cent) and Gulbarga district (25.70 per cent) in 2001.

Rural Areas: Table 3.8 shows an increase in the percentage of main workers from 42.36 per cent in 1981 to 43.13 per cent in 1991, however, declined substantially to 33.33 per cent in 2001 in Hyderabad-Karnataka region. From Table 3.8 it can be seen that during the period 1981-2001, the percentage of main workers of male in the total rural population decreased, whereas there is increase in female main workers between 1981-1991, decreased between 1991-2001. In the case of male main workers' proportion shows that there is decline in their share from 56.96 per cent in 1981 to 52.98 per cent in 1991, further decreased substantially to 45.23 per cent in 2001. Whereas, in case of female main workers, proportion of their share increased from 27.61 per cent in 1981 to 33.08 per cent in 1991, however, declined substantially to 21.17 per cent in 2001. This simply indicates that between the 1991-2001 period, the scope of employment for a major part of a year, i.e., 183 days or more, becomes limited to the rural people in Hyderabad-Karnataka region.

Further, the male-female main workers in all districts of Hyderabad-Karnataka region registered a negative rate of growth during 1991-2001. In Bidar district, the decline of male main workers is more prominent, i.e. from 55.01 per cent to 50.50 per cent between 1981-1991, further, declined to 41.90 per cent during 2001. Again in case of Gulbarga district, the share of main workers for male declined from 57.48 per cent during 1981 to 53.50 per

Table 3.8
Main Worker in Hyderabad-Karnataka region (Rural Areas)

(In percent)

Districts	1981				1991				2001			
	Person	Male	Female	Gender Difference	Person	Male	Female	Gender Difference	Person	Male	Female	Gender Difference
Bidar	39.65	55.01	23.96	31.05	40.00	50.50	29.20	21.30	29.80	41.90	17.20	24.70
Gulbarga	43.93	57.48	30.33	27.15	44.40	53.50	35.10	18.40	34.90	46.70	23.00	23.70
Raichur/Koppal	43.49	58.40	28.53	29.87	45.00	54.95	34.95	20.00	35.30	47.10	23.30	23.80
H-K Region	42.36	56.96	27.61	29.36	43.13	52.98	33.08	19.90	33.30	45.23	21.17	24.06
State	39.63	56.28	22.61	33.67	41.60	55.30	27.40	27.90	38.70	52.23	24.70	27.53

Source: Census of India.

Table 3.9
Main Workers in Hyderabad-Karnataka region (Urban Areas).

(In percent)

Districts	1981				1991				2001			
	Person	Male	Female	Gender Difference	Person	Male	Female	Gender Difference	Person	Male	Female	Gender Difference
Bidar	25.69	42.14	7.74	34.40	25.40	41.20	7.80	33.40	22.90	38.20	6.30	31.90
Gulbarga	28.16	44.63	10.23	34.40	26.60	42.90	9.60	33.30	25.50	40.60	9.30	31.30
Raichur/Koppal	31.40	50.42	13.68	36.74	31.35	48.15	13.75	34.40	29.40	46.47	11.30	35.40
H-K Region	28.42	45.73	10.55	35.18	27.88	44.08	10.38	33.70	25.93	41.83	8.97	32.87
State	29.90	47.71	10.68	37.303	31.40	49.50	12.00	37.50	32.90	51.1	13.50	37.60

Source: Census of India

cent during 1991, further declined to 46.70 per cent during 2001. As the size of female main workers a district-level in Hyderabad-Karnaaka region is concerned, Raichur/Koppal district (23.30 per cent) ranks first followed by the Gulbarga district (23.00 per cent) and Bidar district (17.20 per cent) in 2001. This shows that the ratio of female main workers to male main workers is still lowest in rural areas of Hyderabad-Karnataka region.

Urban Areas: The proportion of main workers in urban areas of Hyderabad-Karnataka region to the population was 28.42 per cent in 1981 which declined to 27.88 per cent and 25.93 per cent in 1991 and 2001, respectively. As per the census 2001, the proportion of main workers was the highest in Raichur/Koppal district (29.40 per cent) followed by the Gulbarga district (25.50 per cent) and Bidar district (22.90 per cent) within the region (Table 3.9). The proportion of main workers among males and females was 41.83 per cent and 8.97 per cent in 2001 respectively in the Hyderabad-Karnataka region showing wide gap in employment among male and females (gender-gap was 32.87 per cent).

Further, the proportion of males as the main workers in Hyderabad-Karnataka region has declined from 45.73 per cent in 1981 to 41.83 per cent in 2001, whereas the proportion of female main workers has increased from 7.67 per cent in 1981 to 10.38 per cent in 1991, however, declined marginally to 8.97 per cent in 2001. The proportion of main workers among males was higher in Raichur district (46.70 per cent) and lower in Bidar district (38.20 per cent) in 2001. As against this, the proportion of main workers among females was higher in Raichur/Koppal district (11.30 per cent) and lower in Bidar district (6.30 per cent) during the same period. The gender difference was higher in Raichur/Koppal district (35.40 per cent) and lower in Gulbarga district (31.30 per cent) in 2001.

MARGINAL WORKERS

Total: The data based on 2001 census shows a noticeable increase in the number of total marginal workers in Hyderabab-Karnataka region. As presented in Table 3.10, the percentage of marginal workers in Hyderabad-Karnataka region has declined from 3.78 in 1981 to 2.65 in 1991, however, increased substantially to 14.40 in 2001. Of this male marginal workers who accounted for 0.52 per cent in 1981 declined to 0.16 per cent in 1991, whereas it increased to 10.33 per cent in 2001. Further, female marginal workers share also declined from 7.11 per cent in 1981 to 5.10 per cent in 1991, however increased marginally to 6.40 per cent in 2001.

From Table 3.10, it can be seen that the percentage of marginal workers have increased in all the districts of Hyderabad-Karnataka region during the period 1991-2001. Bidar, Gulbarga and Raichur/ Koppal districts have recorded the highest increase in percentage points of total marginal workers. In case of Bidar, the increase was by 8.95 percentage points (i.e. from 2.65 per cent to 11.60 per cent), for Gulbarga the increase was by 12.71 percentage points (i.e. from 2.89 per cent to 15.60 per cent), and for Raichur/Koppal by 13.60 percentage points (i.e. from 2.40 per cent to 16.00 per cent) between 1991 to 2001. During the period 1981-1991, in all the districts of Hyderabad-Karnataka region, the proportion of marginal workers decreases. Female registered significant share of marginal workers to total population than male workers during 1981 (i.e. 6.80 per cent female and 0.45 per cent male in Bidar district, 9.20 per cent female and 0.79 per cent male in Gulbarga district and 5.34 per cent female and 0.33 per cent male in Raichur/ Koppal) district. However, if we consider the data of 2001, the share of male marginal workers is significantly increased to 9.00 per cent, 10.80 per cent and 11.20 per cent in Bidar, Gulbarga and Raichur/Koppal districts respectively. As against this female share as marginal workers decreased to 6.50 per cent in Bidar district, 6.20 per cent in Gulbarga district, whereas increased to 6.50 per cent in Raichur/Koppal district. The increase in male marginal workers indicates casualisation of the labour force as there is no employment of a stable nature for the major part of the year in the Hyderabad-Karnataka region.

Rural Areas: The share of marginal workers in Hyderabad-Karnataka region as shown in Table 3.11 constitute 4.53 per cent during 1981, which declined to 3.25 per cent during 1991 (declined by 1.28 percentage points between 1981-1991), however increased substantially to 17.87 per cent during 2001 (increased by 14.62 percentage points between 1991-2001). The increase in share of marginal workers in Karnataka state as a whole was less than Hyderabad-Karnataka region between 1991-2001. The share of male marginal workers was 0.59 per cent in 1981, which declined to 0.32 per cent in 1991, whereas it increased to 12.50 per cent in

Table 3.10

Marginal Workers in Hyderabad-Karnataka region (Total= Rural+Urban).

(In percent)

Districts	1981				1991				2001			
	Person	Male	Female	Gender Difference	Person	Male	Female	Gender Difference	Person	Male	Female	Gender Difference
Bidar	3.58	0.45	6.80	-.6.35	2.65	0.23	5.18	-4.95	11.60	9.00	6.50	2.50
Gulbarga	4.95	0.79	9.20	-8.41	2.89	0.37	5.51	-5.14	15.60	10.80	6.20	4.60
Raichur/Koppal	2.82	0.33	5.34	-5.01	2.40	0.25	4.61	-4.36	16.00	11.20	6.50	4.70
H-K Region	3.78	0.52	7.11	-6.59	2.65	0.16	5.1	-4.94	14.40	10.33	6.40	3.93
State	3.48	0.69	6.38	-5.69	3.35	0.57	6.24	-5.67	11.00	7.90	5.00	2.90

Source: Census of India.

Table 3.11

Marginal Worker in Hyderabad-Karnataka region (Rural Areas).

(In percent)

Districts	1981				1991				2001			
	Person	Male	Female	Gender Difference	Person	Male	Female	Gender Difference	Person	Male	Female	Gender Difference
Bidar	4.19	0.50	7.95	-7.45	3.19	0.27	6.21	-5.94	14.20	10.60	7.20	3.40
Gulbarga	6.16	0.94	11.41	-10.47	3,63	0.43	6.91	-6.48	19.90	13.50	7.20	6.30
Raichur/Koppal	3.25	0.34	6.18	-5.84	2.92	0.27	5.59	-5.32	19.50	13.40	7.50	5.90
H-K Region	4.53	0.59	8.36	-7.77	3.25	0.32	6.24	-5.92	17.87	12.50	7.30	5.20
State	4.54	0.77	8.39	-7.62	4.61	0.71	8.62	-7.91	15.20	10.50	6.00	4.50

Source: Census of India.

2001. Among the female marginal workers, the share was 8.36 per cent in 1981, which declined to 6.24 per cent in 1991, however, increased marginally to 7.30 per cent in 2001. The district-wise data of Hyderabad-Karnataka region for marginal workers for the period 1981-2001 are presented in Table 3.11 Marginal workers can undertake different works during their engagement in productive activity. The report on distribution of workers in the 2001 census shows a noticeable increase in the number of marginal workers in rural areas and also in the percentage of marginal workers to the total population. This may be due to the introduction of new technology in agriculture sector in recent period.

From Table 3.11, it can be seen that percentage of marginal workers has increased in all the districts of Hyderabad-Karnataka region during the period 1991-2001. Bidar, Gulbarga and Raichur/ Koppal districts have recorded the highest increase in percentage points of rural marginal workers. In case of Bidar, the increase was by 11.01 percentage points (i.e. from 3.19 per cent to 14.20 per cent), for Gulbarga the increase was by 16.27 percentage points (i.e. from 3.63 per cent to 19.90 per cent) and for Raichur by 16.58 percentage points (i.e. from 2.92 per cent to 19.50 per cent) between 1991 to 2001. During the period 1981-1991, in all districts of Hyderabad-Karnataka region, the proportion of marginal workers decreases. Female registered significant share of marginal workers to total rural population than male workers during 1981 and 1991. However, if we consider the data of 2001, the share of male marginal workers was significantly increased to 10.60 per cent, 13.50 per cent and 13.40 per cent in Bidar, Gulbarga and Raichur/ Koppal districts respectively. And also, the share of female marginal workers was increased from 6.21 per cent to 7.20 per cent in Bidar district, from 6.91 per cent to 7.20 per cent in Gulbarga district and from 5.59 per cent to 7.50 per cent in Raichur/Koppal district between 1991 to 2001.

Urban Areas: Unlike main workers the proportion of marginal workers of urban areas in Hyderabad-Karnataka region has shown a remarkable increase in 2001 census as compared to the 1991 census (Table 3.12). Marginal workers constitute 6.90 per cent of the urban population in the Hyderabad-Karnataka Region in 2001 as against 0.88 per cent in 1981 and 0.45 per cent in 1991. There is considerable variation in the proportion of marginal workers

Table 3.12
Marginal Worker in Hyderabad-Karnataka region (Urban Areas)

(In percent)

Districts	1981			1991				2001			
	Person	Male	Female	Gender Difference	Person	Male	Female	Gender Difference	Person	Male	Female	Gender Difference
Bidar	0.76	0.23	1.33	-1.10	0.40	0.08	0.74	-0.66	7.10	4.40	2.70	1.70
Gulbarga	0.88	0.30	1.50	-1.20	0.48	0.18	0.80	-0.62	7.50	3.80	3.70	0.10
Raichur/Koppal	0.99	0.28	1.73	-1.45	0.47	0.15	0.80	-0.65	6.10	3.10	3.00	0.10
H-K Region	0.88	0.27	1.52	-1.25	0.45	0.14	0.78	-0.64	6.90	3.77	3.13	0.64
State	0.89	0.52	1.29	-0.77	0.52	0.26	0.79	-0.53	5.60	3.00	2.60	0.40

Source: Census of India.

among the districts in Hyderabad-Karnataka region. It is highest in Gulbarga district with 7.50 per cent followed by Bidar district (7.10 per cent) and Raichur/Koppal district (6.10 per cent) during 2001.

The proportion of male marginal workers in the Hyderabad-Karnataka region has significantly increased from 0.14 per cent in 1991 to 3.77 per cent in 2001. In 1991, there was a fall in male marginal workers to 0.14 per cent from 0.27 in 1981. The highest proportion of male marginal workers among the districts of the region was recorded 4.40 per cent in Bidar district followed by 3.80 per cent in Gulbarga district and 3.10 per cent in Raichur/Koppal district during 2001.

The proportion of marginal workers was considerably lower among the females as compared to the males. The proportion of female marginal workers has declined from 1.52 per cent in 1981 to 0.78 per cent in 1991, however increased substantially to 3.13 per cent in Hyderabad-Karnataka region during 2001. Among the districts, Gulbarga with 3.70 per cent stands first amongst the districts of the region followed by Raichur/Koppal (3.0 per cent) and Bidar (2.70 per cent) in 2001.

SECTORWISE DISTRIBUTION OF WORKERS

The occupation categories considered for the present analysis are cultivators, agricultural labourers, household industry and the rest of categories/workers classified as 'other workers'.

(a) Cultivators

Total: The corresponding data for cultivators in Hyderabad-Karnataka region has declined from 33.56 per cent in 1981 to 31.15 per cent in 1991, further to 27.60 per cent in 2001 (Table 3.13). The proportion of male cultivators in the Hyderabad-Karnataka region declined from 40.65 per cent in 1981 to 37.81 per cent in 1991, further declined to 33.7 per cent in 2001. This may be because of cropping pattern practiced in Region which is female labour intensive. The share of female workers as cultivators moved up from 16.91 per cent in 1981 to 20.87 per cent in 1991, however it has come down to 17.47 per cent in 2001. Further, the decline in the proportion can be seen in all the districts within the region as well as in the State. Among the districts in Hyderabad-Karnataka region, Raichur/Koppal district stood first and constitutes 29.60

Table 3.13
Sector-wise Main Workers in Hyderabad - Karnataka region (Total Rural+ Urban)

(In percent)

Category	Bidar			Gulbarga			Raichur/Koppal			H. K. Region			State		
	1981	1991	2001	1981	1991	2001	1981	1991	2001	1981	1991	2001	1981	1991	2001
(a) Cultivators															
Persons	32.84	29.66	25.8	32.12	30.66	27.40	35.73	33.14	29.60	33.56	31.15	27.60	38.25	34.36	29.50
Male	39.09	34.28	27.9	38.63	37.56	34.90	44.22	41.58	38.30	40.65	37.81	33.7	42.83	37.82	32.20
Female	16.04	26.43	19.9	18.08	18.17	15.90	16.60	18.02	16.60	16.91	20.87	17.47	24.75	26.01	24.60
G. Difference	23.03	7.85	8.00	20.55	19.39	19.00	27.62	23.56	21.70	23.74	16.94	16.23	18.08	11.81	7.60
(b) Agri. Labourers															
Persons	42.18	45.43	37.40	38.91	44.11	39.90	43.12	45.13	43.50	41.40	44.89	40.27	26.78	28.75	26.40
Male	30.42	32.82	26.00	26.54	29.51	23.40	29.96	29.47	27.30	28.97	30.6	25.57	19.01	20.32	17.00
Female	73.88	70.65	59.30	65.61	70.53	65.20	72.77	73.19	67.60	70.75	71.46	64.03	49.72	49.06	43.80
G. Difference	-43.46	-37.83	-33.30	-39.07	-41.02	-41.80	-42.81	-43.72	-40.30	-41.78	-40.86	-38.47	-30.71	-28.74	-26.80
(c) House-hold Workers															
Persons	2.78	2.11	2.40	3.27	2.32	2.40	2.73	2.42	2.60	2.93	2.28	2.47	4.1	2.81	4.00
Male	2.75	2.13	2.10	3.1	2.45	2.20	2.88	2.65	2.60	2.91	2.41	2.30	3.28	2.73	2.50
Female	2.86	2.06	2.80	3.64	2.1	2.80	2.40	2.00	2.60	2.97	2.05	2.73	6.51	3.01	6.60
G. Difference	-0.11	0.07	-0.70	-0.54	0.35	-0.60	0.48	0.65	0.00	-0.06	0.36	-0.43	-3.23	-0.28	-4.10
(d) Other Workers															
Persons	22.20	22.8	35.10	25.7	22.91	30.30	18.42	19.31	24.20	22.11	21.67	29.87	30.87	34.08	40.10
Male	27.76	30.7	44.00	31.73	30.48	39.50	22.94	26.30	31.70	27.48	29.18	38.40	34.88	39.13	48.30
Female	7.22	6.86	18.00	12.67	9.2	16.10	8.23	6.79	13.10	9.37	7.62	15.73	19.02	21.92	25.00
G. Difference	20.54	23.91	26.00	19.06	21.28	23.40	14.71	19.51	18.60	18.11	21.56	22.67	15.86	17.21	23.30

Source: Census of India.

per cent followed by Gulbarga district (27.40 per cent) and Bidar district (25.80 per cent) during 2001. The share of male and female cultivators varied from district to district within the Region. For instance, male cultivators constitutes 38.3 per cent in Raichur/ Koppal district, 34.9 per cent in Gulbarga district and 27.90 per cent in Bidar district during 2001. Similar varied trend in the proportion of female cultivators can be seen in all districts of Hyderabad-Karnatka region; i.e. 19.90 per cent in Bidar district, 16.60 per cent in Raichur/Koppal district and 15.90 per cent in Gulbarga district during the same period.

Rural Areas: In Hyderabad-Karnataka region, the shares of cultivators decreased i.e. from 37.68 per cent to 40.03 per cent over the period 1981-2001 (Table 3.14). Among males, the share decreased from 46.95 per cent to 40.03 per cent during the same period. However, the share of female cultivators increased from 17.90 per cent during 1981 to 19.53 per cent during 1991, but declined to 18.53 per cent during 2001. Results shows that, in Hyderabad-Karnataka region the share of cultivators is lower than those in Karnataka state average. Here also, in Karnataka there was a decrease from 47.81 to 39.10 per cent persons, from 55.32 to 45.90 per cent among males during 1981-2001. Different trend was found in case of females in State, i.e. increased from 28.36 to 30.04 per cent between 1981-1991, decreased slightly to 29.00 per cent between 1991-2001. Further, from Table 3.14 it can be seen that the share of cultivators in three districts of Hyderabad-Karnataka region, further declined in two districts during 1991-2001; the decline was from 36.31 per cent in 1981 to 33.12 per cent in 1991 and to 29.30 per cent in 2001 in the case of Bidar district; the share declined from 39.96 per cent in 1981 to 37.42 per cent in 1991 and to 31.3 per cent in 2001 in the case of Raichur/Koppal district. Whereas, in the case of Gulbarga district, the share declined from 36.78 per cent in 1981 to 30.66 per cent in 1991, however, increased marginally to 32.50 per cent in 2001. The male cultivators share declined from 44.23 per cent in 1981 to 34.30 per cent in 2001 and 50.74 per cent in 1981 to 41.4 per cent in 2001 in Bidar, Raichur/ Koppal districts, respectively. Whereas, in the case of Gulbarga district, the male cultivators share has declined from 45.89 per cent in 1981 to 37.56 per cent in 1991, however, increased marginally to 44.40 per cent in 2001. Further, it can be seen that all district of Hyderabad-Karnataka region presented the decreasing

Table 3.14
Sector Wise Main-Workers in H.K. region (Rural Areas)

(In percent)

Category	Bidar			Gulbarga			Raichur/Koppal			H. K. Region			State		
	1981	1991	2001	1981	1991	2001	1981	1991	2001	1981	1991	2001	1981	1991	2001
(a) Cultivators															
Persons	36.31	33.12	29.30	36.78	30.66	32.50	39.96	37.42	31.30	37.68	33.73	31.03	47.81	43.99	39.10
Male	44.23	39.77	34.30	45.89	37.56	44.40	50.74	48.93	41.40	46.95	42.09	40.03	53.32	50.83	45.90
Female	16.84	21.41	21.30	19.29	18.17	17.20	17.57	19.02	17.10	17.90	19.53	18.53	28.36	30.04	29.00
G. Difference	27.39	18.36	13.00	26.60	19.39	27.20	29.91	33.17	24.30	29.05	22.56	21.50	24.96	20.79	16.90
(b) Agri. Labourers															
Persons	46.39	50.53	43.40	43.95	44.11	47.00	47.02	49.42	45.30	45.79	48.02	45.02	32.37	35.71	34.40
Male	34.16	37.80	31.60	30.92	29.51	29.20	33.36	33.12	29.00	32.81	33.48	29.93	23.62	26.22	23.70
Female	76.45	72.95	62.70	68.99	70.53	69.00	75.41	75.44	61.50	73.62	72.97	64.40	55.04	55.09	50.40
G. Difference	-42.29	-35.15	-31.10	-38.07	-41.02	-39.80	-42.05	-42.32	-32.50	-40.81	-39.49	-34.47	-31.42	-28.87	-26.70
(c) House-hold Workers															
Persons	2.22	1.85	2.20	2.66	2.06	2.00	2.47	2.22	2.50	2.45	2.04	2.23	3.53	2.35	3.40
Male	2.40	2.05	2.10	2.83	2.37	2.20	2.63	2.55	2.50	2.62	2.32	2.27	2.83	2.48	2.30
Female	1.78	1.51	2.40	2.33	1.59	1.90	2.14	1.71	2.40	2.08	1.60	2.23	5.32	2.09	5.00
G. Difference	0.62	0.54	-0.30	0.50	0.78	0.30	0.49	0.84	0.10	0.54	0.72	0.04	-2.49	0.39	-2.70
(d) Other Workers															
Persons	15.08	14.50	25.10	16.61	12.60	18.50	10.55	10.94	20.80	14.08	12.68	21.47	16.29	17.95	23.10
Male	19.21	20.38	32.00	20.36	17.16	24.20	13.27	15.40	27.00	17.61	17.65	27.73	18.23	20.47	28.10
Female	4.93	4.13	13.60	9.39	5.46	11.00	4.88	3.83	11.90	6.40	4.47	12.17	11.28	12.78	15.60
G. Difference	14.28	16.25	18.40	10.97	11.7	13.20	8.39	11.57	15.10	11.21	13.17	15.56	6.95	7.69	12.50

Source: Census of India.

trend for female cultivators during 1991-2001 from 21.41 per cent to 21.30 per cent, 18.17 per cent to 17.20 per cent and 19.02 per cent to 17.10 per cent in Bidar, Gulbarga and Raichur/Koppal districts, respectively. Still the share of cultivators, especially male cultivators, remained the main occupation of rural areas in Hyderabad-Karnataka region.

Urban Areas: The composition of workers among the districts of the Hyderabad-Karnataka region reveals a quite different picture from the one observed in rural areas (Table 3.15). The proportion of cultivators is quite low compared to rural areas. The proportion of cultivators has declined from 9.12 per cent in 1981 to 7.51 per cent in 1991 further to 4.87 per cent in 2001 in Hyderabad-Karnataka region. Further, it may be observed from the Table 3.15 that the proportion of cultivators in all districts of the Hyderabad-Karnataka region was less than 8 per cent during 2001. The highest proportion was recorded in Raichur/Koppal district (6.40 per cent) followed by Gulbarga district (4.60 per cent) and Bidar district (3.60 per cent) during the same period.

The proportion of urban male workers engaged as cultivators is quite low in all the districts of the Hyderabad-Karnataka region and even so it has declined from 9.77 per cent in 1981 to 7.86 per cent in 1991, further to 5.07 per cent in 2001. Further, data reveals that the proportion of cultivators among districts varies from 6.80 per cent in Raichur/Koppal to 4.70 per cent in Gulbarga and 3.10 per cent in Bidar during 2001.

Like in case of urban male workers, the proportion of cultivators among the urban female workers constitutes a small proportion and declined from 6.48 per cent in 1991 to 3.97 per cent in 2001. The proportion varies from 4.90 per cent in Raichur/Koppal district to 3.90 per cent in Gulbarga district and 3.10 per cent in Bidar district during 2001.

(b) Agricultural Labourers

Total: In the Hyderabad-Karnataka region, the percentage of agricultural labourers among males and females there is trend showing a declining from 1991 onwards. In case of Karnataka State as whole, the share of agricultural labourers in respect to persons, males and females decreasing from 1991 onwards (Table 3.13).

In the case of agricultural labourers in Hyderabad-Karnataka region, their proportion has gone up from 41.40 per cent in 1981 to 44.89 per cent in 1991, whereas it has declined to 40.27 per cent in 2001. The proportion of male agricultural labourers in Hyderabad-Karnataka region has increased marginally from 28.97 per cent in 1981 to 30.6 per cent in 1991 and declined to 25.57 per cent in 2001. Among the female agricultural labourers in Hyderabad-Karnataka region, their share was increased marginally from 70.75 per cent in 1981 to 71.46 per cent in 1991, whereas, it has declined to 64.03 per cent in 2001. Thus, the proportion of agricultural labourers was higher among female than among male in Hyderabad-Karnataka region.

Further, in Table 3.13 shows that the proportion of female agricultural labourers was higher in all districts of Hyderabad-Karnataka region; i.e. 67.70 per cent in Raichur/Koppal district, 65.20 per cent in Gulbarga district and 59.30 per cent in Bidar district during 2001. Among the male in Hyderabad-Karnataka region, the highest proportion of agricultural labourers was in Raichur/Koppla district (27.30 per cent) followed by Bidar district (26.00 per cent) and Gulbarga district (23.40 per cent) in 2001. Thus, it is to be noted that all districts in Hyderabad-Karnataka region have the proportion of female agricultural labourers higher than the State proportion. The higher participation in agricultural labour may be attributed to the poverty and illiteracy among the people, especially women.

Rural Areas: Generally, the shares of agricultural labourers in rural areas are higher in Hyderabad-Karnataka region than those in Karnataka state as a whole (Table 3.14). Further, the shares of agricultural labourers were higher than those of cultivators among females both in Hyderabad-Karnataka region during the period under study. Table 3.14 presents that the share of agricultural labourers in rural areas of Hyderabad-Karnataka region was 45.79 per cent in 1981, which increased to 48.02 per cent in 1991, however, it declined to 45.23 per cent in 2001. The share of male agricultural labourers in Hyderabad-Karnataka region has increased marginally from 32.81 per cent in 1981 to 33.48 per cent in 1991, however, declined to 29.93 per cent in 2001. Unlike male agricultural labourers, female show a decreasing trend in respect of agricultural labourers in Hyderabad-Karnataka region during the period under the study. For instance, the share of female agricultural labourers has declined from 73.62 per cent in 1981 to 72.97 per cent in 1991, further to 64.4 per cent in 2001. Among the districts in Hyderabad-Karnataka region, Gulbarga district accounts for the highest share of 47.00 per cent followed by 45.30 per cent in Raichur/Koppal district and 43.40 per cent in Bidar district during 2001. Among the male agricultural labourers the share of Bidar district was highest (31.60 per cent) followed by Gulbarga district (29.20 per cent) and Raichur/Koppal district (29.00 per cent) during the same period. The share of female agricultural labourers ranges from 69.00 per cent in Gulbarga district to 62.70 per cent in Bidar district and 61.50 per cent in Raichur/Koppal district during 2001.

Urban Areas: The proportion of agricultural labourers too in the urban areas of Hyderabad-Karnataka region has declined from 15.18 per cent in 1981 to 14.92 per cent in 1991, further to 9.43 per cent in 2001 (Table 3.15). The district which has recorded highest per cent of agricultural labour in urban areas was Raichur/Koppal (12.90 per cent) followed by Gulbarga (8.50 per cent) and Bidar (6.90 per cent) during 2001.

Like in case of urban male cultivators, the proportion of agricultural labourers in Hyderabad-Karnataka region also registered a decline from 9.98 per cent in 1981 to 9.83 per cent in 1991, further to 5.57 per cent in 2001. The highest proportion of 7.40 per cent in Raichur/Koppal district recorded highest followed by Bidar district (4.70 per cent) and Gulbarga district (4.60 per cent) during 2001.

As in case of rural areas, the proportion of agricultural labourers is higher among urban female workers as compared to males. However, there is sharp fall in the proportion of female urban agricultural labourers in Hyderabad-Karnataka region from 39.02 per cent in 1981 to 38.08 per cent in 1991 (0.94 percentage points), further to 24.67 per cent in 2001 (13.41 percentage points). The proportion of workers varies between 32.70 per cent in Raichur/Koppal district to 22.60 per cent in Gulbarga district and 18.70 per cent in Bidar district according to 2001 census.

(c) Household Industry Workers

For assessing the comparative scenerio of the three censuses (1981, 1991 and 2001), we consider rural household industry in this section. The census defines household industry as an industry conducted by one or more members of the household at home or within the village in rural areas or only within the precincts of the

Table 3.15
Sector Wise Main - Workers in H.K. region (Urban Areas)

(In percent)

Category	Bidar			Gulbarga			Raichur/Koppal			H. K. Region			State		
	1981	1991	2001	1981	1991	2001	1981	1991	2001	1981	1991	2001	1981	1991	2001
(a) Cultivators															
Persons	8.32	6.94	3.60	7.44	6.27	4.60	11.60	9.33	6.40	9.12	7.51	4.87	7.18	5.86	3.51
Male	8.98	7.40	3.70	7.77	6.45	4.70	12.55	9.72	6.80	9.77	7.86	5.07	7.54	6.02	3.93
Female	4.29	4.22	3.10	5.93	5.41	3.90	7.97	9.82	4.90	6.06	6.48	3.97	5.43	5.21	1.98
G. Difference	4.69	3.18	0.60	1.84	1.04	0.80	4.58	-0.10	1.90	3.71	1.38	1.10	2.11	0.81	1.95
(b) Agri. Labourers															
Persons	12.47	11.89	6.90	12.17	11.56	8.50	20.89	21.3	12.90	15.18	14.92	9.43	8.6	8.16	3.53
Male	8.63	8.41	4.70	7.92	7.43	4.60	13.39	13.66	7.40	9.98	9.83	5.57	6.02	5.87	2.56
Female	36.18	32.62	18.70	31.52	31.45	22.60	49.36	50.18	32.70	39.02	38.08	24.67	21.25	17.99	6.89
G. Difference	-27.55	-24.21	-14.00	-23.60	-24.02	-18.00	-35.97	-36.52	-25.30	29.04	28.25	19.10	-15.23	-12.12	-4.33
(c) House-hold Workers															
Persons	6.69	3.78	3.00	6.53	3.70	4.10	4.23	3.49	4.20	5.82	3.66	3.77	5.96	N.A.	4.38
Male	4.74	2.54	2.10	4.27	2.76	2.30	4.08	3.10	3.10	4.36	2.80	2.50	4.55	N.A.	1.75
Female	18.67	11.17	7.60	16.85	8.24	10.90	4.78	4.94	7.90	13.43	8.12	8.80	12.91	N.A.	11.49
G. Difference	-13.93	-8.63	-5.50	-12.58	-5.48	-8.60	-0.70	-1.84	-4.80	-9.07	-5.32	-6.30	-8.36	N.A.	-9.74
(d) Other Workers															
Persons	75.52	77.39	86.50	73.86	78.47	82.80	63.28	65.88	76.50	70.89	73.91	81.93	78.26	71.96	63.59
Male	77.65	81.65	89.50	80.04	83.36	88.40	69.98	73.52	82.60	75.89	79.51	86.83	81.89	N.A.	66.74
Female	40.86	51.99	70.60	45.70	54.9	62.60	37.89	37.06	54.40	41.48	47.98	62.53	60.41	N.A.	54.64
G. Difference	36.79	2.66	18.90	34.34	28.46	25.80	32.09	36.46	28.20	34.41	31.53	24.30	21.48	N.A.	12.10

Source: Census of India.   *N.A.* = Not Available.

house in the urban areas. The main characteristic of a household industry is that the larger population of the workers employed in such an industry should consist of members of the household. Therefore, these industries should not be of the scale of registered factories.

Total: Turning towards Household Industry (HHI) workers, their shares are the lowest, occupying 2 to 3 per cent among persons, males and females, taking all-districts of Hyderabad-Karnataka region into account. Generally the shares are lower in Hyderabad-Karnataka region than Karnataka state as a whole (Table 3.13).

There has been a general decrease in the percentage of household industry workers in the total number of workers between 1981-1991, whereas increase between 1991-2001 at the State level and regional level. It has decreased from 2.93 per cent in 1981 to 2.28 per cent in 1991, whereas increased marginally to 2.47 per cent in 2001 in Hyderabad-Karnataka region. There was continuous decrease in male household industry workers from 2.91 per cent in 1981 to 2.41 per cent in 1991, further to 2.30 per cent in 2001 in the Region. Further, Table 3.13 shows that there was fall in female household industry workers from 2.97 per cent in 1981 to 2.05 per cent in 1991, however, there was increase in female household industry workers to 2.73 per cent in 2001. This increase in household industry workers between 1991-2001, especially female workers, may suggest some sort of revival of household manufacturing in Hyderabad-Karnataka region. While, no district has recorded a increase in the male and female percentage, a increase in the female percentage was noticed in Bidar (from 2.06 per cent to 2.80 per cent) and Raichur (from 2.00 per cent to 2.60 per cent) between 1991-2001.

Rural Areas: In the case of household industry in Hyderabad-Karnataka region, their proportion has gone down from 2.45 per cent in 1981 to 2.04 per cent in 1991, whereas it has gone up marginally to 2.23 per cent in 2001. Further, from Table 3.14, it can be seen that, the share of household industry workers in Hyderabad-Karnataka region declined between 1981-1991 from 2.62 per cent to 2.32 per cent and from 2.08 per cent to 1.60 per cent among male and female, respectively. During 1991-2001, there was marginal decline in the case of male from 2.31 to 2.27 per cent, whereas there was increase in the case of female workers from 1.60 per cent to 2.23 per cent during the same period.

The district-wise distribution of data in Hyderabad-Karnataka region shows that the percentage of Household Industry Workers improved marginally from 2.47 to 2.50 in Raichur/Koppal district during 1981-2001, whereas declined marginally from 2.22 per cent to 2.20 per cent in Bidar district and 2.66 per cent to 2.00 per cent in Gulbarga district during the same period. The highest percentage of male household industry workers was in Raichur/Koppal district (2.50 per cent) followed by Gulbarga district (2.2 per cent) and Bidar district (2.10 per cent) during 2001. The female household industry workers were higher in Raichur/Koppal district (2.40 per cent) and Bidar district (2.40 per cent) followed by Gulbarga district (1.90 per cent) during 2001. The marginal spurt in household industry may be attributed to various self-employment programmes sponsored by the central and state government in the Region. In addition, the Government of Karnataka lays special emphasis on the growth of cottage and small-scale industries because of its greater employment potential. However, all the districts in Hyderabad-Karnataka region have a very low share of house-hold industry workers in the total working population.

Urban Areas: The proportion of workers engaged in household industry in urban areas of Hyderabad-Karnataka region has declined from 5.82 per cent in 1981 to 3.66 per cent in 1991, however, increased marginally to 3.77 per cent in 2001. Raichur/Koppal district with 4.20 per cent has the highest proportion of household workers in the Region followed by Gulbarga district with 4.10 per cent and Bidar district with 3.00 per cent in 2001 (Table 3.15).

The proportion of male household workers in urban areas of Hyderabad-Karnataka region has declined from 4.36 per cent in 1981 to 2.80 per cent in 1991, further to 2.50 per cent in 2001. The highest proportion of urban male workers in household industry is recorded in Raichur/Koppal district with 3.10 per cent followed by Gulbarga district (2.30 per cent) and Bidar district (2.10 per cent) during 2001.

The proportion of female urban workers in the category of household industry has gone down from 13.43 per cent in 1981 to 8.12 per cent in 1991, however, it has gone up marginally to 8.80 per cent in 2001. The highest share of female urban workers in this category recorded in Gulbarga district with 10.90 per cent followed by Raichur/Koppal district (7.90 per cent) and Bidar district (7.60 per cent) in 2001.

(d) Other Workers

According to the definition given in the 2001 census, all workers, i.e. those who have been engaged in some economic activity during the last one year preceding the date of enumeration, but are not cultivators, agricultural labourers or workers; for example, factory workers, plantation workers, employees of government and semi-government organizations, persons engaged in professions like doctor, etc., come under the category of 'other workers'.

Total: Data on 'other workers' in Hyderabad-Karnataka region presented in Table 3.13 shown that there was decline in proportion from 22.67 per cent in 1981 to 21.67 per cent in 1991, however increased substantially, to 29.87 per cent in 2001. Among the male 'other workers', there is continuous rise in proportion from 27.48 per cent in 1981 to 29.18 per cent in 1991, further substantially to 38.40 per cent in 2001. The proportion of female 'other workers' has gone down from 9.37 per cent in 1981 to 7.67 per cent in 1991, however it rose to 15.73 per cent in 2001. These figures clearly bring out the fact that the proportion of 'other workers' in total number of workers shown substantial increase between 1991-2001 both for males and females in Hyderabad-Karnataka region. Further, it is pointed out that what is observed at the Region-level is also visible at the district level. The proportion of 'other workers' is highest in case of Bidar district (35.10 per cent) followed by Gulbarga district (30.30 per cent) and Raichur/Koppal district (24.20 per cent) during 2001. Of this, the proportion of male 'other workers' is highest in Bidar district (44.00 per cent) followed by Gulbarga district (39.50 per cent) and Raichur/Koppal district (31.70 per cent) during the same period. The proportion of female 'other workers' in 2001 constitutes 18.00 per cent, 16.10 per cent and 13.10 per cent in Bidar, Gulbarga and Raichur/Koppal districts, respectively.

Rural Areas: Overall there has been a significant increase in the share of 'other workers' to the total working population during the period 1991-2001 (i.e., from 12.68 per cent to 21.47 per cent) in Hyderabad-Karnataka region (Table 3.14). The district-wise scenario in terms of the share of other workers in the total working population is presented in Table 3.14. The share of 'other workers' in the total working population of Hyderabad-Karnataka region increased from 17.65 per cent to 27.73 per cent (by 10.08 percentage points) in the case of male and from 4.47 per cent to 12.17 per cent (by 7.70 percentage points) in the case of female between 1991-2001. The district-wise distribution of 'other workers' shows that the share of male 'other workers' is highest in Bidar district (i.e., 32.0 per cent) and lowest in Gulbarga district (i.e. 24.20 per cent) during 2001. In case of female workers, the share of Bidar district (i.e., 13.60 per cent) is highest followed by the Raichur/Koppal district (11.90 per cent) and Gulbarga district (11.00 per cent) during the same period. This indicates that the scope of employment in the service sector expanded in recent years in rural areas of Hyderabad-Karnataka region.

Urban Areas: The residuary category of 'other workers' in urban areas of Hyderabad Karnataka region has increased from 70.89 per cent in 1981 to 73.91 per cent in 1991 and further to 81.93 per cent in 2001. Bidar district stands first with 86.50 per cent followed by Gulbarga district (82.80 per cent) and Raichur/Koppala district (76.50 per cent) during 2001 (Table 3.15).

As we can see in the Table 3.15, the male 'other workers' in Hyderabad-Karnataka region has increased from 75.89 per cent in 1981 to 79.51 per cent in 1991 and further to 86.83 per cent in 2001. The proportion of male 'other workers' constitutes 89.5 per cent in Bidar district followed by Gulbarga district (88.40 per cent) and Raichur/Koppal district (82.60 per cent) in 2001.

As in the case of males, other workers constitute a major portion of total urban female workers in Hyderabad-Karnataka region which increased from 41.48 per cent in 1981 to 47.98 per cent in 1991 and to 62.53 per cent in 2001. The highest proportion of 70.60 per cent of the workers is recorded in Bidar district followed by Gulbarga (62.60 per cent) and Raichur/Koppal (54.40 per cent) in 2001.

WOMEN IN THE ORGANISED SECTOR

The organized sector in India comprises of all public sector establishments, i.e., all services under the central, state and local government and occupations in public undertakings in the field of industry, credit financing, public utilities etc. and non-agricultural private sector establishments which employ 10 or more persons.

While the size of the organized sector has been growing steadily over the last few decades, the proportion of women employed in organize sector in Hyderabad-Karnataka region formed 18.07 per cent in 1996, being 18.93 per cent in public sector and 15.37 per cent in private sector during the same period (Table 3.16). The share of female employment in organized sector in 2000 constitutes 20.17 per cent (increased by only 2.10 percentage points); of this 22.08 per cent in public sector and 16.26 per cent in private sector. The district-wise distribution of data shows that female share in organized sector was highest in Gulbarga district (21.91 per cent) followed by the Bidar district (20.41 per cent) and Raichur/Koppal district (20.00 per cent) during 2000. Women employed in public and private sector accounts 22.30 per cent and 14.50 per cent in Bidar district, 22.64 per cent and 18.88 per cent in Gulbarga district, 21.30 per cent and 15.40 per cent in Raichur/ Koppal district, respectively. This while the public sector offer more employment to women as compared to the private sector. Secondly, over the five years period, women's employment in public sector (increased by 3.15 per cent) has been rising faster than the private sector (increased by 0.89 per cent). Thirdly, as public sector employment of women is growing at a much faster rate than the same for the private sector relative importance of the two sectors in share of women's employment is undergoing radical change.

Table 3.16
Employment in Organized Sector of Hyderabad-Karnataka region

(In percent)

Districts	1996									2000								
	Total Organized Sector			Public Sector			Private Sector			Total Organized Sector			Public Sector			Private Sector		
	M	F	G.D.	M	F	G.D.	M	F	G.D.	M	F	G.D.	M	F	G.D.	M	F	G.D.
Bidar	81.92	18.08	63.84	80.40	19.60	60.80	86.65	13.35	73.30	79.59	20.41	59.18	77.70	22.30	55.4	85.50	14.50	71.00
Gulbarga	82.50	17.50	65.00	81.30	18.70	62.60	86.74	13.26	73.48	78.09	21.91	56.18	77.36	22.64	54.72	81.12	18.88	62.24
Raichur/ Koppal	81.36	18.64	62.72	81.50	18.50	63.00	80.49	19.51	60.98	80.00	20.00	59.06	78.70	21.30	57.4	84.60	15.40	69.20
H.K. Region	81.93	18.07	63.86	81.07	18.93	62.14	84.63	15.37	69.26	79.23	20.17	58.46	77.92	22.08	55.84	83.74	16.26	67.48

Source: Women in Karnataka A Regional Analysis of Socio-Economic Indicators-2002.
Note: M=Male, F=Female, G.D.=Gender Difference.

4

Profile of the
Hyderabad-Karnataka Region

The analysis of the women education, employment and gender-discrimination in Hyderabad-Karnataka Region of Karnataka' is based on the knowledge of general as well as some socio- and economic features of the region. Their brief socio-economic profile is presented in the foregoing analysis.

When the State reorganization took place on 1st November 1956, many districts were added to Karanataka state from the neighbouring States of Hyderabad, Bombay and Madras. The three districts viz., Bidar, Gulbarga and Raichur belonging to Hyderabad State were added to the Karnataka state. These three districts together are called as the Hyderabad-Karnataka region (Map). These districts were more backward than other districts included from Bombay and Madras States. The fact finding committee also clearly states in its report that this area is very backward in all most all respects. The total area of this region is 35689 sq. kms (Bidar 5448 sq. kms, Gulbarga 16224 sq. kms and Raichur/Koppal 14017 sq. kms.) which together constitutes about 18.61 per cent of total area of the State. On the basis of a set of socio-economic indicators, it indicated that since 1960-61 Bidar, Gulbarga and Raichur/Koppal districts occupied 17th, 19th and 18th positions respectively in the development.

Bidar, Gulbarga and Raichur districts were the most backward in development at the time of integration. Though intensive efforts were made to develop the whole state including these three districts still the disparities in development levels between this region and others could not be narrowed to desired levels with the passage of time. In order to devote special attention and resources to the development and monitoring of the development of this region a separate board was constituted in the year 1986, known as the Hyderabad-Karnataka Development Board. Still there is much to be desired in the development of this region and Raichur district in particular. A profile of the region would give a clear picture of the resources, level of development, capabilities and special problems.

GULBARGA DISTRICT

Gulbarga is not only the headquarters of the district but also of the division and both the district and the division are called by its name. In former days, Gulbarga was known as 'Kalburgi' which means a 'stony land' or 'stone roofing' or 'a heap of stones in Kannada'.

Location: Gulbarga district is situated in the northern part of Karnataka State. Among the three districts of the former Hyderabad state area which, after the re-organisaion of States, formed part of Mysore state, Gulbarga occupies a central place with Bidar to its north and Raichur to its south. It lies between longitude 76°04' and 77°42' and latitude 16°12' and 17°46'.

Rivers: The main rivers of the district are the Krishna and the Bhima and other rivers flowing in the district are the tributaries of the river Bhima. The Bhima itself is a tributary of the Krishna, which runs in the south of the district, forming a natural boundary between Gulbarga and Raichur districts. Therefore, the entire river system in the district is that of the Krishna.

Soil: Overlying the Deccan traps and the Bhima, there are thick spreads of black soil, some of which are as much as 30 feet thick as seen at Akandhalli, Yetnal, Kachapur and Wadi. In the area occupied by granites, the soil varies from loamy to sandy. Frequently, pebbles of chert, limestone, shale and granites are embedded in the soils. The soil in the area between Allapur, Tandur and Kodangal is coarse gravelly with spread of quartz and felspar.

RAICHUR DISTRICT

The district of Raichur has a hoary past. It has had an eventful and rich history beginning from the days of the Mauryan king Ashok. A number of inscriptions, rock edicts and other records, temples, forts and battle-fields bear testimony to this fact. Lying between two important rivers, the Krishna and the Tungabhadra, this potentially rich tract had been a bone of contention between kingdoms. In the recent past, it was a part of the princely State of Hyderabad, and since the 1st November 1956, it is a constituent district of the Mysore state. The name Raichur (Rayachooru in Kannada) is derived from Raichroor or Rachanoor. Racha means Raja (i.e. king) and Ooru means a place or town. This (Racha+Ooru) or Rachanooru (Racha+Oor) means king's place in Kannada language.

Raichur district is located in the North Earstern part of the State. It lies between 15°09' and 16°34' north latitude and 75°46' and 77°35' east latitude and between major rivers viz., the Krishna and Tungabhadra. The general shape of the district is from the north west towards south east. The district is bounded on the North by Gulbarga district on the west by districts of Bijapur and Dharwad, on the east by the district of Mahabubnagar of Andhra Pradesh and Bellary. The two rivers, the Krishna and Tungabhadra form the entire northern and southern boundaries of the district.

Topography: The undulating black cotton soil strips, cut by numerous nalas, characters the region of the Dharwar schists, which is now practically denuded of trees and presents a monotonous landscape, while the gneissic region is generally more or less broken and covered with a thin mantle of red loamy soil. Gneissic hills, wherever occur, form bold relief in the landscape. The sedimentary formations, which cover a small belt of the region adjoining the confluence of the Krishna and the Tungabhadra rivers, occupy more or less flat plateaus.

Rivers: The important rivers of Raichur district are the Krishna and the Tungabhadra, which form the entire northern and southern boundaries of the district, respectively. They have been associated from time immemorial with religious and cultural activities and have several famous shrines on their banks.

Soils: The reddish sandy soil is confined to the zones of the pink gneisses in the neighbourhood of Gangavati, Kushtagi, Mudgal, Jalhalli, Deodurg and Sirvar. The light grey loamy soil is found near Kavital and certain other places. The reddish brown soil is found in the neighbourhood of Chikhesrur and other localities and the major portion of the district comprises black cotton soil.

Climate: The climate of the district is characterized by dryness for the major part of the year and a very hot summer. The low and highly variable rainfall renders the district liable to drought. The year may be divided broadly into four seasons. The hot season begins by about the middle of February and extends to the end of May. The south-west monsoon season is from June to end of September. October and November are the post-monsoon or retreating monsoon months and the period from December to the middle of February is the cold season.

Temperature: December is the coldest month with the mean daily maximum temperature at 29.3°c (84.8°f) and the mean daily minimum at 17.7°c (63.9°f). The nights are generally cool in the season, but day temperatures sometimes reach 35° to 38°C. The period from about the middle of February to May is one of continuous rise in temperature. May is the hottest month, the mean daily maximum temperature being 39.8°C (103.7°F). The heat is oppressive till the onset of the South-west monsoon by about the first week of June. Thereafter, the weather becomes slightly cooler and continues to be so till the end of the South-west monsoon season.

BIDAR DISTRICT

Bidar is the northern-most district of Karnataka. It is at present relatively a small district, being the remainder of a bigger one, parts of which were transferred to the neighbouring States with effect from the 1st of November 1956 when there was a States' reorganization. Upto that date, the district was a part of the erstwhile Hyderabad state.

The Bidar area had a great past. It was the nucleus of some important royal dynasties which held sway in the ancient and medieval period, and witnessed several upheavals. In the 12th century A.D., it was the immediate scene of the rise of the Sharana (Veerashaiva) movement led by Basaveshwara, Allam Prabhu and others, which bought new epoch with far-reaching consequences in social, religious, literary, cultural and economic fields.

Bidar, the headquarter of the district, is an ancient town. There was a legend association of the name 'Bidar' with 'Vidarbha' because of similarity in the names. Now scholars have identified modern Berar (Varhad) with the ancient kingdom of Vidarbha.

The name of the place appears to be derived from 'bidaru' which mean bamboo in English, and the place, which seems to have been noted for its bamboo clusters in the past, became known as 'Bidarooru' and then 'Bidare', 'Bidar'.

Location: The district of Bidar is situated between 17°35' and 18°25' north latitudes and 76°42' and 77°39' east longtitudes and lies in the extreme north of the State. Its maximum length from east to west is 93.4 kilometres and from north-east to south-east 115.2 kilometres.

General Boundaries: The district is bounded on the east by the Nizamabad and Medak districts of the Andhra Pradesh state, on the north and the west by the Nanded and Osmanabad districts of the Maharashtra state and on the south by the Gulbarga district of the Karntaka state.

Rivers: The district falls under two distinct river basins-the Godavari basin covering about 4411 sq. km. (1703 sq. miles) of area, of which the Manjra river basin covers 1989 sq. km. of area and the Karanja river basin 2422 sq.km and the Krishna basin covering about 585 sq. km. of area of which the Mullamari river basin covers 249 sq. km. and the Gandori nala basin 336 sq. km. The main river of the district is the Manjra which is a tributary of the Godavari. The Karanja, which is a tributary of the Manjra, is another important river of the district.

Climate: The climate of this district is characterized by general dryness-throughout the year except during the south-west monsoon season. The summer season is from about the middle of February to about the first week of June. This is followed by the south-west monsoon season which continues till the end of September. The months of October and November constitute the post-monsoon or retreating monsoon season. The cold season is from December to the middle of February.

Temperature: Temperature begins to decrease from about the end of November. December is the coldest month with the mean daily maximum temperature at 27.3°C (81.1°F) and the mean daily minimum at 16.4°C (61.5°F) during the cold season, temperatures may sometimes go down to about 3°C (37.4°F). From about the middle of February, both day and night temperatures begin to increase rapidly. May is the hottest month with the mean daily maximum temperature at 38.8°C (101.8°F) and the mean daily minimum at 25.8° (78.4°F).

ECONOMIC PROFILE

Agriculture

Agriculture in the region largely depends on Rain and weather conditions. The rainfall in this area is scanty and erratic. A large part of the area therefore is officially recognized as drought prone area.

Irrigation

Hyderabad-Karnataka region is situated in the semi-arid area. Therefore, agriculture is heavily dependent on the rain. In the post independence period the State government laid much stress on the development of irrigation facilities in the region. As a result of this numbering minor, medium and major irrigation projects in the Hyderabad-Karnataka region have increased notable are the Tungabadra Irrigation Project, Upper Krishna Irrigation Project and Karanja Irrigation Project. The Table 4.1 gives the idea about the net irrigated area by major, medium and minor irrigation project in Hyderabad-Karnataka region as on 1999-2000.

Table 4.1
Irrigated area in Hyderabad-Karnataka Region: 1999-2000

Districts	Total Irrigated Area (Hectares)-Medium, Minor, Major	Net Area Sown
Bidar	38,041 (10.22)	3,72,345
Gulbarga	1,57,527 (13.67)	11,52,143
Raichur	1,44,629 (28.71)	5,03,664
Koppal	1,06,901 (30.55)	3,49,942
H-K Region	4,47,098 (18.80)	23,78,094
State	25,47,669 (24.83)	1,02,58,605

Source: Karnataka at a Glance, Bureau of Economics and Statistics, Government of Karnataka, Bangalore, 2001-02.
Note: Figures in brackets indicates percentages.

As on 1999-2000, the total area irrigated by major, medium and minor irrigation projects was 4,47,098 hectares, which accounts 18.80 per cent of net area sown in the region. The district-wise analysis shows that Koppal (30.55 per cent) has larger percentage of area irrigated followed by Raichur (28.71 per cent), Gulbarga (13.67 per cent) and Bidar (10.22 per cent). The net area irrigated in Gulbarga and Bidar districts is lower. Thus, revealing that despite of government efforts to develop irrigation facility in the region, very small percentage of agriculture land is supplied with assured water. This may be due to the delay in the implementation of irrigation projects, technical problems and other hurdles. This is one of the key to the socio-economic backwardness of Hyderabad-Karnataka region.

Cropping Pattern

The cropping system is highly localized and considered as the major source of agricultural production in State. Raichur and Koppal along with Bellary district are considered as the Rice Bowl of Karnataka. Raichur and Koppal districts together product 71.9 lakh tonnes (1999-2000) of rice annually. With regard to cotton production and its marketing, Raichur is recognized as a leading district in the country. Raichur produce 35606 bales of cotton (1999-2000). Similarly Gulbarga is counted as a leading district for product of redgram i.e. 1,81,795 tonnes (1999-2000) which contributes nearly 63 per cent of the total production in the State. Bidar district though small in area is famous for sugarcane cultivation and contributes nearly 6 per cent to the total sugar production (21,40,715 tonnes in 1999-2000) in the State (Referred Karnataka at a Glance 2001-02). Among the rainfed crops Jawar, Bajra and other minor millets are the important ones. Jawar is the staple food of the region and it is grown evenly in all the district of the region.

Of late a shift in agricultural production has been observed and now more emphasis is laid on oilseeds production. Groundnut and Sunflower are the two major oilseeds of the region grown in command area where as sesamum and safflower are grown in rainfed area. Minor oilseed crops like castor in Raichur, niger in Bidar and linseed in Gulbarga district are localized and grown in small areas.

The area under horticulture and forest is very less and scatter. However, Banana and Mango are the important fruit crops. Grape cultivation is confined to Koppal taluk of Koppal district, Aland of Gulbarga district and Basavakalyan taluk of Bidar district. The cultivation of vegetables is localized around towns and cities only. Onion is extensively grown in Gulbarga district (Referred Karnataka at a Glance).

Population

The population figures of Hyderabad-Karnataka region shown in the Table 4.2 reveals that in 1991, the total population of the region was 6147852, by 2001 it has increased to 7467940. The district-wise distribution of population shows that Gulbarga is the largest district (41.85%) in the region followed by Raichur (22.07%), Bidar (20.10%) and Koppal (15.98%) during 2001.

Table 4.2
Total Population of Hyderabad-Karnataka Region

District	1991	2001
Bidar	12,55,796 (20.43)	15,01,374 (20.10)
Gulbarga	25,82,169 (42.00)	31,24,858 (41.85)
Raichur	13,51,809 (21.99)	16,48,212 (22.07)
Koppal	9,58,078 (15.58)	11,93,496 (15.98)
H-K Region	61,47,852 (100.00)	74,67,940 (100.00)

Source: Census of India.
Note: Figures in brackets indicates the percentages.

Table 4.3
Density of Population in Hyderabad-Karnataka
Region: 1981-2001

Districts	1981	1991	2001
Bidar	183	230	276
Gulbarga	128	159	193
Raichur	127	165	241
Koppal	-	-	166
H-K Region	135	171	219
State	194	235	275

Source: Census of India, 1981-2001.

Density: The density of population in Hyderabad-Karnataka region in 1991 was 171, by 2001 it increased to 219, which is lower than the State average of 275. The district-wise density of population shows that Bidar district is the most densely (276) populated district followed by Raichur district (241), Gulbarga district (193) and Koppal (166) in the region during 2001 (Table 4.3). This shows that the population in the region is not uniformly distributed.

Sex Ratio: Sex ratio presented in the Table 4.4 for Hyderabad-Karnataka region shows that in 1991 the sex ratio was 968 as against the State average of 960. In 2001 the sex ratio in Hyderabad-Karnataka region remains same i.e., 968 which is higher than the State average of 964.

The district-wise sex ratio in Hyderabad-Karnataka region shows that Koppal district has highest sex ratio of 982 followed by Raichur district(980), Gulbarga district (964) and Bidar district (948) in 2001.

Table 4.4
Sex ratio of Hyderabad-Karnataka Region: 1981-2001

Districts	1981	1991	2001
Bidar	968	952	948
Gulbarga	981	962	964
Raichur	988	978	980
Koppala	989	981	982
H-K Region	981	968	968
State	963	960	964

Source: Census of India, 1981-2001.

HUMAN DEVELOPMENT INDEX

The Human Development Index for the Hyderabad-Karnataka region (Table 4.5) shows that all the districts of Hyderabad-Karnataka region (0.56) have low Human Development Index score when compared to the State average (0.63) in 1998. Further, there is disparity among the districts of Hyderabad-Karnataka region. Bidar and Gulbarga districts with HDI score of 0.57 tops the Table whereas Raichur/Koppal district with the HDI score of 0.54 is the last district in the region.

DEVELOPMENT INDEX

The composite index of development presented for the Hyderabad-Karnataka region for different time points helps to understand the level of backwardness of the region (Table 4.6). All districts of study region have improved upto 1976-77 (76.34), however declined during 1998-99 (69.61). This shows that physical level of development covering various sectors and sub-sectors vary from period to period.

Table 4.5
Human Development Index (HDI) of
Hyderabad-Karnataka Region

Districts	1991	1998
Bidar	0.42	0.57
Gulbarga	0.41	0.57
Raichur/Koppal	0.40	0.54
H-K Region	0.41	0.56
State	0.47	0.63

Source: High Power Committee for Redressal of Regional Imbalance, Government of Karnataka, Bangalore, 2002.

Table 4.6
Composite Index of Development of
Hyderabad-Karnataka Region

Districts	1960-61	1971-72	1976-77	1998-99
Gulbarga	60.10	63.19	66.83	66.44
Bidar	64.28	86.85	85.86	69.22
Raichur/Koppal	63.04	80.53	76.34	73.17
H-K Region	62.47	76.86	76.34	69.61
State	100.00	100.00	100.00	100.00

Source: High Power Committee for Redressal of Regional Imbalance, Government of Karnataka, Bangalore, 2002.

The profile of Hyderabad-Karnataka region gives the ideas that the region is situated in the northern plain of Karnataka state. The climate is mostly semi-arid and the Region is spread between three river basins of South India i.e. Tungabadra, Krishna and Godavari basins. The region has good mineral resource bases. Agriculture is the mainstay of the population. However, due to heavy dependency on rain, sub-division and fragmentation of agricultural land and lack of diversification in the cropping pattern have hampered the agriculture development. Though the region has been endowed with valuable natural resources, such as gold, manganese, iron ore, limestone etc., their exploitation is not upto the mark due to poor industrial base. The infrastructure facility has also not been developed properly. Thus, the region has all the characters of an underdeveloped area.

5

Socio-economic Profile of the Women Respondents in Hyderabad-Karnataka Region

In this chapter data concerning the rural-urban background, education and occupational status, age-structure, caste, marital status, of the women respondents are being analysed. The aim of this exploration is to find out the ascriptive status of the working women in their traditional social structure and also to investigate their mobility towards achieved status on the parameters of education, occupation etc.

In any research analysis, the discussion of the socio-economic background of the respondents is an essential undertaking, because such a discussion provides the study with a proper perspective and brings out the social composition and the economic status of the respondents. In the context of the present study, this discussion about all these is more relevant, as it throws light not only on the social origin of the working women and their socio-economic status in Hyderabad-Karnataka region.

RURAL-URBAN BACKGROUND

Rural-urban differentiation has played a vital role in shaping individual's life chances and life styles. The level and quantum of achievement differ widely on the basis of one's residential background. Early specialization and availability of socio-economic opportunity for upward mobility differ widely in the rural and urban communities. This also results in a differential mobility pattern among rural and urban dwellers. The chances of upward mobility for women is comparatively higher in urban community than in the rural. Because of the socio-cultural constraints in rural areas, the chances of getting education and entering into modern occupations by women are almost negligible. Whereas, urban women enjoy not only a liberal atmosphere but also opportunities and institutions which facilitate their entry into the job market. For present and purposive study 150 women respondents were selected separately from urban and rural areas (Table 5.1) of each district comprising Bidar, Gulbarga, Koppal and Raichur of Hyderabad-Karnataka region.

Table 5.1
**Rural-urban Background of Women Respondents in
Hyderabad-Karnataka Region**

District	Urban	%	Rural	%	Total	%
Bidar	150	50.00	150	50.00	300	100.00
Gulbarga	150	50.00	150	50.00	300	100.00
Raichur	150	50.00	150	50.00	300	100.00
Koppal	150	50.00	150	50.00	300	100.00
H-K Region	600	50.00	600	50.00	1200	100.00

Source: Field study.

AGE STRUCTURE

Age is the key variable in understanding the socio-economic status of an individual. Biologically age signifies the physical and mental maturity of an individual. Age denotes the status of an individual in a group, be that his/her family, kinship or other larger and organized groups of society.

In terms of occupations, age has got some more significant role to play. In most of the occupational activities, a certain preparatory period is required, which is generally the period of childhood and early adulthood. In the modern industrialized society this preparatory period is devoted to education and to the learning of sophisticated skills through specialized training programmes. Thus, till 25 or so, one has to complete educational and professional training programmes, and prepare for entering into the field of employment. This means that he/she has to spend his/her childhood and early adulthood in education or in professional training, after completion of which, he/she becomes

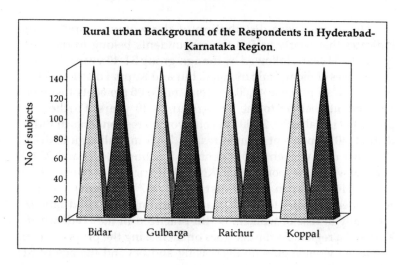

eligible for jobs. As regards women, the requirement of age is same as for men.

Keeping in view the relevance of age the data regarding the age structure of the women in the sample have been discussed (Table 5.2). Nearly 15.25 per cent of the 1200 women respondents of our study area are in the age-group of 11-20 years. Nearly half of the women (i.e. 48.33 per cent) are concentrated in the 21-30 years age-group. 27.58 per cent of the respondents are between 31-40 years age-group. There are relatively fewer women in the 41-50 and 51 and above age-groups (7.50 per cent and 1.33 per cent, respectively).

Table 5.2
Age Structure of Women Respondents in Hyderabad-Karnataka Region (in years)

District	11-20	%	21-30	%	31-40	%	41-50	%	51+	%	Totals
Bidar	83	27.67	122	40.67	72	24.00	16	5.33	7	2.33	300
Gulbarga	36	12.00	143	47.67	91	30.33	28	9.33	2	0.67	300
Raichur	30	10.00	147	49.00	93	31.00	26	8.67	4	1.33	300
Koppal	34	11.33	168	56.00	75	25.00	20	6.67	3	1.00	300
H-K Region	183	15.25	580	48.33	331	27.58	90	7.50	16	1.33	1200

Chi-square=9.9576, <0.05, S
Source: Field study.

The district-wise distribution of the women respondents indicates that nearly half of the respondents belong to the age-group 21-30 years, followed by the age-group 31-40 years. Among the samples of Bidar, Gulbarga, Raichur and Koppal districts, 40.67 per cent, 47.67 per cent, 49.00 per cent and 56.00 per cent of women respondents belong to the age-group 21-30 years. Further, as presented in Table 5.2, 24.00 per cent women respondents in Bidar district, 30.33 per cent women respondents in Gulbarga district, 31.00 per cent women respondents in Raichur district and 25.00 per cent women respondents in Koppal district are between 31-40 years. However, in Bidar district (27.67 per cent) women respondents belong to 11-20 years indicating that child labour, especially in case of women, is still practiced in the Hyderabad-Karnataka region. As the age goes on increasing the proportion of employed women goes on decreasing and beyond the age of 51 years very few women are employed.

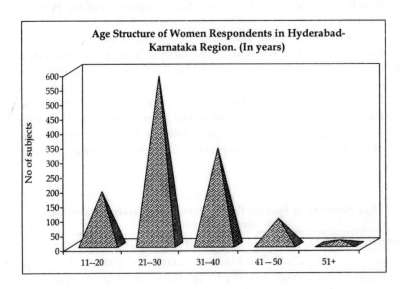

Further, examination of the distribution of data reveals that the mean-age of women respondents in rural areas is 28.89 years and in urban areas is 29.91 years (Table 5.3). Among the district-wise working women in rural areas, mean age in Bidar, Gulbarga, Koppal and Raichur districts are 26.33 years, 28.46 years, 30.89

years and 29.89 years, respectively. The corresponding averages for the ages of the women respondents in urban areas women respondents of Bidar, Gulbarga, Koppal and Raichur districts are 29.29 years, 31.42 years, 27.91 years and 31.03 years, respectively. At each socio-economic level the mean age of rural women respondents is less than urban areas.

Table 5.3
Mean age of women respondents in Hyderabad-Karnataka Region (in years)

District	Rural		Urban		Total		T-value
	Mean	SD	Mean	SD	Mean	SD	
Bidar	26.33	8.75	29.29	9.99	27.81	9.49	-2.7363, $p < 0.01$, S
Gulbraga	28.46	7.61	31.42	8.00	29.94	7.94	-3.2828, $p < 0.01$, S
Koppal	30.89	8.43	27.91	6.75	29.40	7.76	3.3736, $p < 0.01$, S
Raichur	29.89	7.99	31.03	8.03	30.46	8.02	-1.2326, $p > 0.05$, NS
H-K Region	28.89	8.36	29.91	8.37	29.40	8.38	-2.1184, $p < 0.05$, S
	F=8.7128, $p<0.01$, S		F=5.7685, $p<0.01$, S		F= 5.6722, $p<0.01$, S		

Source: Field study.

These results show that the present sample consists of such working women who predominantly belong to the younger age group. This signifies that the entrance of women into the job market and especially into the male-dominated occupational field is comparatively a recent phenomenon in Hyderabad-Karnataka region.

CASTE

One of the important elements of our social structure is caste system. This caste system has not only ordained a differentiated social structure on the basis of ascriptive criterion of birth and ritualistic hierarchy but it has also prescribed a rigidly defined pattern of social interaction, commensality, reciprocity and mutual obligations. This system has also put restrictions on inter-marriage among different castes and the performance of religious sacraments and deeds have been defined in term of caste status.

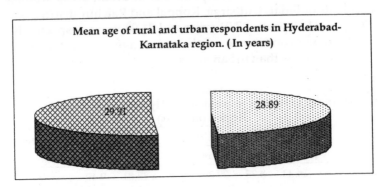

Mean age of rural and urban respondents in Hyderabad-Karnataka region. (In years)

One of the important features of caste system in traditional society has been its close association with occupation. Each caste in traditional society has been assigned with a particular occupation and some time the very name of caste used to suggest its occupation as well. Every new generation followed its traditional caste occupation and there used to be more or less no shift in occupation or in the economic status of the people, even after the change of generations. It is only in recent time that this close proximity between caste and occupation is becoming loose. People, irrespective of caste, are entering into different occupations depending upon their achievement, skill, ability and performance. In contemporary society, there exists a theoretical equality of opportunity, where individuals, irrespective of caste, creed, sex or religion can enter into any occupational field of their choice.

Recent changes in our society with regard to economic and educational opportunities have provided a conducive atmosphere, where women from different stratum of society can achieve higher educational status and can also enter into better occupational fields. In order to understand the socio-economic status of the working women, as also to explore the broader pattern of the mobility and the social change in the contemporary in Hyderabad-Karnataka region, the respondents of the present study have been asked to specify their caste status (Table 5.4). In our sample, 22.50 per cent respondents belong to scheduled caste and tribe (of this 21.00 per cent in Bidar and Gulbarga districts, 20 per cent in Raichur district and 28 per cent in Koppal district), 12.00 per cent women respondents belong to minority (of this 15.00 per cent in Bidar district, 12.00 per cent in Gulbarga district, 10.67 per cent in Raichur district and 10.33 per cent in Koppal district), 27.58 per cent respondents belong to Other Backward Classes (of this 27.33 per cent in Bidar, 27.00 per cent in Gulbarga, 28.33 per cent in Raichur and 27.67 per cent in Koppal), 37.92 per cent respondents of the total women respondents chosen for study belong to the General Merit or Upper Castes such as Brahmins, Lingayats, Vokkaligas, Kshatriyas etc., (of this 36.67 per cent in Bidar district, 40.00 per cent in Gulbarga district, 41 per cent in Raichur district and 34.00 per cent in Koppal district).

Table 5.4
Caste status of Women Respondents in Hyderabad-Karnataka Region

District	SC	%	Mino-rity	%	OBC	%	Upper Caste	%	Total	%
Bidar	63	21.00	45	15.00	82	27.33	110	36.67	300	100.00
Gulbarga	63	21.00	36	12.00	81	27.00	120	40.00	300	100.00
Raichur	60	20.00	32	10.67	85	28.33	123	41.00	300	100.00
Koppal	84	28.00	31	10.33	83	27.67	102	34.00	300	100.00
H-K region	270	22.50	144	12.00	331	27.58	455	37.92	1200	100.00

Chi-square=11.3942, >0.05, NS

Source: Field study.

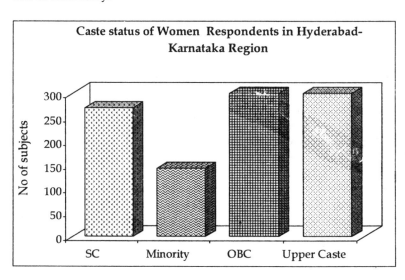

Caste status of Women Respondents in Hyderabad-Karnataka Region

Our data with regard to the caste of respondents suggest some very significant facts. Firstly, that the traditional association of the caste and occupation is no more relevant today. Now women belonging to different castes are successfully entering into different occupations. Secondly, intermediate groups are coming up. Women belonging to Kshatriya, Lingayats, Vokkaliga caste groups in Hyderabad-Karnataka region are increasingly represented in modern occupations. Thirdly, though the traditional hegemony of the upper caste in the field of occupation and education is shattered, yet it has not been vanished. They still constitute a significant portion in the prestigious job situations.

EDUCATIONAL STATUS

Education is one of the major tools which provides individuals the necessary qualifications to fulfill economic roles and consequently improve their socio-economic status. In the case of women education, particularly, higher education, has much importance as it provides them not only requisite equipment and training for their future economic participation, but it also acts as a revolutionary force which is expected to liberate them from their subjugation and exploitation.

As with regard to relevance of female education for women, it may be said that it is the only channel through which women can find their rightful place in the society. Education gives not only a modern outlook and regional perspective but it also liberates individual from insularism and dogmatism. Moreover, education fosters a sense of independence and develops initiative in women, which were hitherto unknown to them in the traditional society. Women's entrance into the job market as well as their participation in the broader socio-cultural and political context of the society have become feasible only because of education.

For the present study, we have chosen only educated female employees those who have education above the 4th standard and involved in one or other economic activities. Examination of the educational status of the respondents in the study area is presented in Table 5.5. The break up of educational levels shows that 28.83 per cent of the respondents had education up to primary level, 22.25 per cent up to secondary level, 12.25 per cent up to PUC (pre-university) level, 12.17 per cent respondents possess under-graduation, 5.50 per cent had post-graduation level and 19.00 per

Table 5.5
Educational Status of Women Respondents in Hyderabad-Karnataka Region

District	Prim	%	Sec	%	PUC	%	UG	%	PG	%	Profe-ssional	%	Total	%
Bidar	84	28.00	71	23.67	42	14.00	47	15.67	18	6.00	38	12.66	300	100.00
Gulbarga	95	31.67	65	21.67	31	10.33	42	14.00	22	7.33	45	15.00	300	100.00
Raichur	76	25.33	65	21.67	31	10.33	34	11.33	19	6.33	75	25.00	300	100.00
Koppal	91	30.33	66	22.00	36	12.00	23	7.67	8	2.67	76	25.33	300	100.00
H-K region	346	28.83	267	22.25	140	11.67	146	12.17	67	5.58	234	19.50	1200	100.00

Chi-square = 79.4707, <0.05, S

Source: Field study.

cent completed professional courses (i.e. TCH, B.Ed, ITI, Polytechnic etc.). But critical examination of the data showed that majority of women those who had education upto primary and secondary level indicating less preference given to female education in Hyderabad-Karnataka region.

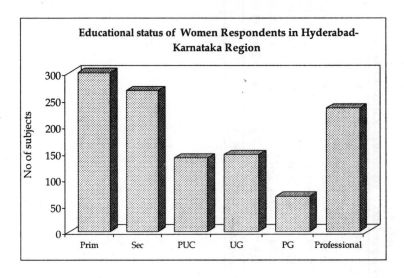

A cross comparison of the data on the basis of districts in Hyderabad-Karnataka region also reveals that the majority of women respondents who were selected for the study did their education upto primary and secondary level. Some were educated upto Post-graduation and 'professional courses'. In this respect, 28.00 per cent women respondents in Bidar district, 31.67 per cent women respondents in Gulbarga district, 25.33 per cent women respondents in Koppal district, 30.33 per cent women respondents in Raichur district had primary education. Further, 23.67 per cent in Bidar district, 21.67 per cent in Gulbarga district, 21.67 per cent in Raichur district and 22.00 per cent in Koppal district did the education upto secondary level. However, it is found that 10.67 per cent in Bidar district, 15.00 per cent in Gulbarga district, 25.00 per cent in Koppal district and 25.33 per cent in Raichur district completed 'professional courses'. This shows that the women prefers to undergo professional courses to join as Teachers in either private or government schools.

OCCUPATIONAL STATUS

In modern urban industrial society, occupation and income are two very important factors in the determination of an individual's status. Not only the nature of occupation and amount of income but even individual's specialization in it are the important contributing factors in deciding his/her socio-economic status. The achieved criteria of education, occupation and income have become important bases of status determination of women in contemporary society. In recent times, not only women's participation in economic life has increased, but women are also entering into such occupational fields, which are hitherto dominated by men, and in these new occupational fields, inspite of hard-competition with the latter, they are successfully attaining high positions.

The exploration into the occupational status of the respondents reveals that 16.42 per cent respondents belong to the agriculture, and 36.83 per cent respondents belong to self-employed category. In the present sample, the second major occupational group is the government employees. There are 31.83 per cent respondents who are in this category. The last occupational group in the present study is related to the private employees who are employed in the various private business agencies or entrepreneurs. There are 14.92 per cent respondents who belong to this category (Table 5.6).

Table 5.6
Occupational Status of Women Respondents in Hyderabad-Karnataka Region

Districts	Agricul-ture	%	Self	%	Pri-vate	%	Govt.	%	Total	%
Bidar	51	17.00	138	46.00	53	17.67	58	19.33	300	100.00
Gulbarga	48	16.00	66	22.00	106	35.33	80	26.67	300	100.00
Raichur	59	19.67	92	30.67	78	26.00	71	23.67	300	100.00
Koppal	78	20.00	107	35.67	52	17.33	63	21.00	300	100.00
H-K region	236	19.67	403	33.58	289	24.08	272	22.67	1200	100.00
Chi-square=67.2758, <0.05, S										

Source: Field study.

The district-wise exploration into the occupational status of the women respondents that 17.00 per cent women respondents in Bidar district, 16.00 per cent women respondents in Gulbarga district, 19.67 per cent women respondents in Raichur district and 26.00 per cent women respondents in Koppal district belong to the agriculture sector. There are 46.00 per cent women respondents in Bidar district, 22.00 per cent women respondents in Gulbarga district, 30.67 per cent women respondents in Raichur district and 35.67 per cent women respondents in Koppal district who are self-employed. Among the women respondents who are working in private/business sector constitute 17.67 per cent women respondents in Bidar district, 35.33 per cent women respondents in Gulbarga district, 26.00 per cent women respondents in Raichur district and 17.33 per cent women respondents in Koppal district. The fourth important occupational group in the present is that of women as Government employees. There are 19.33 per cent women respondents in Bidar district, 26.67 per cent women respondents in Gulbarga district, 23.67 per cent women respondents in Raichur district and 21.00 per cent women respondents who belong to this category.

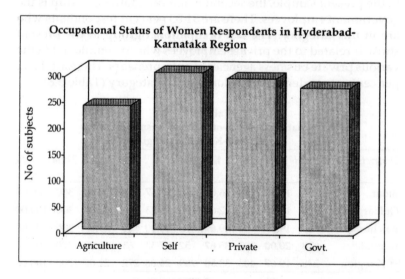

The analysis of data pertaining to the occupational status of the respondents very clearly indicates that women's participation in occupational life is becoming increasingly diversified and they are achieving top positions in male–dominated occupational fields as well. However, their representation in Hyderabad-Karnataka region is still very marginal.

SIZE OF THE FAMILY

Size of the family generally depicts the load and liability on the head of the household, although there could be more than one earner in a household. Here, size of the family stands for the number of persons living together in a household. To have a clear picture of the varying size of the households in the sample, the household are classified into four groups namely, households having 1-2, 3-4, 5-6, and 7+ members (Table 5.7). Majority of the households are found to have 3-4 and 5-6 members (49.67 per cent and 33.33 per cent respectively) in rural areas. Households with 1-2 members constitute 11.00 per cent and 7+ members constitute 6.00 per cent. The size of the household in urban areas of study region upto 2 and 3-4 members constitute 11.00 per cent and 49.17 per cent, respectively. Further, Table 5.7 shows that between 5-6 members and 7+ members constitute 32.00 per cent and 7.83 per cent respectively. The larger size of the family indicate that the rural people generally have larger family members.

It is quite obvious from the district-wise distribution of data for rural areas as 52.67 per cent women respondents in Bidar district, 37.33 per cent in Gulbarga district, 61.33 per cent in Raichur district had an average household size of 3-4 members. Further, the study also shows in case of Urban areas that 46.67 per cent in Bidar district, 41.33 per cent in Gulbarga district, 70.67 per cent in Koppal district and 38.00 per cent in Raichur district the households average size of family was between 3-4 members.

The mean size of the family is 4.29 for the sampled respondents in the rural area and 4.20 for the urban areas, although it varies with district-wise. It is 4.27 for Bidar district, 4.38 for Gulbarga district, 3.83 for Koppal district and 4.66 for Raichur district in rural areas. Further, mean size of the family for urban areas constitute 4.03 in Bidar district, 4.53 in Gulbarga district, 3.94 in Koppal district and 4.29 in Raichur district (Table 5.8). Thus, the larger size of the households in rural areas indicate that the rural people generally prefer larger family members, especially in backward region like Hyderabad-Karnataka region.

Table 5.7
Family Size of Women Respondents in Hyderabad-Karnataka Region

Family size	Bidar		Gulbarga		Koppal		Raichur		H-K Region	
	Rural	Urban	Rural	Urban	Rural	Urban	Rural	Urban	Rural	Urban
Upto 2	21 (14.00)	22 (14.67)	12 (8.00)	18 (12.00)	17 (11.33)	13 (8.67)	16 (10.67)	13 (8.67)	66 (11.00)	66 (11.00)
3-4	79 (52.67)	70 (46.67)	56 (37.33)	62 (41.33)	92 (61.33)	106 (70.67)	71 (47.33)	58 (38.00)	298 (49.67)	295 (49.17)
5-6	38 (25.33)	44 (29.33)	73 (48.67)	56 (37.33)	37 (24.67)	28 (18.67)	52 (34.67)	64 (42.67)	200 (33.33)	192 (32.00)
7+	12 (8.00)	14 (9.33)	9 (6.00)	14 (9.33)	4 (2.67)	3 (2.00)	11 (7.33)	16 (10.67)	36 (6.00)	47 (7.83)
Total	150 (100.00)	150 (100.00)	150 (100.00)	150 (100.00)	150 (100.00)	150 (100.00)	150 (100.00)	150 (100.00)	600 (100.00)	600 (100.00)

Source: Field study.
Note: Figures in brackets denotes percentages.

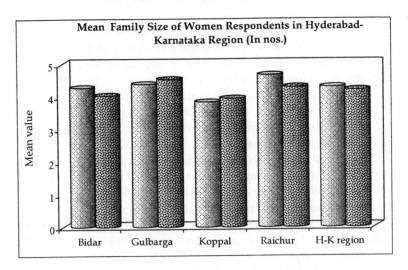

Mean Family Size of Women Respondents in Hyderabad-Karnataka Region (In nos.)

Table 5.8
Mean Family Size of Women Respondents in Hyderabad-Karnataka region (In nos.)

District	Rural		Urban		Total		T-value
	Mean	SD	Mean	SD	Mean	SD	
Bidar	4.27	1.64	4.03	1.71	4.15	1.68	-2.0655, $p < 0.05$, S
Gulbarga	4.38	1.61	4.53	1.38	4.45	1.50	2.6541, $p < 0.01$, S
Koppal	3.83	1.15	3.94	1.23	3.88	1.19	2.3434, $p < 0.01$, S
Raichur	4.66	1.51	4.29	1.44	4.48	1.48	1.6311, $p > 0.05$,NS
H-K region	4.29	1.51	4.20	1.47	4.24	1.49	-0.9874, $p > 0.05$, NS
	F = 5.1561, $p < 0.01$,S		F = 8.1293, $p < 0.01$,S		F = 11.0147, $p < 0.01$,S		-0.9874, $p > 0.05$,NS

Source: Field study.

MARITAL STATUS

Marriage has been one of the important determinants of an individual's status in society. Marriage give social prestige and make them to involve in many conjugal, familial and social roles. In our society marriage is considered as an important sacrament of life and without it, many religious duties and social obligations would not be fulfilled. Unmarried life was almost unthinkable in traditional Indian society. Moreover, many social and religious customs prevailing in traditional society encourage to early marriages. Widespread illiteracy or low literacy level in traditional society encourage to early marriage of girls. All these social taboos and religious sanctions made the position of the women in the traditional society very pathetic.

Table 5.9 shows the distribution of sampled women respondents' marital status. Among the 1200 respondents, a majority of 899 (74.92 per cent) women respondents are married, 301 (25.08 per cent) are unmarried. Married respondents constitute higher percentage in Koppal district (80.00 per cent) followed by Gulbarga district (79.67 per cent), Raichur district (76.00 per cent) and Bidar district (64.00 per cent. Among the unmarried respondents on district –wise, 36.00 per cent are in Bidar district, 24.00 per cent in Raichur district, 20.33 per cent in Gulbarga district and 20.00 per cent in Koppal district.

Table 5.9
Marital Status of Women Respondents in Hyderabad-Karnataka Region

District	Married	%	Unmarried	%	Total
Bidar	192	64.00	108	36.00	300
Gulbarga	239	79.67	61	20.33	300
Raichur	228	76.00	72	24.00	300
Koppal	240	80.00	60	20.00	300
H-K Region	899	74.92	301	25.08	1200
Chi-square = 26.9402, < 0.05, S					

Source: Field study.

AGE AT MARRIAGE

In contemporary society, many changes are taking place in the institution of marriage. One of these relates to the age of marriage. With the expansion of education and entrance of women in the field of employment, the age of marriage is rising. As regards the 461 married women respondents in rural areas of Hyderabad-Karnataka region 5.86 per cent got married between 10-15 years of age, 71.37 per cent between 16-20 years of age, 16.48 per cent between 21-25 years of age, 11.43 per cent between 26-30 years of age and 0.65 per cent above 31 years of age (Table 5. 10). The data clearly shows that the child marriages are still prevalent in the rural areas of Hyderabad-Karnataka region. This practice can be attributed to the extension of rural norms or to the need to protect the chastity of young girls in the rural areas.

Looking at the age of the marriage in the urban areas, it is found that 7.54 per cent of the females got married between 10-15 years of age. Those who married between the age of 16-20 years constitute 40.87 per cent, between the age of 21-25 years constitute 38.58 per cent and those between the age of 26-30 years constitute only 10.73 per cent and 2.28 per cent in the 31 and above years age group.

The data clearly shows that among the women respondents in urban area also child marriage is as prevalent as among the rural women respondents in Hyderabad-Karnataka region. This data further supports that the late marriage in urban areas (for example between 21-25 and 26-30 years age group) is practiced.

According to the district-wise distribution of data for rural areas shows that 61.29 per cent women respondents in Bidar district, 75.21 per cent women respondents in Gulbarga district, 73.39 per cent women respondents in Koppal district and 73.17 per cent women respondents in Raichur district married at the age between 16-20 years. Further, the present study reveals for Urban areas that 54.55 per cent women respondents in Bidar district, 27.12 per cent women respondents in Gulbarga district, 47.41 per cent women respondents in Koppal district and 36.19 per cent women respondents in Raichur district married between the age 16-20 years. The next major share of married women respondents for both rural-urban areas is between age-group of 21-25 years. This shows that the percentage of women respondents age at marriage was highest between 16-20 years and 21-25 years and it decreases with the higher age-groups in all districts of study region.

In Table 5.11, it has been found that mean age at marriage constitutes 19.73 years in rural areas of Hyderabad-Karnataka region (i.e., 19.81 years in Bidar, 19.57 years in Gulbarga, 20.13 years in Koppal and 19.39 years in Raichur district). Whereas, the distribution of data in urban areas reveals that mean age at marriage in Hyderabad-Karnataka region accounts 21.60 years

Table 5.10
Age at Marriage of Women Respondents in Hyderabad-Karnataka Region (In Years)

Age (Years)	Bidar		Gulbarga		Koppal		Raichur		H-K region	
	Rural	Urban	Rural	Urban	Rural	Urban	Rural	Urban	Rural	Urban
10-15	10	13	5	11	4	2	8	7	27	33
	(10.75)	(13.13)	(4.13)	(9.32)	(3.23)	(1.71)	(6.50)	(6.67)	(5.86)	(7.54)
16-20	57	54	91	32	91	55	90	38	329	179
	(61.29)	(54.55)	(75.21)	(27.12)	(73.39)	(47.41)	(73.17)	(36.19)	(71.37)	(40.87)
21-25	19	21	20	55	16	48	21	45	76	169
	(20.43)	(21.21)	(16.53)	(46.61)	(12.90)	(41.38)	(17.07)	(42.86)	(16.48)	(38.58)
26-30	7	6	4	19	11	10	4	12	26	47
	(7.53)	(6.06)	(3.31)	(16.10)	(8.87)	(8.62)	(3.25)	(11.43)	(5.64)	(10.73)
31+	0	5	1	1	2	1	0	3	3	10
	(0.00)	(5.05)	(0.81)	(0.85)	(1.61)	(0.86)	(0.00)	(2.86)	(0.65)	(2.28)
Total	93	99	121	118	124	116	123	105	461	438
	(100.00)	(100.00)	(100.00)	(100.00)	(100.00)	(100.00)	(100.00)	(100.00)	(100.00)	(100.00)

Chi-square = 89.4738, <0.05, S

Source: Field study.
Note: Figures in brackets denotes percentage.

(i.e.,20.96 years in Bidar district, 21.93 years in Gulbarga district, 21.78 years in Koppal district and 21.72 years in Raichur district). Thus, the mean age at marriage is higher in urban areas than rural areas. It seems that employment is playing a significant role in this context.

Table 5.11
Mean Age at Marriage of Women Respondents in Hyderabad-Karnataka region (In years)

District	Rural		Urban		Total		T-value
	Mean age	SD age	Mean age	SD age	Mean age	SD age	
Bidar	19.81	3.737	20.96	6.179	20.4	5.162	-1.5525, $p > 0.05$,NS
Gulbraga	19.57	2.918	21.93	4.373	20.74	3.885	-4.9230, $p < 0.01$, S
Koppal	20.13	3.851	21.78	3.296	20.93	3.681	-3.5663, $p < 0.01$, S
Raichur	19.39	3.064	21.72	4.362	20.46	3.889	-4.7236, $p < 0.01$, S
H-K region	19.73	3.398	21.60	4.605	20.63	4.14	-7.0744, $p < 0.01$, S
	F= 1.0837, $p>0.05$, NS		F=0.9260, $p>0.05$, NS		F= 0.7810, $p>0.05$, NS		

Source: Field study.

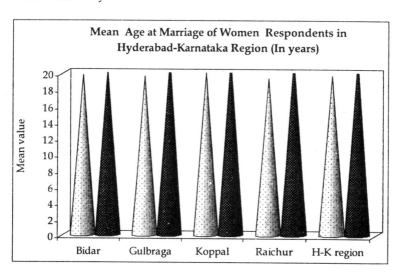

Mean Age at Marriage of Women Respondents in Hyderabad-Karnataka Region (In years)

NUMBER OF CHILDREN

In order to understand the familial responsibilities of the married working women, the respondents have been asked to state the number of their children. It may be noted that working women in both rural and urban areas in the present study conform to this pattern (Table 5.12). Among the working women the mean number of children for the rural respondents is 2.35 (i.e. 2.26 in Bidar, 2.45 in Gulbarga, 2.24 in Koppal and 2.46 in Raichur district). However, mean number of children for urban women respondents is lower than rural women respondents i.e., 2.20 (2.70 in Bidar, 2.05 in Gulbarga, 1.87 in Koppal and 2.19 in Raichur district). The results show that mean number of children is higher in rural areas than urban areas of study region.

Table 5.12
Mean N0umber of Children of Women respondents in Hyderabad-Karnataka Region (In nos.)

District	Rural		Urban		Total		T-value
	Mean	SD	Mean	SD	Mean	SD	
Bidar	2.26	1.17	2.70	1.51	2.4894	1.37	-2.0655, $p < 0.05$, S
Gulbraga	2.45	1.12	2.05	1.00	2.25	1.08	2.6541, $p < 0.01$, S
Koppal	2.24	1.09	1.87	1.14	2.06	1.13	2.3434, $p < 0.01$, S
Raichur	2.46	1.22	2.19	1.04	2.33	1.15	1.6311, $p > 0.05$, NS
H-K region	2.35	1.15	2.20	1.21	2.28	1.18	2.0388, $p < 0.05$, S
	F= 1.0333, $p>0.05$, NS		F=8.0613, $p<0.01$, S		F= 4.2037, $p<0.01$, S		

Source: Field study.

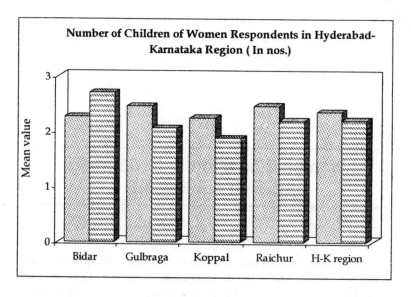

Number of Children of Women Respondents in Hyderabad-Karnataka Region (In nos.)

6

Women Education in Hyderabad Karnataka Region

The hypothesis underlying this section of the study was fairly straight forward: There are discriminations and restrictions with regard to the pattern of education and accessibility. The study attempted to find major biases against women in access to schooling, continuing education opportunities in the Hyderabad-Karnataka region. The study also attempted to explore dimensions like medium of education, educational institutions, girls school and co-education, drop-outs and reasons etc.

MEDIUM OF EDUCATION

Argueably, the central issues in Indian education has been the language of education, in other words, the medium of education. Invariably, the medium of education is determined by the economic and social benefits that are likely to accrue to the learner. Be it basic education or higher education, the medium of education is determined on the basis of a complex mix of factors. What is significant is that in contexts where specialized education is restricted to a small section of the society, the question of medium is sorted out more easily. Once, education is universalized the problem of medium takes on several unpredictable implications. It is quite clear that in a multilingual country like India, education has been delivered through different mediums at different levels for different clientele groups.

English continued to hold sway as an important vehicle for education, administration and inter-state communication. In view of the expanding knowledge and the concept of world as the global village, the hold of the English language on the Indian mind continued to tighten. Economic benefits of education through the medium of English became more and more evident and all parents perceived English-medium education as the only route to success (Daswani C.J., 2001).

The distribution of data about the medium of education of the female respondents in rural areas of Hyderabad-Karnataka region reveals that 90.17 per cent of sample women respondents completed/studied their primary education with Kannada medium (regional language) followed by the 87.63 per cent in secondary level. As against this, in urban areas, 80.67 per cent of female respondents in primary level and 80.71 per cent in secondary level studied with Kannada medium (Table 6.1).

Distribution of data by district about the medium of education reveal that majority of the women respondents in all districts of Hyderabad-Karnataka region (i.e., 88.00 per cent and 78.00 per cent in Bidar district; 88.67 per cent and 79.33 per cent in Gulbarga district; 91.33 per cent and 84.67 per cent in Koppal district; and 92.67 per cent and 80.67 per cent in Raichur district studied their primary education with regional language Kannada in rural and urban areas, respectively. The percentage of the women respondents studied in regional language Kannada in secondary level constitutes 88.46 and 22.32 in Bidar district, 85.37 and 76.42 in Gulbarga district, 84.27 and 82.68 in Koppal district and 91.75 and 77.50 in Raichur district of rural and urban areas, respectively. This shows that the majority of respondents who studied in regional language made them to work in low-end/low-wages jobs in Hyderabad-Karnataka region.

INDEPENDENT/CO-EDUCATION

It is very difficult to assess how female educational opportunity, aside from potential constraints on access, is affected by single-sex as compared with co-educational schooling because of the enormous disparities in the quality of the schools and the social backgrounds of students in them in many educational systems. In principles schooling within a female environment which affords girls appropriate role models, freedom from the social pressures of competing with males, and enables them to assume leadership positions might provide an incentive to excel-academically, to

Table 6.1
Medium of Education of Women Respondents in
Hyderabad-Karnataka Region

EducationLevel	Bidar		Gulbarga		Koppal		Raichur		H-K Region	
	Rural	Urban	Rural	Urban	Rural	Urban	Rural	Urban	Rural	Urban
Primary:										
Kannada	132	117	133	119	137	127	139	121	541	484
	(88.00)	(78.00)	(88.67)	(79.33)	(91.33)	(84.67)	(92.67)	(80.67)	(90.17)	(80.67)
Engligh	18	33	17	31	13	23	11	29	59	116
	(12.00)	(22.00)	(11.33)	(20.67)	(8.67)	(15.33)	(7.33)	(19.33)	(9.83)	(19.33)
Total	150	150	150	150	150	150	150	150	600	600
	(100.00)	(100.00)	(100.00)	(100.00)	(100.00)	(100.00)	(100.00)	(100.00)	(100.00)	(100.00)
Secondary:										
Kannada	92	87	70	94	75	105	89	93	326	389
	(88.46)	(77.68)	(85.37)	(76.42)	(84.27)	(82.68)	(91.75)	(77.50)	(87.63)	(80.71)
English	12	25	12	29	14	22	08	27	46	93
	(11.54)	(22.32)	(14.63)	(23.58)	(15.73)	(17.32)	(8.25)	(22.50)	(12.37)	(19.29)
Total	104	112	82	123	88	127	95	120	372	482
	(100.00)	(100.00)	(100.00)	(100.00)	(100.00)	(100.00)	(100.00)	(100.00)	(100.00)	(100.00)

Source: Field study.
Note: Figures in brackets denotes percentages.

pursue non-traditional academic subjects and to develop more expansive aspirations for higher education and for professional careers.

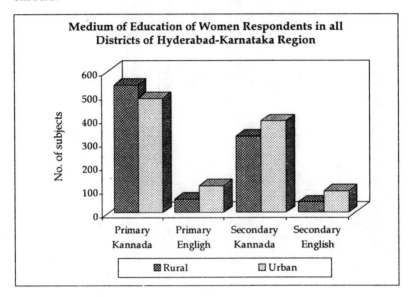

To explore the role of gender-discrimination of female educational history in Hyderabad-Karnataka region, a little further, we asked female respondents to state the type of school/college they studied (Table 6.2). There are 24.33 per cent female respondents studied their primary education in girls independent school and 75.67 per cent studied in co-education schools in rural areas of Hyderabad-Karnataka region. Further, 37.63 per cent female respondents studied secondary education in independent schools and 62.37 per cent in co-education schools.

Whereas, in case of Urban areas of Hyderabad-Karnataka region, 19.50 per cent and 80.50 per cent female respondents in primary education level, 32.78 per cent and 67.01 per cent in secondary level completed in independent and co-education schools, respectively. This shows that in the Hyderabad-Karnataka region, number of independent/separate schools for girls are less.

Cross-tabulation of data on the basis of districts reveals that majority of the women respondents who studied their primary level in co-education, i.e. 76.67 per cent and 73.33 per cent in Bidar

Table 6.2
Type of School in which Women Respondents Studied in Hyderabad-Karnataka Region

EducationLevel	Bidar		Gulbarga		Koppal		Raichur		H-K Region	
	Rural	Urban	Rural	Urban	Rural	Urban	Rural	Urban	Rural	Urban
Primary:										
Independent	35	40	37	35	32	16	42	26	146	117
	(23.33)	(26.67)	(24.67)	(23.33)	(21.33)	(10.67)	(28.00)	(17.33)	(24.33)	(19.50)
Coeducation	115	110	113	115	118	134	108	124	454	483
	(76.67)	(73.33)	(75.33)	(76.67)	(78.67)	(89.33)	(72.00)	(82.67)	(75.67)	(80.50)
Total	150	150	150	150	150	150	150	150	600	600
	(100.00)	(100.00)	(100.00)	(100.00)	(100.00)	(100.00)	(100.00)	(100.00)	(100.00)	(100.00)
Secondary:										
Independent	35	37	32	39	33	36	43	46	140	158
	(33.65)	(33.04)	(39.02)	(31.71)	(33.71)	(28.35)	(44.33)	(38.33)	(37.63)	(32.78)
Coeducation	69	75	50	84	59	91	54	74	232	324
	(66.35)	(66.96)	(60.97)	(68.29)	(66.29)	(71.65)	(55.67)	(61.67)	(62.37)	(67.22)
Total	104	112	82	123	88	127	95	120	372	482
	(100.00)	(100.00)	(100.00)	(100.00)	(100.00)	(100.00)	(100.00)	(100.00)	(100.00)	(100.00)

Source: Field study.
Note: Figures in brackets denotes percentages.

district, 75.33 per cent and 76.67 per cent in Gulbarga district, 78.67 per cent and 89.33 per cent in Koppal district and 72.00 per cent and 82.67 per cent in Raichur district in rural and urban areas respectively. Further, it is found that 66.35 and 66.96 per cent in Bidar district, 60.97 and 68.29 per cent in Gulbarga district, 66.29 and 71.65 per cent in Koppal district, 55.67 and 61.67 per cent in Raichur district studied their secondary level education in co-education schools in rural and urban areas, respectively.

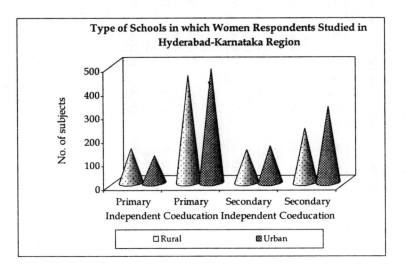

TYPE OF MANAGEMENT

At primary education level, 79.50 per cent female respondents studied in Government schools and 20.50 per cent in private school in rural areas of Hyderabad-Karnataka region. At secondary education level, 66.13 per cent women respondents have studied in Government schools and 33.87 per cent women respondents in private schools (Table 6.3).

Whereas, in urban areas, 72.83 per cent female respondents at primary education level followed by the 63.90 per cent at secondary level have studied in government schools. Further, 27.17 per cent at primary level, 45.64 per cent at secondary level have studied in private schools.

Table 6.3 depicts the district-wise distribution of women respondents education level studied in different managements/

Table 6.3
Type of Management in which Women Respondents Studied in Hyderabad-Karnataka Region

EducationLevel	Bidar		Gulbarga		Koppal		Raichur		H-K Region	
	Rural	Urban	Rural	Urban	Rural	Urban	Rural	Urban	Rural	Urban
Primary:										
Government	133	124	113	95	120	125	111	93	477	437
	(88.67)	(82.67)	(75.33)	(63.33)	(80.00)	(83.33)	(74.00)	(62.00)	(79.50)	(72.83)
Private	17	26	37	55	30	16	39	57	123	163
	(11.33)	(17.33)	(24.67)	(36.67)	(20.00)	(16.67)	(26.00)	(38.00)	(20.50)	(27.17)
Total	150	150	150	150	150	150	150	150	600	600
	(100.00)	(100.00)	(100.00)	(100.00)	(100.00)	(100.00)	(100.00)	(100.00)	(100.00)	(100.00)
Secondary:										
Government	70	73	48	66	60	75	68	74	246	308
	(67.31)	(65.18)	(58.54)	(53.66)	(67.42)	(59.06)	(70.10)	(61.67)	(66.13)	(63.90)
Private	34	39	34	57	29	52	29	46	126	174
	(32.69)	(34.82)	(41.46)	(46.34)	(32.58)	(40.94)	(29.90)	(38.33)	(33.87)	(36.10)
Total	104	112	82	123	88	127	95	120	372	482
	(100.00)	(100.00)	(100.00)	(100.00)	(100.00)	(100.00)	(100.00)	(100.00)	(100.00)	(100.00)

Source: Field study.
Note: Figures in brackets denotes percentages.

schools. As is evident from the Table 6.3 that majority of the women respondents who had their primary and secondary level education from Government schools. For instance, of the total women respondents chosen for the study, 88.67 and 82.67 per cent in Bidar district, 75.33 and 63.33 per cent in Gulbarga district, 80.00 and 83.33 per cent in Koppal district and 74.00 and 62.00 per cent in Raichur district studied in Government schools in rural and urban areas, respectively. Similar trend is found in case of secondary school. For instance, 67.31 and 65.18 per cent in Bidar district, 58.54 and 53.66 per cent in Gulbarga district, 67.42 and 59.06 per cent in Koppal district and 70.10 and 61.67 per cent in Raichur district studied their secondary education in Government schools in rural and urban areas, respectively.

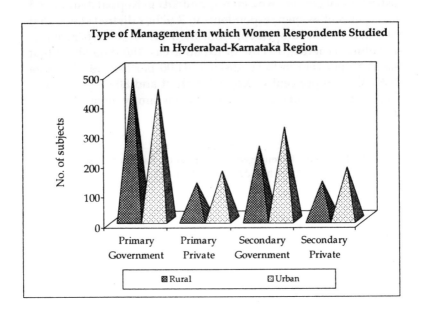

ENCOURAGEMENT FROM FAMILY MEMBERS

While data on the education level, medium and management are important backgrounds of the women respondents, their statements regarding the encouragement or discouragement that they received from their family members offer yet another facet of the home environment. Encouragement or discouragement would, one imagines, have a considerable effect on the students motivation, perseverance and performance.

It is unsatisfactory to note that the overwhelming majority (67.00 per cent) women respondents stated that their family members did not encourage them in their education in rural areas of Hyderabad-Karnataka region (Table 6.4). However, in urban areas, 72.00 per cent of women respondents expressed that they received encouragement from their family members during their education period. District-wise break-down of data shows the similar trend in rural and urban areas of all districts in Hyderabad-Karnataka region. For instance, in case of rural areas it is clear from the Table that 62.00 per cent women respondents in Bidar district, 76.67 per cent women respondents in Gulbarga district, 64.00 per cent women respondents in Koppal district and 65.33 per cent women respondents in Raichur district stated that they had no encouragement from their family members while schooling. Whereas, in case of urban areas, the data show that the 61.33 per cent in Bidar district, 84.00 per cent in Gulbarga district, 62.00 per cent in Koppal district and 80.67 per cent in Raichur district had encouragement from family members while studying.

Table 6.4
Did you have Encouragement from your Family Members while Attending School?

District	Rural			Urban		
	Yes	No	Total	Yes	No	Total
Bidar	57 (38.00)	93 (62.00)	150 (100.00)	92 (61.33)	58 (38.67)	150 (100.00)
Gulbarga	35 (23.33)	115 (76.67)	150 (100.00)	126 (84.00)	24 (16.00)	150 (100.00)
Koppal	54 (36.00)	96 (64.00)	150 (100.00)	93 (62.00)	57 (38.00)	150 (100.00)
Raichur	52 (34.67)	98 (65.33)	150 (100.00)	121 (80.67)	29 (19.33)	150 (100.00)
H-K Region	198 (33.00)	402 (67.00)	150 (100.00)	432 (72.00)	168 (28.00)	150 (100.00)
Chi-square = 9.4320, <0.05, S						

Source: Field study.
Note: Figures in brackets denotes percentages.

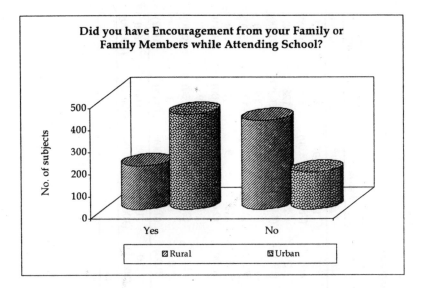

Did you have Encouragement from your Family or Family Members while Attending School?

WHO ENCOURAGED YOUR EDUCATION?

Further, the women respondents in the present study have been asked to state the person/family member who encouraged their education. It has been found from the Table 6.5 that in Hyderabad-Karnataka region 71.83 per cent and 67.00 per cent women respondents stated that they had been encouraged by father followed by mother (21.33 per cent and 22.00 per cent) in rural and urban areas, respectively. Grand father/mother (3.17 per cent in rural areas and 5.00 per cent in urban areas) and uncle/aunt (2.00 per cent in rural areas and 3.33 per cent in urban areas) had been encouraged respondents education. Thus, it is clear that family members of the women respondents were main who encouraged their education.

The distribution of data on the basis of district reveal that except Bidar district, father had played dominant role in Gulbarga district (86.00 per cent and 75.33 per cent), in Koppal district (78.00 per cent and 64.67 per cent), in Raichur district (78.00 per cent and 64.97 per cent) for rural and urban areas respectively. In Bidar district, mother for rural areas (46.67 per cent) and father for Urban areas (63.63 per cent) were important persons who encourage the women respondents education.

Table 6.5
Who Encouraged your Education?

Person	Bidar		Gulbarga		Koppal		Raichur		H-K Region	
	Rural	Urban	Rural	Urban	Rural	Urban	Rural	Urban	Rural	Urban
1. Father	68 (45.33)	95 (63.33)	129 (86.00)	113 (75.33)	117 (78.00)	97 (64.67)	117 (78.00)	97 (78.00)	431 (71.83)	402 (67.00)
2. Mother	70 (46.67)	47 (31.33)	16 (10.67)	27 (18.00)	21 (14.00)	29 (19.33)	21 (14.00)	29 (19.33)	128 (21.33)	132 (22.00)
3. Grand-father/ mother	9 (6.00)	6 (4.00)	0 (0.00)	2 (1.33)	5 (3.33)	11 (7.33)	5 (3.33)	11 (7.33)	19 (3.17)	30 (5.00)
4. Uncle/aunt	2 (1.33)	1 (0.67)	2 (1.33)	1 (0.67)	4 (2.67)	9 (6.00)	4 (2.67)	9 (6.00)	12 (2.00)	20 (3.33)
5. Brother	1 (0.67)	0 (0.00)	2 (1.33)	7 (4.67)	3 (2.00)	4 (2.67)	3 (2.00)	4 (2.67)	9 (1.50)	15 (2.50)
6. Others	0 (0.00)	1 (0.67)	1 (0.67)	0 (0.00)	0 (0.00)	0 (0.00)	0 (0.00)	0 (0.00)	1 (0.18)	1 (0.17)
Total	150 (100.00)	150 (100.00)	150 (100.00)	150 (100.00)	150 (100.00)	150 (100.00)	150 (100.00)	150 (100.00)	600 (100.00)	600 (100.00)

Chi-square = 6.9300, >0.05, NS

Source: Field study.
Note: Figures in brackets denotes percentages.

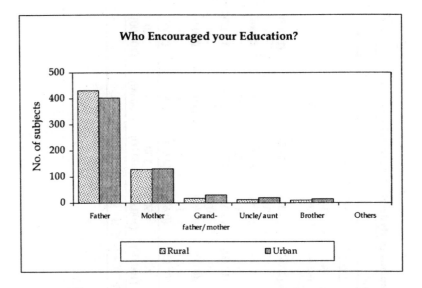

MODE OF TRAVEL DURING THE STUDY PERIOD

The mode of travel to school by the women respondents is important from the point of facilities available at home and village/ cities with regard to school/colleges. Women respondents were asked to specify the mode of travel during their study period (Table 6.6). It is found that 88.00 per cent in rural areas and 69.17 per cent in urban areas traveled/attended their schools/colleges by walk. Only 5.33 per cent and 5.83 per cent of women respondents in rural areas used bicycles and bus services, respectively. Whereas, in case of urban areas, 15.17 per cent and 13.17 per cent used bicycles and bus services respectively. Walking and availing of bus facility was a common practice in both the rural and urban areas, however, bicycles were also utilized by the women respondents in urban areas of Hyderabad-Karnataka region.

Similar trend were observed in all districts of Hyderabad-Karnataka region. For instance, an overwhelming per cent of women respondents who went to school by walk constitutes 89.33 per cent and 84.00 per cent in Bidar district, 90.00 per cent and 63.33 per cent in Gulbarga district, 82.00 per cent and 62.67 per cent in Koppal district, 90.67 per cent and 66.67 per cent in Raichur district in rural and urban areas respectively. The women respondents who attended school by bicycle constitutes 3.33 per

Table 6.6
Mode of Travel During the Study period of Women Respondents in Hyderabad-Karnataka Region.

Person	Bidar		Gulbarga		Koppal		Raichur		H-K Region	
	Rural	Urban	Rural	Urban	Rural	Urban	Rural	Urban	Rural	Urban
1. Walk	134 (89.33)	126 (84.00)	135 (90.00)	95 (63.33)	123 (82.00)	94 (62.67)	136 (90.67)	100 (66.67)	528 (88.00)	415 (69.17)
2. Bicycle	5 (3.33)	12 (8.00)	6 (4.00)	23 (15.33)	16 (10.67)	34 (22.67)	5 (3.33)	22 (14.67)	32 (5.33)	91 (15.17)
3. Car	0 (0.00)	1 (0.67)	0 (0.00)	2 (1.33)	0 (0.00)	2 (1.33)	0 (0.00)	1 (0.67)	0 (0.00)	6 (1.00)
4. Bus	8 (5.33)	10 (6.67)	9 (6.00)	28 (18.67)	10 (6.67)	18 (12.00)	8 (5.33)	23 (15.33)	35 (5.83)	79 (13.17)
5. Train	0 (0.00)	0 (0.00)	0 (0.00)	0 (0.00)	0 (0.00)	0 (0.00)	0 (0.00)	0 (0.00)	0 (0.00)	0 (0.00)
6. Any other	3 (2.00)	1 (0.67)	0 (0.00)	2 (1.33)	1 (0.67)	2 (1.33)	1 (0.67)	4 (2.67)	5 (0.83)	9 (1.50)
Total	150 (100.00)	150 (100.00)	150 (100.00)	150 (100.00)	150 (100.00)	150 (100.00)	150 (100.00)	150 (100.00)	150 (100.00)	150 (100.00)

Chi-square = 65.9670, < 0.05, S

Source: Field study.
Note: Figures in brackets denotes percentages.

cent and 8.00 per cent in Bidar district, 4.00 per cent and 15.33 per cent in Gulbarga district, 10.67 per cent and 22.67 per cent in Koppal district and 3.33 per cent and 14.67 per cent in Raichur district in rural and urban areas, respectively. Only in urban areas of Gulbarga district (18.67 per cent), in Koppal district (12.00 per cent) and Raichur district (15.33 per cent) attended school by bus. This shows that the less importance given to women education and facilities extended to complete their education.

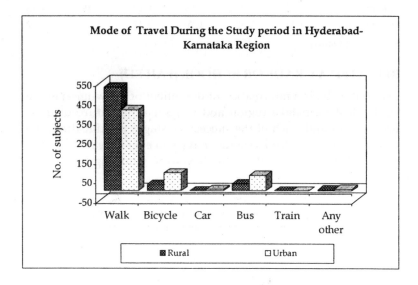

DISTANCE BETWEEN SCHOOL AND HOME

The findings have indicated that a mean distance between school and home of women respondents in rural areas was 1.47 kms and 1.70 kms in urban areas of Hyderabad-Karnataka region (Table 6.7). The district-wise distribution of data for rural areas shows that mean distance was 1.26 kms in Bidar district, 2.05 kms in Gulbarga district, 1.45 kms in Koppal district and 1.13 km in Raichur district. With regard to the mean distance in urban areas, it was 1.38 kms in Bidar district, 2.02 kms in Gulbarga district, 1.54 km in Koppal district and 1.84 kms in Raichur district. (Gulbarga city is big one, therefore traveling from one place to another for education purpose has made distance more).

Table 6.7
**Average Distance between School and Home of Women Respondents
in Hyderabad-Karnataka Region**

District	Rural		Urban		Total	
	Mean (in km)	SD (in km)	Mean (in km)	SD (in km)	Mean (in km)	SD (in km)
Bidar	1.26	3.99	1.38	3.21	1.32	3.61
Gulbarga	2.05	10.05	2.02	1.71	2.04	7.20
Koppal	1.45	1.83	1.54	2.24	1.50	2.04
Raichur	1.13	1.33	1.84	1.49	1.49	1.45
H-K region	1.47	5.52	1.70	2.27	1.58	4.22

Source: Field study.

REPEATED A GRADE OR SCHOOL (FAILED)

In order to obtain a information of the caliber of the women in the Hyderabad-Karnataka region and to gauge the nature of their progress through each of the successive stages of education, the respondents were asked 'whether have you ever repeated a grade or school (failed) upto the year they were studying in school/college.

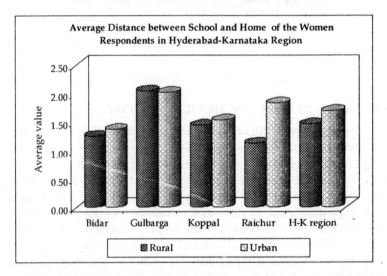

As evident from Table 6.8 the majority of women respondents (83.00 per cent in rural areas and 84.83 per cent in urban areas) in

Hyderabad-Karnataka region have/had not failed (at all) during their academic career. Only 17.00 per cent in rural areas and 15.17 per cent in urban areas have failed/repeated their grade. Further, table 8 indicates the district-wise breakdown of the data on women respondents performance during the study period. The largest per centage (22.00) women respondents in rural areas of Gulbarga district followed by Raichur district (19.33), Koppal district (15.33) and Bidar district (11.33) have failed during their study period. In case of Urban areas, the women respondents who repeated class/ failed were highest in Koppal district (23.33) followed by Bidar district (15.33), Raichur district (14.67) and Gulbarga district (7.33).

Table 6.8
Repeated a Grade or School by Women Respondents in
Hyderabad-Karnataka Region

Districts	Rural			Urban		
	Yes	No	Total	Yes	No	Total
Bidar	17	133	150	23	127	150
	(11.33)	(88.67)	(100.00)	(15.33)	(84.66)	(100.00)
Gulbarga	33	117	150	11	139	150
	(22.00)	(78.00)	(100.00)	(7.33)	(92.67)	(100.00)
Koppal	23	127	150	35	115	150
	(15.33)	(84.67)	(100.00)	(23.33)	(76.67)	(100.00)
Raichur	29	121	150	22	128	150
	(19.33)	(80.67)	(100.00)	(14.67)	(85.33)	(100.00)
H-K region	102	498	600	91	509	600
	(17.00)	(83.00)	(100.00)	(15.17)	(84.83)	(100.00)
	Chi-square=6.9454, NS >0.05,			Chi-square=14.9516, <0.05, S		

Source: Field study.
Note: Figures in brackets denotes percentages.

DESIRABLE LEVEL OF EDUCATION

First of all, it is interesting to see that as far as basic schooling is concerned, the largest percentage of men and women, and an equal percentage of both aggress that girls must complete their matriculation. Almost three times as many hold this vie for girls compared to boys. This is partly because a significant proportion of both men and women perceive a PUC or degree level education as necessary for boys; it is also because a large percentage of both genders believe boys should have the choice of studying up to whatever level they wish- a choice only half as many would give girls.

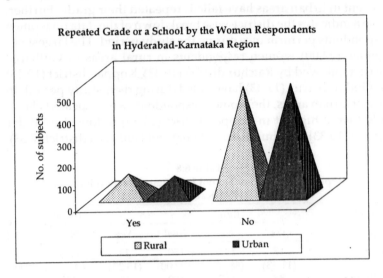

Keeping this in view, the women respondents were asked to state 'whether your parents thought that girls must study as much as you want' (Table 6.9). The data collected in this regard indicates that only 36.00 per cent women respondents in rural areas and 57.83 per cent women respondents in urban areas of Hyderabad-Karnataka region stated that their 'parents thought that girls must study as much as they want'. This could indicate that the 'women's resentment of the lack of opportunity to study in their own childhood, as well as the impact of the growing awareness of women's equal right to education in urban areas.

District-wise distribution of data reveals that 39.33 per cent in Raichur district pronounced highest in terms of desirable level of education followed by the Koppal (38.00 per cent), Gulbarga (34.00 per cent) and Bidar (32.67 per cent) in rural areas. However, it is significant to note that in Bidar district (61.33 per cent) women respondents expressed that their parents thought that girls must study as much as they want followed by Raichur district (59.33 per cent), Koppal district (57.33 per cent) and Gulbarga district (53.33 per cent) in urban areas. Since, in urban areas of Hyderabad-Karnataka region campaigning for literacy and school enrollment has been targeted at women, this could reflect parents perception that the girls should get education as much as they want.

Table 6.9
Desirable level of Education of Women Respondents in Hyderabad-Karnataka Region

Districts	Rural			Urban		
	Yes	No	Total	Yes	No	Total
Bidar	49	101	150	92	58	150
	(32.67)	(67.33)	(100.00)	(61.33)	(38.67)	(100.00)
Gulbarga	51	99	150	80	70	150
	(34.00)	(66.00)	(100.00)	(53.33)	(46.67)	(100.00)
Koppal	57	93	150	86	64	150
	(38.00)	(62.00)	(100.00)	(57.33)	(42.67)	(100.00)
Raichur	59	91	150	89	61	150
	(39.33)	(60.67)	(100.00)	(59.33)	(40.67)	(100.00)
H-K Region	216	384	600	347	253	600
	(36.00)	(64.00)	(100.00)	(57.83)	(42.17)	(100.00)
	Chi-square=1.9516, >0.05, NS			Chi-square=2.1526, >0.05, NS		

Source: Field study.
Note: Figures in brackets denotes percentages.

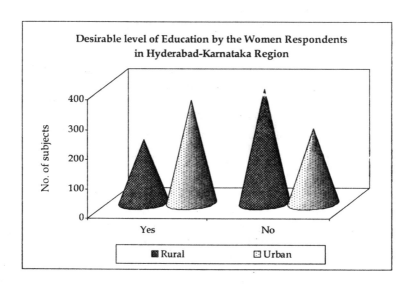

Desirable level of Education by the Women Respondents in Hyderabad-Karnataka Region

DROP-OUT

At the outset, data of the women respondents who dropped their primary education is presented in Table 6.10 for the purpose of analysis, drop-out rate was worked out for grades I-IV, V to VII. Of the 1200 women respondents chosen for the present study, 228 and 118 women respondents had primary education (I-VII standard) in rural and urban areas respectively. In rural areas, of the 228 women respondents, 64 (28.07 per cent) dropped their education at lower primary level (between I-IV standard) and 170 (71.93 per cent) dropped their education at higher primary level (between V-VII standard). Whereas, in case of Urban areas of Hyderabad-Karnataka region, 48 (40.68 per cent) and 70 (59.32 per cent) women respondents dropped their education at lower primary level (between I-IV standard) and higher primary level (V-VII standard), respectively.

Table 6.10
Drop-out of Women Respondents in Primary Education in Hyderabad-Karnataka Region

Districts	Rural			Urban		
	I-IV	V-VII	Total	I-IV	V-VII	Total
Bidar	6	40	46	16	22	38
	(13.04)	(86.96)	(100.00)	(42.11)	(57.80)	(100.00)
Gulbarga	29	39	68	12	15	27
	(42.65)	(57.35)	(100.00)	(31.58)	(68.42)	(100.00)
Koppal	15	46	61	12	18	30
	(24.59)	(75.41)	(100.00)	(44.44)	(55.56)	(100.00)
Raichur	14	39	53	8	15	23
	(26.42)	(73.58)	(100.00)	(34.78)	(65.22)	(100.00)
H-K region	64	164	228	48	70	118
	(28.07)	(71.93)	(100.00)	(40.68)	(59.32)	(100.00)
	Chi-square = 12.7314, < 0.05, S			Chi-square = 0.5278, > 0.05, NS		

Source: Field study.
Note: Figures in brackets denotes percentages.

The distribution of data according to the district for rural areas in Hyderabad-Karnataka reveals that 6 (13.04 per cent) women respondents in Bidar, 29 (42.65 per cent) women respondents in Gulbarga, 14 (22.22 per cent) in Koppal and 15 (24.59 per cent) in

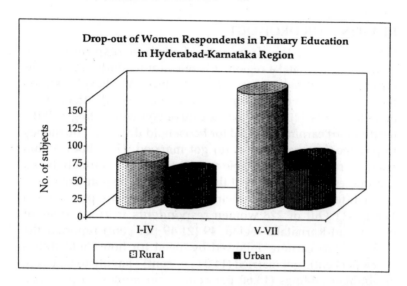

Raichur district stopped their education at lower primary level (between I-IV standard). Further, it is found that 40 (86.96 per cent) women respondents in Bidar district, 39 (57.35 per cent) women respondents in Gulbarga district, 39 (73.58 per cent) women respondents in Koppal district and 46 (75.41 per cent) women respondents in Raichur district dropped their education at higher primary level (between V-VII standard). This significant drop-out at higher primary level could be to non-availability of Higher Primary schools in their village/s.

As against this, in Urban areas, when grades I-IV are taken into consideration, it is found that 16 (42.11 per cent) women respondents in Bidar district, 12 (44.44 per cent) women respondents in Gulbarga district, 8 (34.78 per cent) women respondents in Koppal district, 17 (40.00 per cent) women respondents in Raichur district dropped their education. When, grades V-VII are taken into consideration, it is found that there is steep increase in women respondents drop-outs. For instance, 22 (57.80 per cent) women respondents in Bidar district, 15 (55.56 per cent) women respondents in Gulbarga district, 18 (60.00 per cent) women respondents in Koppal district and 15 (65.22 per cent) women respondents in Raichur district stopped their study at higher primary level (between V-VII standard).

REASONS FOR DROP-OUT

While studying the drop-outs of women respondents in Hyderabad-Karnataka region, it is relevant to study the reasons for drop-outs at the primary education level. We have classified these reasons into eight categories: (1) absence or death of either or both parents; (2) having to take care of younger siblings; (3) the need to start earning; (4) need for household duties; (5) no money to pay fee/purchase books; (6) got married; (7) school within village/area was not available and (8) failed in examination and lost interest. The data reveal that the women respondents have given different reasons for their drop-out which are presented in Table 6.11 Out of 228 women respondents in rural areas of Hyderabad-Karnataka region, 49 (21.49 per cent) reported the 'need to start earning' followed by 'need for household duties (18.86 per cent); 'got married (14.04 per cent)'; having to take care of younger siblings (13.60 per cent)'; 'no money to pay fee/ purchase books (11.40 per cent) and 'school within village/areas was not available (14.04 per cent)'. When we asked the same question to 118 women respondents who dropped their education at primary level in urban areas, it is found that they had to discontinue their education due to 'the need to start earning (37.29 per cent)' followed by 'having to take care of younger siblings

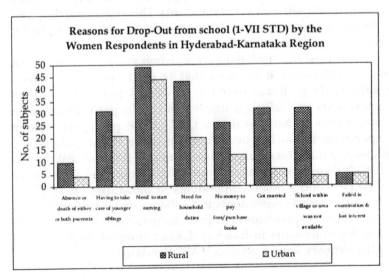

Table 6.11
Reasons for Drop-out from School (1-VII STD) by Women Respondents in Hyderabad-Karnataka Region

Reasons	Bidar		Gulbarga		Koppal		Raichur		H-K Region	
	Rural	Urban	Rural	Urban	Rural	Urban	Rural	Urban	Rural	Urban
1. Absence or death of either or both paerents	03 (6.52)	01 (2.63)	05 (7.35)	02 (7.41)	02 (3.77)	00 (0.00)	00 (0.00)	01 (4.35)	10 (4.39)	04 (3.39)
2. Having to take care of younger siblings	06 (13.04)	04 (10.53)	09 (13.24)	04 (14.81)	06 (11.32)	06 (20.00)	10 (16.39)	07 (30.43)	31 (13.60)	21 (17.80)
3. Need to start earning	09 (19.57)	16 (42.11)	14 (20.59)	09 (33.33)	11 (20.75)	11 (36.67)	15 (24.59)	08 (34.78)	49 (21.49)	44 (37.29)
4. Need for household duties	08 (17.39)	06 (15.79)	11 (16.18)	05 (18.52)	13 (24.53)	04 (13.33)	11 (18.03)	05 (21.74)	43 (18.86)	20 (16.95)
5. No money to pay fees/ purchase books	05 (10.87)	05 (13.16)	07 (10.29)	03 (11.12)	07 (13.22)	04 (13.33)	07 (11.48)	01 (4.35)	26 (11.40)	13 (11.02)
6. Got married	06 (13.04)	04 (10.52)	10 (14.71)	02 (7.41)	08 (15.09)	01 (3.33)	08 (13.11)	00 (0.00)	32 (14.04)	07 (5.93)
7. School within village or area was not available	09 (19.57)	01 (2.63)	10 (14.71)	01 (3.70)	06 (11.32)	02 (6.67)	07 (11.48)	00 (0.00)	32 (14.04)	04 (3.38)
8. Failed in examination & lost interest	00 (0.00)	01 (2.63)	02 (2.93)	01 (3.70)	00 (0.00)	02 (6.67)	03 (4.92)	01 (4.35)	05 (2.18)	05 (4.24)
Total	46 (100.00)	38 (200.00)	68 (100.00)	27 (100.00)	53 (100.00)	30 (100.00)	61 (100.00)	23 (100.00)	228 (100.00)	118 (100.00)

Chi-square=17.3400, <0.05, S

Source: Field study.
Note: Figures in brackets denotes percentages.

(17.80 per cent)'; 'need for household duties (16.95 per cent); 'no money to pay fees/purchase books (11.02 per cent)' and 'got married (5.93 per cent)'. An analysis of the reasons for the drop-outs of the women in both rural and urban areas of Hyderabad-Karnataka region are mainly for 'need for household duties', 'to start earning', 'got married' and 'having to take care of younger siblings' and 'no money to pay fees/purchase books' The distribution of data according to districts of Hyderabad-Karnataka region also shows the same reasons. It seems that the poor economic condition of their parents and domination of traditional conditions in the region compel them to discontinue their education and engage in various economic activities to supplement the meager family income instead of going to schools.

7

Employment Status of Women in Hyderabad-karnataka Region

It is almost universally accepted that women primary role is that of a home maker and it is for the men to provide subsistence to their family. But in recent years, specially after Independence, the traditional status and roles of women in Indian society are gradually changing. Few of the most important causes of such changes are the spread of education among women and the entrance of the educated women in the field of employment. Although, the traditional images of women as helpers to their men-fold- as wives, mothers and home-makers have not changed completely yet, the emergence of women as independent earners and as self-seeking individual entities are being felt increasingly. Their roles and status are undergoing remarkable changes. More specifically, their education and employment outside the home have led to the upliftment of their social status, but at the same time have widened the area of conflicts and tensions, both inside and outside the home. Employed women, as such, are confronting with the problem of striking a balance between home and work.

Occupation has provided a new social prestige to the women, specially their achievement in the performance of occupational roles newly recognised. Several studies have shown for that the woman employee whatever be the job she holds, is equal in efficiency and performance as the male employee in identical employment situations (Sengupta 1974; Srivastava 1978; Arora 1963; Kumuda Ranjan 1993; Srilatha Batliwala 1998; Mira Seth 2001 etc.). Some of the studies even indicate that in certain respects, the women employee is even more efficient. In matters of reliability, promptness and punctually, she has been found to have an edge over her male counterpart (Ranade and Ramachandran, 1970; Kapur 1974; Savitri Arputhamurthy 1990; Abhalakshmi Singh 2005; Anil Bhuimali 2004; Chhaya Shukla 2003 etc.).

In order to understand the extent of women education, employment, income and consequences of these on family, the occupational and economic achievements and obstacles of the working women in Hyderabad-Karnataka region this study is undertaken. The data pertaining to the occupational career of the respondents are being investigated. The reasons for women entering into employment, motivating agent in job selection, in-job improvement of qualification, etc., are investigated in the present study. Even the attitudes of their husband towards their employment achievement and interpersonal behaviour in the outside job also investigated.

OCCUPATIONAL STATUS

The exploration into the occupational status of the 600 women respondents in rural areas of Hyderabad-Karnataka reveals that 214 (35.67 per cent) women respondents belong to the self-employed occupation, 176 (29.33 per cent) women respondents belong to agriculture, 111 (18.50 per cent) women belong to Government employees and 99 (16.50 per cent) women respondents belong to private sector/business sector (Table 7.1). Further, among the sample of 600 women respondents from urban areas in Hyderabad-Karnataka region, 189 (31.50 per cent) are self-employed, 60 (10.00 per cent) women respondents are agriculturist, 161 (26.83 per cent) women respondents are Government employees and 190 (31.67 per cent) women respondents are working in private sector/businesses. The district-wise distribution of data for rural and urban areas is presented in Table 7.1 reveals the same trend about occupational status of women respondents in Hyderabad-Karnataka region.

The analysis of data pertaining to the occupational status of the respondents clearly indicates that women's participation in the occupational life is becoming increasingly diversified and they are achieving top positions in male-dominated occupational fields as well. However, their representation is still very small in Hyderabad-Karnataka region.

Table 7.1
Occupation Categories of Women Respondents in Hyderabad-Karnataka region

Occupation	Bidar		Gulbarga		Koppal		Raichur		H-K region	
	Rural	Urban	Rural	Urban	Rural	Urban	Rural	Urban	Rural	Urban
Self employed	77 (51.33)	61 (40.67)	30 (20.00)	36 (24.00)	52 (34.67)	55 (36.67)	55 (36.66)	37 (24.67)	214 (35.67)	189 (31.50)
Agriculture	35 (23.33)	16 (10.67)	39 (26.00)	9 (6.00)	51 (34.00)	27 (18.00)	51 (34.00)	8 (5.33)	176 (29.33)	60 (10.00)
Government	19 (12.67)	39 (26.00)	33 (22.00)	47 (31.33)	31 (20.66)	32 (21.33)	28 (18.67)	43 (28.67)	111 (18.50)	161 (26.83)
Private	19 (12.67)	34 (22.66)	48 (32.00)	58 (38.67)	16 (10.67)	36 (24.00)	16 (10.67)	62 (41.33)	99 (16.50)	190 (31.67)
Total	150 (100.0)	150 (100.0)	150 (100.0)	150 (100.0)	150 (100.0)	150 (100.0)	150 (100.0)	150 (100.0)	600 (100.0)	600 (100.0)
	Chi-square = 20.0753, p<0.05, S		Chi-square = 22.6889, p<0.05, S		Chi-square =17.1569, p<0.05, S		Chi-square = 65.1569, p<0.05, S		Chi-square = 96.4130, p<0.05, S	

Source: Primary data.
Note: Figures in brackets denotes percentages.

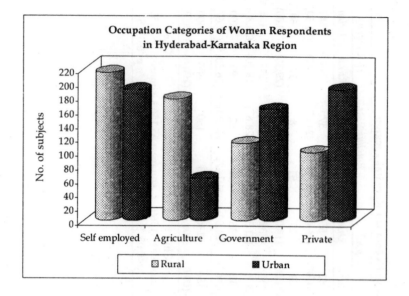

EDUCATION LEVEL OF EMPLOYED WOMEN

Exploring the status consistency of working women respondents in the present study, their educational status has been studied in the region (Table 7.2). It is observed that in rural areas of Hyderabad-Karnataka region, 38.00 per cent women respondents were educated upto primary level, 26.67 per cent women respondents studied upto secondary level and 9.33 per cent women respondents had Pre-university (PUC) education. And 7.33 per cent were graduate, 2.50 per cent women respondents were post-graduates and 16.17 per cent women respondents completed 'professional courses'.

The distribution of data about the educational status of working women respondents for urban areas in Hyderabad-Karnataka region has revealed that 19.67 per cent were educated upto primary level, 17.83 per cent upto secondary level, 14.00 per cent upto tertiary (PUC) level, 17.00 per cent upto graduation, hardly 8.67 per cent upto post-graduation and 22.83 per cent completed 'professional courses'.

Among districts in Hyderabad-Karnataka region, it is found that female respondents in rural areas who are employed had primary level education constituted 30.67 per cent in Bidar district,

Table 7.2
Education level of Women Respondents in Hyderabad-Karnataka Region
Occupation Categories of Women Respondents in Hyderabad-Karnataka region

Education level	Bidar		Gulbarga		Koppal		Raichur		H-K region	
	Rural	Urban	Rural	Urban	Rural	Urban	Rural	Urban	Rural	Urban
Primary	46 (30.67)	38 (25.33)	68 (45.33)	27 (18.00)	61 (40.67)	30 (20.00)	53 (35.33)	23 (15.33)	228 (38.00)	118 (19.67)
Secondary	48 (32.00)	23 (15.33)	42 (28.00)	23 (15.33)	27 (18.00)	39 (26.00)	43 (28.67)	22 (14.67)	160 (26.67)	107 (17.83)
PUC	15 (10.00)	27 (18.00)	13 (8.67)	18 (12.00)	12 (8.00)	24 (16.00)	16 (10.67)	15 (10.00)	56 (9.33)	84 (14.00)
UG	16 (10.67)	31 (20.66)	9 (6.00)	33 (22.00)	8 (5.33)	15 (10.00)	11 (7.36)	23 (15.33)	44 (7.33)	102 (17.00)
PG	10 (6.66)	8 (5.33)	1 (0.67)	21 (14.00)	2 (1.33)	6 (4.00)	2 (1.33)	17 (11.33)	15 (2.50)	52 (8.67)
Professional	15 (10.00)	23 (15.33)	17 (11.33)	28 (18.67)	40 (26.67)	36 (24.00)	25 (16.67)	50 (33.34)	97 (16.17)	137 (22.83)
Total	150 (100.0)	150 (100.0)	150 (100.0)	150 (100.0)	150 (100.0)	150 (100.0)	150 (100.0)	150 (100.0)	600 (100.0)	600 (100.0)
	Chi-square = 19.6870, $p < 0.05$, S		Chi-square = 58.6400, $p < 0.05$, S		Chi-square = 21.0832, $p < 0.05$, S		Chi-square = 43.0697, $p < 0.05$, S		Chi-square=101.4032, $p < 0.05$, S	

Source: Primary data.
Note: Figures in brackets denotes percentages.

45.33 per cent in Gulbarga district, 40.67 per cent in Koppal district and 35.33 per cent in Raichur district. As against this, in Urban areas, female respondents constituted 25.33 per cent, 18.00 per cent, 20.00 per cent and 35.33 per cent in Bidar, Gulbarga, Koppal and Raichur districts, respectively. Among the secondary level educated women respondents in rural areas of these district were 32.00 per cent in Bidar , 28.00 per cent in Gulbarga, 18.00 per cent in Koppal and 28.67 per cent in Raichur. Whereas, in Urban areas, the women respondents who had secondary level of education accounts 15.33 per cent in Bidar and Gulbarga districts, 26.00 per cent in Koppal and 14.67 per cent in Raichur district. Among the pre-university level women respondents in rural areas, 10.00 per cent are in Bidar district, 8.67 per cent in Gulbarga district, 8.00 per cent in Koppal district and 10.67 per cent in Raichur district. Whereas, in Urban areas, female respondents who completed pre-university education constitutes 18.00 per cent, 12.00 per cent, 16.00 per cent and 10.00 per cent in Bidar, Gulbarga, Koppal and Raichur districts, respectively. Among those who have completed Graduation in rural areas, 10.67 per cent are in Bidar district, 6.00 per cent in Gulbarga district, 5.33 per cent in Koppal district and 7.33 per cent in Raichur district. As against this in Urban areas, 20.68 per cent are in Bidar district, 22.00 per cent are in Gulbarga district, 10.00 per cent are in Koppal district, 15.33 per cent are in Raichur district. Among those respondents who had Post-graduation degrees in rural areas, 6.66 per cent are in Bidar district, 0.67 per cent in Gulbarga district, 1.33 per cent are in Koppal district and 1.33 per cent are in Raichur district. Whereas, in urban areas, they constituted 5.33 per cent, 14.00 per cent, 4.00 per cent and 11.33 per cent in Bidar, Gulbarga, Koppal and Raichur districts respectively. Further, table reveals that the respondents who had 'Professional courses' education in rural areas constituted 10.00 per cent in Bidar, 11.33 per cent in Gulbarga, 26.67 per cent in Koppal and 16.67 per cent in Raichur district. As against this, in urban areas, female respondents constituted 15.33 per cent, 18.67 per cent, 24.00 per cent and 33.33 per cent in Bidar, Gulbarga, Koppal and Raichur districts respectively. Thus, it is clear that in most of the cases in both rural and urban areas of Hyderabad-Karnataka region, the lower educated working women and 'Professionals" (like TCH and B.Ed, etc.) constituted more. This may be due to the backwardness of the region less importance given to female education and dominating traditional culture and immediate employment opportunities in schools as teachers.

AT WHAT AGE YOU ENTERED INTO THE FIRST WORK OR JOB?

Employees in an organization can be classified as young, middle aged and old. Generally, the job performance of older and younger employees would be nearly the same. Yet, the composition of the age of employee may be mature enough but may not be mature enough in performance of his/her job. The middle-aged employee is supposed to be active and enough mature.

We have asked to state at what age respondent has entered the first work/job. Table 7.3 presents the mean age of women respondent when they entered the first work/job. The mean age of women respondents when they entered the work/job was 17.87 years in rural areas and 20.76 years in urban areas. The district-wise distribution of data for rural areas further, reveals that mean age of women respondents when they entered work/job was 15.04 years in Bidar district, 17.60 years in Gulbarga district, 19.46 years in Koppal district and 19.38 years in Raichur district. As against this in Urban areas, mean age constitutes 18.77 years in Bidar district, 22.90 years in Gulbarga district, 20.04 years in Koppal district and 21.34 years in Raichur district. Examining the mean age of women respondents when they entered in first work or job, it is found that the higher mean-ages are represented in urban areas than rural areas. Because poverty compelled them to take work earlier in rural areas and higher education may be reason for late entry by women in urban areas.

NATURE OF ACTIVITY

An analysis of the employment of working women with regard to permanent, temporary, daily wages, i.e., nature of employment is made here. 371(61.83 per cent) women respondents held regular jobs, 140 (23.33 per cent) women respondents held seasonal jobs and 89 (14.83 per cent) women respondents held irregular jobs in rural areas of Hyderabad-Karnataka region (Table 7.4). In Urban areas, 470 (78.33 per cent) women respondents were permanent employed, 66(11.00 per cent) women respondents as temporary and 64 (10.67 per cent) women respondents employment was based on daily wages.

Table 7.3:

At what Age you Entered into the First Work or Job? (In Years)

District	Rural		Urban		Total		T-value
	Mean	SD	Mean	SD	Mean	SD	
Bidar	15.04	10.99	18.77	9.76	16.91	10.44	1.8793, p>0.05.NS
Gulbraga	17.60	8.05	22.90	5.82	20.25	7.49	-6.5383, p<0.01, S
Koppal	19.46	5.61	20.04	5.18	19.75	5.41	-2.7746, p<0.05,S
Raichur	19.38	8.22	21.34	7.21	20.36	7.80	-7.0577, p<0.01, S
H-K Region	17.87	8.03	20.76	7.58	19.32	8.72	-5.4476, p<0.01, S
	F = 29.5809, p < 0.01, S		F = 105.8632, p < 0.01, S		F = 78.7722, p < 0.01, S		

Source: Field survey.

Table 7.4
Nature of Economic Activity of Women Respondents in Hyderabad-Karnataka Region

Nature of Activity	Bidar		Gulbarga		Koppal		Raichur		H-K region	
	Rural	Urban	Rural	Urban	Rural	Urban	Rural	Urban	Rural	Urban
Permanent	75 (50.00)	97 (64.67)	104 (69.33)	128 (85.33)	88 (58.67)	107 (71.33)	104 (69.33)	138 (92.00)	371 (61.83)	470 (78.33)
Temporary	38 (25.33)	18 (12.00)	26 (17.33)	15 (10.00)	48 (32.00)	28 (18.67)	28 (18.67)	5 (3.3)	140 (23.33)	66 (11.00)
Daily wages	37 (24.67)	35 (23.33)	20 (13.33)	7 (4.67)	14 (9.33)	15 (10.00)	18 (12.00)	7 (4.67)	89 (14.83)	64 (10.67)
Total	150 (100.0)	150 (100.0)	150 (100.0)	150 (100.0)	150 (100.0)	150 (100.0)	150 (100.0)	150 (100.0)	600 (100.0)	600 (100.0)
	Chi-square=10.0124, $p<0.05$, S		Chi-square=11.6932, $p<0.05$, S		Chi-square=7.1489, $p<0.05$, S		Chi-square=25.6472, $p<0.05$, S		Chi-square=42.3214, $p<0.05$, S	

Source: Primary data.
Note: Figures in brackets denotes percentages.

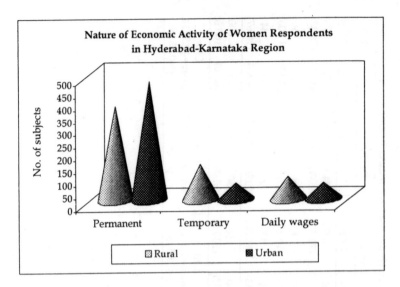

REASONS TO START THE WORK

Job selection is a complicated phenomenon. In modern competitive society, the jobs are numerous and the individual has the option to choose one or the other job. However, each job has got its own specific requirements and mandatory qualifications need to be fulfilled by the individual candidate. As the job situation at any given point of time in society is limited in number and the persons aspiring for those positions will be more. This results into meritocracy and achievements orientation in the society. At ideal level it is the meritorious would succeed in the competitions. In reality many pulls and pressures take place and the individuals with political connections and personal influences get through. In this competitive atmosphere the selection of a job becomes a very complicated process especially in traditional society and backward region. Many would like to enter into the job market only for the sake of economic gains and security. There may be others who strive for power and prestige, and , therefore, would opt for a particular job and reject others. Keeping this background in view, in the present study an attempt has been made to explore the most important factors which were influenced/forced women to start working. It has been found from the Table 7.5 that of the 600 sample in rural areas, 45.50 per cent women respondents have started to work in order to have more money to support their families. Further, in rural areas, 23.67 per cent women respondents have stated that they have selected their jobs because of economic independence. There are 9.67 per cent and 10.50 per cent women respondents who have started the working outside due to laid off of work by their father/brothers/husband and break up of joint family, respectively. There are 3.83 per cent women respondents who because of the death of father/husband have taken up their present job. There are 1.00 per cent women respondents who had no alternative except to join the present job because of desertion by husband. Some of the respondents i.e., 3.83 per cent have stated that just because of their drunkard father/husband they have gone for the jobs. Thus, it is clear that the job selection by respondents in rural areas in the present study has been governed by two factors; these are (1) 'need for more money' and (2) 'need for economic independence'.

The distribution of data according to the district in rural areas in Hyderabad-Karnataka region, women respondents reveals that in 44.00 per cent in Bidar district, 46.00 per cent in Gulbarga district, 44.00 per cent in Koppal district and 48.00 per cent in Raichur district, stated that the main reason for the working outside is due to 'need for more money' to support their families.

The response of the women respondents engaged in the various economic activities reveals that it is hardly a matter of choice for women in the urban areas of Hyderabad-Karnataka region. An overwhelming majority of 41.50 per cent women started working because they needed economic independence and 39.00 per cent reported that they need money. Several other reasons cited by the respondents also emphasize the economic determinant of their participation, such as, male member laid off his work (3.67 per cent respondents), death of parents or husband (3.50 per cent) and desertion by husband (1.33 per cent). A few women also mentioned the break-up of joint family and drunkard father/husband (3.83 per cent and 2.67 per cent respectively) as determinants of their economic participation (Table 7.5).

The distribution of data on the basis of district in urban areas of Hyederabad-Karnataka region reveals that in Bidar district (45.33 per cent and 34.67 per cent), in Gulbarga district (33.33 per cent and 43.33 per cent), in Koppal district (46.00 per cent and 38.00 per cent), in Raichur district (48.00 per cent and 21.33 per

Table 7.5

Reasons to start the Work by Women Respondents in Hyderabad-Karnataka Region

Reasons	Bidar		Gulbarga		Koppal		Raichur		H-K region	
	Rural	Urban	Rural	Urban	Rural	Urban	Rural	Urban	Rural	Urban
1. Father/brother/ husband laid off work	5 (3.33)	5 (3.33)	24 (16.00)	3 (2.00)	7 (4.67)	5 (3.33)	22 (14.67)	9 (6.00)	58 (9.67)	22 (3.67)
2. Death of father/ husband	9 (6.00)	6 (4.00)	3 (2.00)	7 (4.68)	6 (4.00)	3 (2.00)	5 (3.33)	5 (3.33)	23 (3.83)	21 (3.50)
3. Desertion of husband	2 (1.33)	4 (2.67)	0 (0.00)	3 (2.00)	3 (2.00)	0 (0.00)	1 (0.67)	1 (0.68)	6 (1.00)	8 (1.33)
4. Need for more money	66 (44.00)	68 (45.33)	69 (46.00)	50 (33.33)	66 (44.00)	69 (46.00)	72 (48.00)	47 (31.33)	273 (45.50)	234 (39.00)
5. Need for economic independence	36 (24.00)	52 (34.67)	39 (26.00)	65 (43.33)	35 (23.33)	57 (38.00)	32 (21.33)	75 (50.00)	142 (23.67)	249 (41.50)
6. Break-up of joint family	25 (16.68)	12 (8.00)	11 (7.33)	2 (1.33)	18 (12.00)	7 (4.67)	9 (6.00)	2 (1.33)	63 (10.50)	23 (3.83)
7. Drunkard father/ husband	5 (3.33)	3 (2.00)	4 (2.67)	5 (3.33)	11 (7.33)	6 (4.00)	3 (2.00)	2 (1.33)	23 (3.83)	16 (2.67)
8. Any other	2 (1.33)	0 (0.00)	0 (0.00)	15 (10.00)	4 (2.67)	3 (2.00)	6 (4.00)	9 (6.00)	12 (2.00)	27 (4.50)
Total	150 (100.0)	150 (100.0)	150 (100.0)	150 (100.0)	150 (100.0)	150 (100.0)	150 (100.0)	150 (100.0)	600 (100.0)	600 (100.0)
	Chi-square = 18.4856, p<0.05, S		Chi-square = 52.7392, p<0.05, S		Chi-square =15.0009, p<0.05, S		Chi-square = 57.5444, p<0.05, S		Chi-square=92.0333, p<0.05, S	

Source: Primary data.
Note: Figures in brackets denotes percentages.

cent) 'need for more money' and 'economic independence' has been described as the most dominating factors in the selection of jobs.

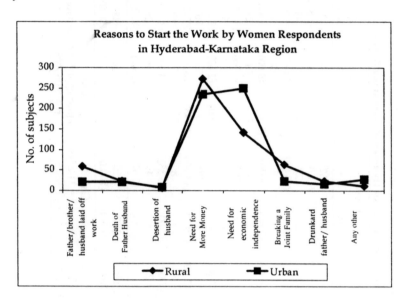

REASONS TO CHOOSE THE PRESENT JOB

Further, the women respondents have been asked to state the reasons to choose the present job. It has been found from Table 7.6 that in rural areas, 33.83 per cent respondents have selected the present job because it is 'very easy' and 27.17 per cent respondents stated that the 'supplementary job' is not available'. As against this, in urban areas, 41.33 per cent respondents stated that they have chosen the present job because it is 'very easy' and 16.17 per cent respondents stated that because of 'easy employment opportunity'. Thus, it is clear that the job-selection by female in both rural and urban areas of Hyderabad-Karnataka region has been governed by three reasons like: (i) very easy job; (ii) supplementary job is not available and (iii) easy employment opportunity. This, further, shows the lack of competitiveness among the female in the region.

The district-wise distribution of data for rural areas reveals that, the women respondents from Bidar district have stated that

Table 7.6

Reasons to Choose the present Job by Women Respondents in Hyderabad-Karnataka Region

Reasons	Bidar		Gulbarga		Koppal		Raichur		H-K region	
	Rural	Urban	Rural	Urban	Rural	Urban	Rural	Urban	Rural	Urban
1. Very easy job	55 (36.67)	66 (44.00)	42 (28.00)	60 (40.00)	55 (36.67)	62 (41.33)	51 (34.00)	60 (40.00)	203 (33.83)	248 (41.33)
2. Easy employment opportunity	38 (25.33)	19 (12.67)	11 (7.33)	29 (19.33)	20 (13.33)	27 (18.00)	25 (16.67)	22 (14.67)	94 (15.67)	97 (16.17)
3. Easy accessibility	5 (3.33)	14 (9.33)	3 (2.00)	25 (16.67)	4 (2.68)	9 (6.00)	5 (3.33)	12 (8.00)	17 (2.83)	60 (10.00)
4. More attractive wages	7 (4.67)	3 (2.00)	5 (3.33)	10 (6.67)	2 (1.33)	15 (10.00)	7 (4.67)	14 (9.33)	21 (3.50)	42 (7.00)
5. Heredetary	13 (8.67)	15 (10.00)	12 (8.00)	3 (2.00)	17 (11.33)	5 (3.33)	15 (10.00)	4 (2.67)	57 (9.50)	27 (4.50)
6. Supplementary job not available	25 (16.67)	25 (16.67)	59 (39.33)	18 (12.00)	44 (29.33)	20 (13.33)	35 (23.33)	23 (15.33)	163 (27.17)	86 (14.33)
7. Less wage paid in other jobs	5 (3.33)	5 (3.33)	4 (2.68)	3 (2.00)	3 (2.00)	8 (5.33)	7 (4.67)	5 (3.33)	19 (3.17)	21 (3.50)
8. Any other	2 (1.33)	3 (2.00)	14 (9.33)	2 (1.33)	5 (3.33)	4 (2.67)	5 (3.33)	10 (6.67)	26 (4.33)	19 (3.17)
Total	150 (100.0)	150 (100.0)	150 (100.0)	150 (100.0)	150 (100.0)	150 (100.0)	150 (100.0)	150 (100.0)	600 (100.0)	600 (100.0)
	Chi-square = 13.5393, $p > 0.05$, NS		Chi-square = 65.2819, $p < 0.05$, S		Chi-square = 31.2549, $p < 0.05$, S		Chi-square = 0.8039, $p > 0.05$, NS		Chi-square=49.9271, $p < 0.05$, S	

Source: Primary data.
Note: Figures in brackets denotes percentages.

they have selected present job because of 'very easy' (36.67 per cent women respondents), and 'easy employment opportunity' (25.33 per cent women respondents) followed by Gulbarga district-it is 'supplementary job is not available' (39.33 per cent women respondents) and 'very easy job' (28.00 per cent women respondents). In case of Koppal district, respondents stated that they have selected the present job because it is 'very easy' (36.67 per cent women respondents) and 'supplementary job is not available' (29.33 per cent women respondents). In the similar way, respondents in Raichur district stated that it is because of 'very easy job' (34.00 per cent respondents) and 'supplementary job is not available' (23.33 per cent respondents), therefore they have selected the present job.

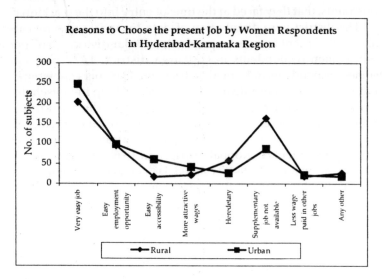

Further, the district-wise distribution of data for urban areas, it is found that 44.00 per cent women respondents in Bidar, 40.00 per cent women respondents in Gulbarga, 41.33 per cent women respondents in Koppal and 40.00 per cent women respondents in Raichur stated that they have chosen the present job because it is 'very easy'. This indicates the lack of competitiveness to acquire the job among women respondents and lack of employment opportunities in both rural and urban areas of all districts in Hyderabad-Karnataka region.

CONSTRAINTS FACED AT THE TIME OF ENTRY INTO WORK PLACE

In the present study, the respondents have been asked to state what kind of constraints did they face at the time of entering into workplace. It has been found (Table 7.7) that in rural areas, 16.33 per cent women respondents stated 'lack of crèche facilities (care takers of children)' and 41.67 per cent women respondents stated 'lack of help in the household' are two important constraints they faced at the time of entry into workforce. Whereas, in urban areas, 24.00 per cent women respondents stated 'lack of help in the household', 24.50 per cent women respondents stated 'lack of crèche facilities (care taker)' and 13.83 per cent women respondents stated 'lack of education (desirable level)' are important constraints, that they faced at the time of entry into the workforce.

The district-wise distribution of data for rural areas reveals that 42.00 per cent women respondents in Bidar district, 38.67 per cent women respondents in Gulbarga district, 47.33 per cent women respondents in Koppal district and 38.67 per cent women respondents in Raichur district stated 'lack of help in household' was an important restraint for entering into the workforce. Secondly, 16.67 per cent women respondents in Bidar district, 14.67 per cent women respondents in Gulbarga district, 17.33 per cent women respondents in Koppal district and 16.67 per cent women respondents in Raichur district stated 'lack of crèche facilities' was an abstacle while entering the workforce.

In case of urban areas, it has been found that in Bidar district 32.00 per cent of women respondents stated 'lack of crèche facilities' and 20.00 per cent respondents stated 'inadequate information' were important restraints. In Gulbarga district, 24.00 per cent women respondents stated 'lack of help in the household' and 22.00 per cent women respondents stated 'lack of crèche facilities' were important constraints. In Koppal district 32.00 per cent and 26.67 per cent women respondents stated 'lack of help in the household' and 'lack of crèche facilities' were important constraints respectively. Further, in Raichur district, it has been found that 'lack of help in the household (30.00 per cent women respondents) and lack of crèche facilities (17.33 per cent women respondents) were important constraints they confronted while entering into workforce. In the case of women the working outside is seriously affected by their domestic roles and familial obligations in the Region.

Table 7.7

Constraints Faced at the Time of Entry into Work Force by Women Respondents in Hyderabad-Karnataka Region

Constraints	Bidar		Gulbarga		Koppal		Raichur		H-K region	
	Rural	Urban	Rural	Urban	Rural	Urban	Rural	Urban	Rural	Urban
1. Lack of crèche facilities	25 (16.67)	48 (32.00)	22 (14.67)	33 (22.00)	26 (17.33)	40 (26.67)	25 (16.67)	26 (17.33)	98 (16.33)	147 (24.50)
2. Lack of help in the household	63 (42.00)	15 (10.00)	58 (38.67)	36 (24.00)	71 (47.33)	48 (32.00)	58 (38.67)	45 (30.00)	250 (41.67)	144 (24.00)
3. Social and caste taboos	13 (8.67)	12 (8.00)	18 (12.00)	8 (5.33)	6 (4.00)	3 (2.00)	16 (10.67)	5 (3.33)	53 (8.83)	28 (4.67)
4. Competition with men	9 (6.00)	5 (3.33)	12 (8.00)	15 (10.00)	7 (4.67)	8 (5.33)	9 (6.00)	12 (8.00)	37 (6.17)	40 (6.67)
5. Lack of skill	12 (8.00)	8 (5.33)	7 (4.67)	17 (11.33)	7 (4.67)	15 (10.00)	14 (9.33)	19 (12.67)	40 (6.67)	59 (9.83)
6. Lack of education	11 (7.33)	28 (18.67)	17 (11.34)	15 (10.00)	19 (12.67)	21 (14.00)	12 (8.00)	19 (12.67)	59 (9.83)	83 (13.83)
7. Inadequate information	17 (11.33)	30 (20.00)	11 (7.33)	18 (12.00)	12 (8.00)	15 (10.00)	11 (7.33)	16 (10.67)	51 (8.50)	79 (13.17)
8. Any other	0 (0.00)	4 (2.67)	5 (3.33)	8 (5.33)	2 (1.33)	0 (0.00)	5 (3.33)	8 (5.33)	12 (2.00)	20 (3.33)
Total	150 (100.0)	150 (100.0)	150 (100.0)	150 (100.0)	150 (100.0)	150 (100.0)	150 (100.0)	150 (100.0)	600 (100.0)	600 (100.0)
	Chi-square=49.7289, p<0.05, S		Chi-square=17.4802, p<0.05, S		Chi-square=12.3376, p>0.05, NS		Chi-square=11.0848, p>0.05, NS		Chi-square=56.2168, p<0.05, S	

Source: Primary data.
Note: Figures in brackets denotes percentages.

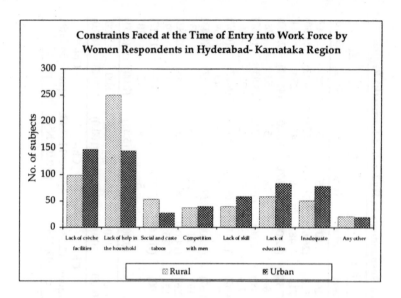

DURATION OF STAY IN THE PROFESSION/OCCUPATION

Data concerning the respondents' period of stay in their profession/occupations reveal that most of the women respondents are comparatively new entrants in Hyderabad-Karnataka region (Table 7.8). The study results shows that in rural areas 52.83 per cent of women respondents in Hyderabad-Karnataka region (of this 68.00 per cent in Bidar district, 51.33 per cent in Gulbarga district, 44.67 per cent in Koppal district and 47.30 per cent in Raichur district) were in their occupations for 5 years or less. The period of stay of 23.33 per cent women respondents ranges from 6-10 years, 12.00 per cent women respondents between 11-15 years, 7.33 per cent women respondents have their stay period between 16-20 years, while 4.50 per cent respondents have been working since more than 20 years in their jobs or occupations.

The distribution of data for the respondents of urban areas in Hyderabad-Karnataka reveals that the job in which most of the women respondents have spent is the shortest duration of time of 5 years or less(58.17 per cent); of this 68.00 per cent in Bidar district, 54.67 per cent in Gulbarga district, 56.00 per cent in Koppal district and 54.00 per cent in Raichur district. This is, further, followed by 22.66 per cent (6-10 years), 9.16 per cent (11-15 years), 6.50 per

Table 7.8

Duration of Stay in the Profession/occupation by the Women Respondents in Hyderabad-Karnataka Region

Years	Bidar		Gulbarga		Koppal		Raichur		H-K region	
	Rural	Urban	Rural	Urban	Rural	Urban	Rural	Urban	Rural	Urban
1 – 5	102 (68.00)	102 (68.00)	77 (51.33)	82 (54.67)	67 (44.67)	84 (56.00)	71 (47.30)	81 (54.00)	317 (52.83)	349 (58.17)
6 – 10	31 (20.67)	28 (18.67)	41 (27.33)	35 (23.33)	22 (14.67)	35 (23.33)	46 (30.70)	38 (25.30)	140 (23.33)	136 (22.67)
11 – 15	12 (8.00)	13 (8.67)	20 (13.33)	13 (8.67)	24 (16.00)	16 (10.67)	16 (10.70)	13 (8.70)	72 (12.00)	55 (9.16)
16 – 20	3 (2.00)	5 (3.33)	11 (7.33)	12 (8.00)	18 (12.00)	9 (6.00)	12 (8.00)	13 (8.70)	44 (7.33)	39 (6.50)
21 & above	2 (1.33)	2 (1.33)	1 (0.68)	8 (5.33)	19 (12.66)	6 (4.00)	5 (3.30)	5 (3.30)	27 (4.50)	21 (3.50)
Total	150 (100.0)	150 (100.0)	150 (100.0)	150 (100.0)	150 (100.0)	150 (100.0)	150 (100.0)	150 (100.0)	600 (100.0)	600 (100.0)
	Chi-square=0.7239, p>0.05, NS		Chi-square=2.1378, p>0.05, NS		Chi-square=16.2388, p<0.05, S		Chi-square=2.2001, p>0.05, NS		Chi-square=5.3887, p>0.05, NS	

Source: Primary data
Note: Figures in brackets denotes percentages.

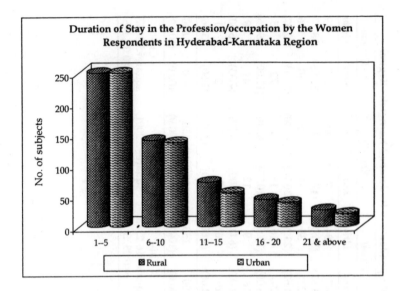

Duration of Stay in the Profession/occupation by the Women Respondents in Hyderabad-Karnataka Region

cent (16-20 years) and 3.50 per cent women respondents (more than 20 years). One of the possible explanations for this phenomenon may be that in Hyderabad-Karnataka region, women have recently started for getting formal education and therefore, most of them started their work/job recently, and therefore fall in the duration of 1-5 and 6-10 years.

TRAINING/APPRENTICE

According to Campbell, "Training courses are typically designed for a short term, stated set purpose, such as the operation of some piece(s) of machinery, while development involves a broader education for long term purpose". Training is the process of assisting personnel in increasing their efficiency and effectiveness at work. It can improve and update their professional knowledge by way of developing administrative skills relevant to their work. Efficiency of personnel can be improved by cultivating appropriate behaviour and attitudes towards work and people. Training makes personnel independent and enables them to understand/perform their job efficiently.

Thus, working in different fields requires knowledge, skill and techniques. To know about the improvement of women respondents knowledge and skill who are working in different fields are asked to state whether you have undergone any apprentice course or training. It has been found from Table 7.9 that 15.83 per cent women respondents in rural areas and 20.50 per cent women respondents in urban areas in Hyderabad-Karnataka region had training after their involvement in economic activities. As is evident from the Table 7.9 in rural areas 24.00 per cent women respondents in Bidar district have undergone training followed by 16.00 per cent women respondents in Raichur district, 14.67 per cent in Gulbarga district and 8.67 per cent women respondents in Bidar district.

Table 7.9
**Training/apprentice Received by the Women Respondents
in Hyderabad-Karnataka Region**

Districts	Rural			Urban		
	Training	*No training*	*Total*	*Training*	*No training*	*Total*
Bidar	36	114	150	25	125	150
	(24.00)	(76.00)	(100.00)	(16.67)	(83.33)	(100.00)
Gulbarga	22	128	150	35	115	150
	(14.67)	(85.33)	(100.00)	(23.33)	(76.67)	(100.00)
Koppal	13	137	150	28	122	150
	(8.67)	(91.33)	(100.00)	(18.67)	(81.33)	(100.00)
Raichur	24	126	150	35	115	150
	(16.00)	(84.00)	(100.00)	(23.33)	(76.67)	(100.00)
H-K region	95	505	600	123	477	600
	(15.83)	(84.17)	(100.00)	(20.50)	(79.50)	(100.00)
	Chi-square = 6.2725, p > 0.05, NS			Chi-square = 6.8441, p > 0.05, NS		

Source: Field study
Note: Figures in brackets denotes percentages.

On further analyzing the data it was found that in Urban areas 23.33 per cent women respondents in Gulbarga and Raichur districts, 18.67 per cent women respondents are in Koppal district and 16.67 per cent women respondents are in Bidar district who had skill-oriented training. This shows that there is less encouragement for knowledge/skill improvement for women in backward region i.e., Hyderabad-Karnataka.

DISTANCE BETWEEN THE PLACE OF RESIDENCE AND WORKING PLACE

In certain case, the respondents had to waste more time on commuting. This is because the distance between the workplace and residence was considerable. If time spend on this is saved, it can b e devoted for domestic and other work. Respondents having own house had to travel a lot whereas those residing in rented house chose the place of residence to suit their convenience. This is severe in Hyderabad-Karnataka region because of under development of infrastructure.

Table 7.10
Mean Distance of Working place of Women Respondents in
Hyderabad-Karnataka Region (in Kms.)

District	Rural		Urban		Total		T-value
	Mean	SD	Mean	SD	Mean	SD	
Bidar	1.65	3.53	2.96	4.10	2.38	3.90	-2.7367, $p<0.01$, S
Gulbraga	4.11	6.24	5.25	7.66	4.86	7.20	-0.8306, $p>0.05$,NS
Koppal	4.57	6.69	5.08	5.16	4.81	6.03	-0.6171, $p>0.05$,NS
Raichur	2.94	4.09	4.06	5.52	3.66	5.07	-1.5472, $p>0.05$,NS
H-K region	3.32	5.34	4.34	5.56	3.93	5.48	-2.4488, $p<0.01$, S
	F=6.6182, $p<0.01$, S		F=4.3530, $p<0.01$, S		F= 10.2295, $p<0.01$, S		

Source: Field study.

Table 7.10 reveals that urban women respondents who are working in different fields have to travel a low when compared with rural women respondents. For instance, mean distance between the place of residence and working place in rural areas accounts 3.32 kms and 4.34 kms in Urban areas of Hyderabad-Karnataka region. District-wise distribution of data for rural areas reveals that men distance in Bidar constitutes 1.65 kms followed by 4.11 kms in Gulbarga, 4.57 kms in Koppal and 2.94 kms in Koppal. Whereas, in case of urban areas, mean distance constitutes 2.96 kms in Bidar district, 5.25 kms in Gulbarga district, 5.08 kms in Koppal district and 4.06 kms in Raichur district. Thus, most of the women respondents have to travel an average distance of 4 kms in both rural and urban areas in Hyderabad-Karnataka region.

EFFECT OF WORKING OUTSIDE ON THE UPBRINGING OF CHILDREN

Working women will have to face many problems in their domestic life. One of these relates to the upbringing of younger/children. The children require the company of their parents, more particularly of their mothers in their early childhood. Working women will have to spend a considerable amount of their time outside the home and therefore, the younger children become neglected. Sometimes this may result into a maladjusted personality of the younger ones. Therefore, the presence of elder members in the family or of close relatives provides the necessary psychological support and care of the younger ones. An adverse effect on care and socialization of the younger ones becomes visible where these are also lacking. To enquire into this dimension, women respondents in the present study have been asked to state the effect of working outside on the upbringing of their children (Table 7.11). It has been found that 25.81 per cent women respondents in rural areas and 31.05 per cent women respondents in urban areas stated that their working outside has been effecting adversely on the upbringing children. It becomes evident that as many as 26.88 per cent women respondents in Bidar district, 22.22 per cent women respondents in Gulbarga district, 37.90 per cent women respondents in Koppal and 20.33 per cent women respondents in Raichur district, women respondents in rural areas admit that their working outside, has affected the upbringing of their children in one way or the other. Some of these women respondents have further complained that their absence has resulted into improper food intake, ill-health, education and irregular dietary habits among their children. Barring these cases, 73.12 per cent women respondents in Bidar district, 77.78 per cent in Gulbarga district, 62.10 per cent in Koppal and 79.67 per cent women respondents in Raichur district have made adjustment between their working life and domestic needs. Therefore, these respondents do not feel any adverse effect on the upbringing of their children due to their working outside.

Table 7.11

Do you feel that the Effect of your Working Outside has been Adverse on the Upbringing Children? (Married Women Respondents)

Districts	Rural			Urban			Total		
	Yes	No	Total	Yes	No	Total	Yes	No	Total
Bidar	25 (26.88)	68 (73.12)	93 (100.00)	28 (28.28)	71 (71.72)	99 (100.00)	53 (27.60)	139 (72.40)	192 (100.00)
Gulbarga	22 (22.22)	99 (77.78)	121 (100.00)	31 (26.27)	87 (73.73)	118 (100.00)	53 (22.18)	186 (77.82)	239 (100.00)
Koppal	47 (37.90)	77 (62.10)	124 (100.00)	42 (36.21)	74 (63.79)	116 (100.00)	89 (37.08)	151 (62.92)	240 (100.00)
Raichur	25 (20.33)	98 (79.67)	123 (100.00)	35 (33.33)	70 (66.67)	105 (100.00)	60 (26.32)	168 (73.68)	228 (100.00)
H-K region	119 (25.81)	342 (74.19)	461 (100.00)	136 (31.05)	302 (68.95)	438 (100.00)	255 (28.36)	644 (71.64)	899 (100.00)
	Chi-square=15.1343, p<0.05, S			Chi-square=3.30940, p>0.05NS			Chi-square=14.0095, p<0.05, S		

Source: Field study.

Note: Figures in brackets denotes percentages.

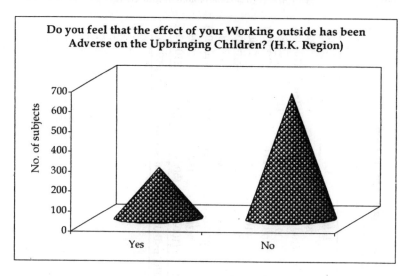

Do you feel that the effect of your Working outside has been Adverse on the Upbringing Children? (H.K. Region)

Further, the distribution of data on district-wise of the respondents in urban areas reveals that the proportion of those working women who feel that there are no adverse effects on the upbringing of their child due to their working outside, is comparatively higher in the Gulbarga district (73.73 per cent) and the proportion of those who feel that it has affected adversely in lower is higher in Koppal district (36.21 per cent).

INADEQUACY OF TIME SPENT WITH HUSBAND

Another important problem with the married working women is her strict time schedule which allocates less time to family obligations and particularly lesser time to spend with her husband. Inquiring into this aspect in rural areas of Hyderabad-Karnataka region (Table 7.12), it has been found that 53.36 per cent women respondents (of this 34.41 per cent women respondents in Bidar district, 56.20 per cent women respondents in Gulbarga district, 61.29 per cent women respondents in Koppal district and 56.91 per cent women respondents in Raichur district) have complained that they did not find sufficient time to spend with their husbands. There are 46.64 per cent women respondents in Hyderabad-Karnataka region (of this 65.59 per cent women respondents in Bidar district, 43.80 per cent women respondents in Gulbarga district, 38.71 per cent women respondents in Koppal district and

Table 7.12

Do you feel that because of your Engagements in the Job you find Inadequate time to spend with your Husband? (Married Women Respondents)

Districts	Rural			Urban			Total		
	Yes	No	Total	Yes	No	Total	Yes	No	Total
Bidar	32 (34.41)	61 (65.59)	93 (100.00)	37 (37.37)	62 (62.63)	99 (100.00)	69 (35.94)	123 (64.06)	192 (100.00)
Gulbarga	68 (56.20)	53 (43.80)	121 (100.00)	52 (44.07)	66 (55.93)	118 (100.00)	120 (50.21)	119 (49.79)	239 (100.00)
Koppal	76 (61.29)	48 (38.71)	124 (100.00)	54 (46.55)	62 (53.45)	116 (100.00)	130 (54.17)	110 (45.83)	240 (100.00)
Raichur	70 (56.91)	53 (43.09)	123 (100.00)	65 (61.91)	40 (38.09)	105 (100.00)	135 (59.21)	93 (40.79)	228 (100.00)
H-K region	246 (53.36)	215 (46.64)	461 (100.00)	208 (47.49)	230 (52.51)	438 (100.00)	454 (50.50)	445 (49.50)	899 (100.00)
	Chi-square=17.5695, p<0.05, S			Chi-square=13.4070, p<0.05, S			Chi-square=24.5075, p<0.05, S		

Source: Field study.

Note: Figures in brackets denotes percentages.

43.09 per cent women respondents in Raichur district) who have reported that in spite of their working outside, they find adequate time for spending with their husbands. Thus, it is clear that the married working women in the study area, because of their heavy work schedule, are not satisfied with the time they spend with their husbands.

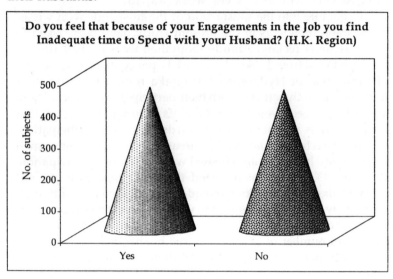

Do you feel that because of your Engagements in the Job you find Inadequate time to Spend with your Husband? (H.K. Region)

In case of urban areas of Hyderabad-Karnataka region 47.49 per cent women respondents stated that they did not find sufficient time to spend with their husband. The district-wise distribution of data in urban areas reveals about the inadequacy of time spent with husband has been reported by more women respondents in Raichur (61.90 per cent) followed by Koppal (46.55 per cent), Gulbarga (44.07 per cent) and Bidar (37.37 per cent). The proportion of those who have no complaint against adequacy of time spent with husband is comparatively higher in Bidar district (62.63 per cent) followed by Gulbarga district (62.63 per cent), Koppal district (53.45 per cent) and Raichur (39.09 per cent).

HUSBAND'S ATTITUDE TOWARDS WIFE'S OCCUPATION

Marital harmony of working women depends on several factors. One of these is the husband's economic life. If the husband is of conservative nature and feels jealous of wives' working among male colleagues, then wives' working outside may become a source of discontentment and strife between the spouses. There may be husbands who may like the economic participation of wife but not its consequences in the form of neglect of domestic duties and responsibilities of the wife. Such husbands may also develop a dissatisfaction with their wives' work (Kapadia).

To enquire into the satisfaction of the husbands with wives' work, the respondents of the present study have been asked to state husbands' feeling/attitude about their work participation. It has been found from Table 7.13 that 61.17 per cent married women in rural areas of Hyderabad-Karnataka region feel that their husbands are fully satisfied with their participation in work. There are 38.83 per cent women respondents who have reported that their husbands are not satisfied towards their work participation. Further, it has been found in urban areas that 56.62 per cent women respondents' husbands are satisfied with their work participation. Whereas, 43.38 per cent reported that their husbands are not satisfied about their working outside. Thus, it is clear that though in majority of the cases working women have the support and approval of their husbands in work participation yet there are a significant number of cases where the husbands are against the work participation of their wives. Objection of husbands are related to the wives' neglect of domestic duties, adverse effect on their children's education, improper care of elders of the family and participation in male company.

District-wise distribution of data about the satisfaction of husbands with wives' work participation is most pronounced in Bidar district (66.67 per cent) followed by Koppal district (64.52 per cent), Raichur district (61.79 per cent) and Gulbarga district (52.89 per cent) in rural areas. The proportion of those respondents whose husbands object towards their work participation is comparatively higher in Gulbarga district (47.11 per cent) followed by Raichur district (38.21 per cent), Koppal district (35.48 per cent) and Bidar (33.33 per cent).

As against this, in urban areas, the proportion of those respondents whose husbands are satisfied with their work participation is comparatively higher in Koppal district (64.66 per cent) followed by Bidar district (62.63 per cent), Gulbarga district (56.78 per cent) and Raichur district (41.90 per cent). Further, data reveals that the proportion of those who have reported that their

Table 7.13

How would you Describe the Attitude of your Husband Towards your Occupational Status?
(Married Women Respondents)

Districts	Rural			Urban			Total		
	He is not satisfied	He is satisfied	Total	He is not satisfied	He is satisfied	Total	He is not satisfied	He is satisfied	Total
Bidar	31 (33.33)	62 (66.67)	93 (100.00)	37 (37.37)	62 (62.63)	99 (100.00)	68 (35.42)	124 (64.58)	192 (100.00)
Gulbarga	57 (47.11)	64 (52.89)	121 (100.00)	51 (43.22)	67 (56.78)	118 (100.00)	108 (45.19)	131 (54.81)	239 (100.00)
Koppal	44 (35.48)	80 (64.52)	124 (100.00)	41 (35.34)	75 (64.66)	116 (100.00)	85 (35.42)	155 (64.58)	240 (100.00)
Raichur	47 (38.21)	76 (61.79)	123 (100.00)	61 (58.10)	44 (41.90)	105 (100.00)	108 (47.37)	120 (52.63)	228 (100.00)
H-K region	179 (38.83)	282 (61.17)	461 (100.00)	190 (43.38)	248 (56.62)	438 (100.00)	369 (41.05)	530 (58.95)	899 (100.00)
	Chi-square=5.2777, p>0.05, NS			Chi-square=13.7614, p<0.05, S			Chi-square=11.1184, p<0.05, S		

Source: Field study.
Note: Figures in brackets denotes percentages

husbands are not satisfied with their work participation is comparatively higher in the Raichur district (58.10 per cent) followed by Gulbarga district (43.22 per cent), Bidar district (37.37 per cent) and Koppal district (35.34 per cent). In order to keep the family happiness intact the association of attitudes of husband and wife is very significant. Thus, it is clear that the proportion of those respondents whose husbands are indifferent to their work participation is comparatively higher in urban areas than rural areas in Hyderabad-Karnataka region.

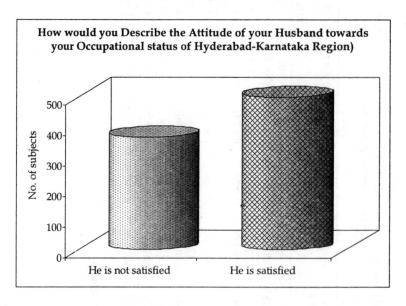

OVERALL SATISFACTION WITH MARRIED LIFE

After having enquired into the various facts of working women's marital and familial life, they have been further asked to express their opinion about the overall satisfaction in their married life (Table 7.14). The data collected in rural areas of Hyderabad-Karnataka region in this regard indicates that 55.10 per cent women respondents in the present study are fully satisfied with their marital life and 44.90 per cent women respondents are dis-satisfied with it. In this regard, 56.62 per cent women respondents who are satisfied and 43.38 per cent women respondents are totally dissatisfied with their marital life in urban areas. The distribution

Table 7.14

How would you Describe your Satisfaction with your Marital Life?
(Married Women Respondents)

Districts	Rural			Urban			Total		
	Satisfied	Dis-satisfied	Total	Satisfied	Dis-satisfied	Total	Satisfied	Dis-satisfied	Total
Bidar	50 (53.76)	43 (46.24)	93 (100.00)	57 (57.58)	42 (42.42)	99 (100.00)	107 (55.73)	85 (44.27)	192 (100.00)
Gulbarga	68 (56.20)	53 (43.80)	121 (100.00)	74 (62.71)	44 (37.29)	118 (100.00)	142 (59.41)	97 (40.59)	239 (100.00)
Koppal	60 (48.39)	64 (51.61)	124 (100.00)	55 (47.41)	61 (52.59)	116 (100.00)	115 (47.92)	125 (52.08)	240 (100.00)
Raichur	76 (61.79)	47 (38.21)	123 (100.00)	62 (59.05)	43 (40.95)	105 (100.00)	138 (60.53)	90 (39.47)	228 (100.00)
H-K region	254 (55.10)	207 (44.90)	461 (100.00)	248 (56.62)	190 (43.38)	438 (100.00)	502 (55.84)	397 (44.16)	899 (100.00)
	Chi-square=4.6089, p>0.05, NS			Chi-square=6.0744, p>0.05, NS			Chi-square=9.3798, p<0.05, S		

Source: Field study.
Note: Figures in brackets denotes percentages.

of data points out that though a half of the women respondents in the present study are satisfied with their married life, yet there are many cases of marital disharmony and dissatisfaction in the present study.

District-wise distribution of data mentions that the satisfaction with married life is most pronounced in the Raichur (61.79 per cent) followed by Gulbarga (56.20 per cent), Bidar (53.76 per cent) and Koppal (48.39 per cent) in rural areas. Further, it is significant to note that the marital dissatisfaction is most prominent in Koppal district (51.61 per cent), Bidar district (46.24 per cent), Gulbarga district (43.80 per cent) and Raichur district (38.21 per cent).

The district-wise distribution of data of the women respondents for urban areas reveals about the satisfaction with the marriage is most pronounced in the Gulbarga district (62.71 per cent) followed by Raichur district (59.05 per cent), Bidar district (57.58 per cent) and Koppal district (57.58 per cent). There are 52.59 per cent women respondents in Koppal district are dissatisfied with their marriages. These women respondents are followed by Bidar district (42.42 per cent), Raichur district (40.95 per cent) and Gulbarga district (37.29 per cent) who are dissatisfied with their married life.

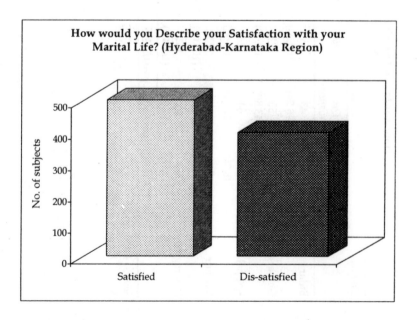

IN-JOB IMPROVEMENT OF QUALIFICATION

Occupational absolution is a phenomenon which is characteristic of the contemporary work organization. Every day so fast progress is occurring in the scientific and professional knowledge that after every five or ten years it will become outdated and one's knowledge is going to become retrograded in comparison with the advancement taking place in one's specialized field. Therefore, continuous updating of knowledge has become an essential part of the occupational life (Dubin 1971). Moreover, career mobility through promotion, refresher course, departmental examinations and additional academic/professional qualifications also implied that in job improvement of qualification is necessary. In top jobs where the chances of career mobility are extremely wide, in such jobs, improvement of qualification becomes a basic pre-requisite for future mobility.

The women in our study are educated and employed in various fields and have achieved their economic position because of their educational achievement. Therefore, they know fully well the value of education and how it contributes to the upward economic mobility. They also know the consequences of higher and technical education of women in both economic and non-economic fields such as promotion, adjustment in marital family life and placement in social life. Therefore, in the present study the working women have been asked that whether they have improved their education/professional qualification after entering into the job. Our explorations suggest that the only 17.00 per cent women respondents have improved their education/professional qualifications and 83.00 per cent respondents reported that they have not improved their education/professional qualifications in rural areas. Even in urban areas, only 22.33 per cent women respondents in the sample have enhanced their academic professional qualification during their occupational career (Table 7.15).

District-wise data of the women respondents in rural areas reveals that education/professional qualification have been improved by more respondents in Raichur district (24.67 per cent) and Gulbarga district (24.00 per cent) followed by Koppal district (10.00 per cent) and Bidar district (9.33 per cent). The proportion of those women respondents who have not improved educational/professional qualification after the entry into job comparatively is

Table 7.15

Improvement of Education/professional Qualification by Women Respondents in Hyderabad-Karnataka Region.

Districts	Rural			Urban			Total		
	Yes	No	Total	Yes	No	Total	Yes	No	Total
Bidar	14 (9.33)	136 (90.67)	150 (100.00)	6 (4.00)	144 (96.00)	150 (100.00)	20 (6.67)	280 (93.33)	300 (100.00)
Gulbarga	36 (24.00)	114 (76.00)	150 (100.00)	53 (35.33)	97 (64.67)	150 (100.00)	89 (29.67)	211 (70.33)	300 (100.00)
Koppal	15 (10.00)	135 (90.00)	150 (100.00)	16 (10.67)	134 (89.33)	150 (100.00)	31 (10.33)	269 (89.67)	300 (100.00)
Raichur	37 (24.67)	113 (75.33)	150 (100.00)	59 (39.33)	91 (60.67)	150 (100.00)	96 (32.00)	204 (68.00)	300 (100.00)
H-K Region	102 (17.00)	498 (83.00)	600 (100.00)	134 (22.33)	466 (77.67)	600 (100.00)	236 (19.67)	964 (80.33)	1200 (100.00)
	Chi-square= 4.3390,df=3, p>0.05,NS			Chi-square= 58.2330,df=3, p<0.01, S			Chi-square= 39.0150,df=3, p<0.01, S		

Source: Field study.

Note: Figures in brackets denotes percentages.

higher in Bidar district (90.67 per cent) and Koppal district (90.00 per cent) followed by the Gulbarga district (76.00 per cent) and Koppal district (75.33 per cent).

The district-wise data of the women respondents in urban areas mentions that the proportion of those who have improved education/professional qualification is comparatively higher in the Raichur district (39.33 per cent) and Gulbarga district (35.33 per cent) and of those who have not improved level of education/ professional qualification is comparatively higher in Bidar district (96.00 per cent) and Koppal district (89.33 per cent).

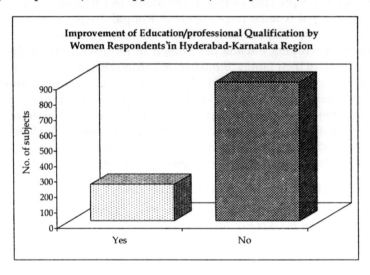

Thus, it is clear that majority of the women respondents in present study have not improved their education/professional qualifications after their entry into job in both rural and urban areas of Hyderabad-Karnataka region. In most of the cases non-availability of the opportunity or facilities for qualification improvement indicate that there is no inclination among these women respondents for career improvement. Therefore, there is need for them to improve their qualification/training in backward region like Hyderabad-Karnataka.

IMPROVED LIVING CONDITIONS OF THE FAMILY

Further, the female respondents have been asked to state whether their working outside has helped in improving the living conditions of the family in any way. In case of rural areas of Hyderabad-Karnataka region, it has been found that 74.67 per cent of respondents have stated that their working outside has improved their family's living conditions and 25.33 per cent women respondents have stated that their working outside still has not improved their family's living conditions (Table 7.16). Whereas, in case of urban areas, 76.00 per cent of women respondents family's conditions have improved and 24.00 per cent respondents family's conditions have not been improved from their working outside. 60.00 per cent women respondents in Bidar district, 81.33 per cent women respondents in Gulbarga district, 80.00 per cent women respondents in Koppal district and 77.33 per cent women respondents in Raichur district in rural areas stated that their working outside has helped in improving the living conditions of their family. Similarly, in urban areas, 48.67 per cent women respondents in Bidar district, 81.33 per cent women respondents in Gulbarga district, 86.00 per cent women respondents in Koppal district and 88.00 per cent women respondents in Raichur district favoured this question. This shows that women in one or other way contributing to their family income which helps in improving their family conditions.

WHETHER SATISFIED WITH THE PRESENT JOB?

The extent of job satisfaction among women is an important aspect of their labour market experiences, for it may satisfy the degree to which they have made a successful accommodation to the work. Further, the employees' satisfaction or dissatisfaction with a particular situation or job factor is a function of the discrepancy between his/her expectations and actual achievements.

After having enquired into the different points of female work, the respondents have been asked to express their overall satisfaction with present job (Table 7.17). The data collected in this regard indicates that 54.50 per cent women respondents are fully satisfied with their present job and 45.50 per cent are totally dissatisfied with their present job in rural areas of Hyderabad-Karnataka region. Whereas, in urban areas, 64.33 per cent of women respondents are satisfied and 36.67 per cent of women respondents are not satisfied with their present job. There are 36.67 per cent women respondents in rural areas in Bidar district, 72.00 per cent women respondents in Gulbarga district, 38.67 per cent

Table 7.16
Improvement of Living Conditions of Women Respondents' Family in
Hyderabad-Karnataka Region

Districts	Rural			Urban			Total		
	Yes	No	Total	Yes	No	Total	Yes	No	Total
Bidar	90 (60.00)	60 (40.00)	150 (100.00)	73 (48.67)	77 (51.33)	150 (100.00)	163 (54.33)	137 (45.67)	300 (100.00)
Gulbarga	122 (81.33)	28 (18.67)	150 (100.00)	122 (81.33)	28 (18.67)	150 (100.00)	244 (81.33)	56 (18.67)	300 (100.00)
Koppal	120 (80.00)	30 (20.00)	150 (100.00)	129 (86.00)	21 (14.00)	150 (100.00)	249 (83.00)	51 (17.00)	300 (100.00)
Raichur	116 (77.33)	34 (22.67)	150 (100.00)	132 (88.00)	18 (12.00)	150 (100.00)	248 (82.67)	52 (17.33)	300 (100.00)
H-K Region	448 (74.67)	152 (25.33)	600 (100.00)	456 (76.00)	144 (24.00)	600 (100.00)	904 (75.33)	296 (24.67)	1200 (100.00)
	Chi-square= 23.4020,df=3, p<0.01, S			Chi-square= 83.8450,df=3, p<0.01, S			Chi-square= 95.1810,df=3, p<0.01, S		

Source: Field study.
Note: Figures in brackets denotes percentages.

Table 7.17
Satisfaction with present Job by Women Respondents in Hyderabad-Karnataka Region

Districts	Rural			Urban			Total		
	Satisfied	Not satisfied	Total	Satisfied	Not satisfied	Total	Satisfied	Not satisfied	Total
Bidar	55 (36.67)	95 (63.33)	150 (100.00)	47 (31.33)	103 (68.67)	150 (100.00)	102 (34.00)	198 (66.00)	300 (100.00)
Gulbarga	108 (72.00)	42 (28.00)	150 (100.00)	126 (84.00)	24 (16.00)	150 (100.00)	234 (78.00)	66 (22.00)	300 (100.00)
Koppal	58 (38.67)	92 (61.33)	150 (100.00)	90 (60.00)	60 (40.00)	150 (100.00)	148 (49.33)	152 (50.67)	300 (100.00)
Raichur	106 (70.67)	44 (29.33)	150 (100.00)	123 (82.00)	27 (18.00)	150 (100.00)	229 (76.33)	71 (23.67)	300 (100.00)
H-K Region	327 (54.50)	273 (45.50)	600 (100.00)	386 (64.33)	214 (35.67)	600 (100.00)	713 (59.42)	487 (40.58)	1200 (100.00)
	Chi-square=68.7370,df=3, $p<0.01$, S			Chi-square=118.1060,df=3, $p<0.01$, S			Chi-square=171.5900,df=3, $p<0.01$, S		

Source: Field study.
Note: Figures in brackets denotes percentages.

women respondents in Koppal district and 70.67 per cent women respondents in Raichur district are satisfied with the present job. As against this, in urban areas, 31.33 per cent women respondents in Bidar district, 84.00 per cent women respondents in Gulbarga district, 60.00 per cent women respondents in Koppal district and 82.00 per cent women respondents in Raichur district are satisfied with their present job. Thus, it is clear from the table that majority of women respondents in Bidar and Koppal district from both rural and urban areas are not satisfied with their job. This shows the women respondents who work in low-end jobs are not satisfied in the Hyderabad-Karnataka region.

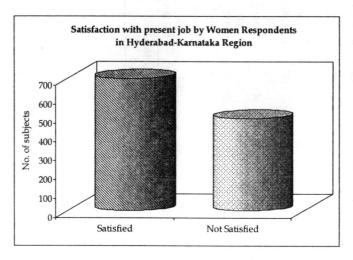

DO YOU HAVE LEAVE FACILITY?

Women respondents in the present study have been asked to state whether they have leave facility. It has been found that in rural areas only 28.50 per cent women respondents in Hyderabad-Karnataka region (of this 18.67 per cent women respondents in Bidar district, 27.33 per cent women respondents in Gulbarga district, 38.00 per cent women respondents in Koppal district and 30.0 per cent women respondents in Raichur district) have the leave facility (Table 7.18). Whereas, 71.50 per cent women respondents in Hyderabad-Karnataka region (of this 81.33 per cent, 72.67 per cent, 62.00 per cent and 70.00 per cent in Bidar, Gulbarga, Koppal and Raichur districts, respectively) do not have leave facility. As

Table 7.18

Leave Facility Given to Women Respondents in Hyderabad-Karnataka Region

Districts	Rural			Urban			Total		
	Yes	No	Total	Yes	No	Total	Yes	No	Total
Bidar	28 (18.67)	122 (81.33)	150 (100.00)	53 (35.33)	97 (64.67)	150 (100.00)	81 (27.00)	219 (73.00)	300 (100.00)
Gulbarga	41 (27.33)	109 (72.67)	150 (100.00)	88 (58.67)	62 (41.33)	150 (100.00)	129 (43.00)	171 (57.00)	300 (100.00)
Koppal	57 (38.00)	93 (62.00)	150 (100.00)	66 (44.00)	84 (56.000)	150 (100.00)	123 (41.00)	177 (59.00)	300 (100.00)
Raichur	45 (30.00)	105 (70.00)	150 (100.00)	94 (62.67)	56 (37.33)	150 (100.00)	139 (46.33)	161 (53.67)	300 (100.00)
H-K Region	171 (28.50)	429 (71.50)	600 (100.00)	301 (50.17)	299 (49.83)	600 (100.00)	472 (39.33)	728 (60.67)	1200 (100.00)
	Chi-square =14.0270,df=3, p< 0.01, S			Chi-square = 29.1940,df=3, p < 0.01, S			Chi-square = 27.3240,df=3, p < 0.01, S		

Source: Field study.

Note: Figures in brackets denotes percentages.

against this, in urban areas, 50.17 per cent women respondents in Hyderabad-Karnataka region (of this 35.33 per cent in Bidar district, 58.67 per cent in Gulbarga district, 44.00 per cent in Koppal district and 62.67 per cent in Raichur district) have leave facility.

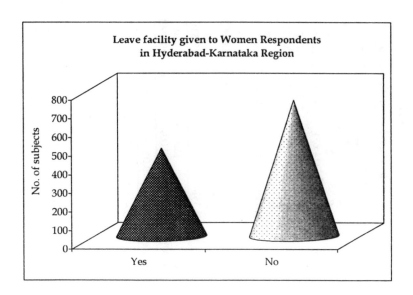

MONTHLY INCOME

In the present study, considerable income variation has been found in the income status of women respondents in Hyderabad-Karnataka region (Table 7.19). In case of rural areas, 41.50 per cent women respondents possess a monthly income of upto Rs.1000, 32.67 per cent of women respondents possess a monthly income Rs.1001-2000, 11.33 per cent women respondents possess income of Rs.2001-5000, 13.33 per cent women respondents possess income of Rs.5001-10000, and only 1.17 per cent of women respondents possess income of Rs.10000 and above. Whereas, in case of urban areas, 19.33 per cent of women respondents belong to the income group of upto Rs.1000, 27.17 per cent women respondents belong to income between Rs.1001-2000, 30.50 per cent women respondents belong to income between Rs.2001-5000, 18.67 per cent women respondents belong to income between Rs.5001-10000

Table 7.19
Monthly Income of Women Respondents in Hyderabad-Karnataka Region

Income Group (Rs.)	Bidar		Gulbarga		Koppal		Raichur		H-K Region	
	Rural	Urban	Rural	Urban	Rural	Urban	Rural	Urban	Rural	Urban
Upto Rs. 1000	71 (47.33)	64 (42.67)	60 (40.00)	14 (9.33)	60 (40.00)	22 (14.67)	58 (38.67)	16 (10.67)	249 (41.50)	116 (19.33)
Rs. 1001-2000	51 (34.00)	41 (27.33)	55 (36.67)	40 (26.67)	38 (25.33)	35 (23.33)	52 (34.67)	47 (31.33)	196 (32.67)	163 (27.17)
Rs. 2001-5000	16 (10.67)	15 (10.00)	10 (6.67)	58 (38.67)	30 (20.00)	64 (42.67)	12 (8.00)	46 (30.67)	68 (11.33)	183 (30.50)
Rs. 5000-10000	12 (8.00)	29 (19.33)	25 (16.66)	25 (16.66)	17 (11.33)	28 (18.66)	26 (17.33)	30 (20.00)	80 (13.33)	112 (18.67)
Rs. 10000 and above	00 (0.00)	1 (0.67)	00 (0.00)	13 (8.67)	5 (3.33)	01 (0.67)	2 (1.33)	11 (7.33)	07 (1.17)	26 (4.33)
Total	150 (100.00)	150 (100.00)	150 (100.00)	150 (100.00)	150 (100.00)	150 (100.00)	150 (100.00)	150 (100.00)	600 (100.00)	600 (100.00)

Chi-square = 81.3646, $p < 0.05$, S

Source: Field study.
Note: Figures in brackets denotes percentages.

and only 4.33 per cent of women respondents belong to income group of Rs.10000 and above.

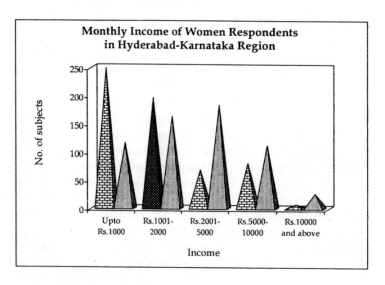

Examining the district-wise monthly income structure of the women respondents in rural areas, it is found that in Bidar district 47.33 per cent have less than Rs. 1000 monthly income, 34.00 per cent have Rs. 1001-2000, 10.67 per cent have Rs. 2001-5000, and only 8.00 per cent respondents have Rs. 5001 to 10000 monthly income. In case of Gulbarga district, 40.00 per cent respondents have less than Rs. 1000 monthly income, 36.67 per cent have between Rs. 1001-2000, 6.66 per cent have Rs. 2001-5000, and 16.67 per cent have monthly income between Rs. 5001-10000. Further, in Koppal and Raichur districts, 40.00 per cent and 38.67 per cent have income less than Rs. 1000, 25.33 per cent and 34.67 per cent have between Rs. 1001-2000 monthly income, respectively. The income between Rs. 2001-5000 constitutes 20.00 per cent and 8.00 per cent, between Rs. 5001-10000 constitutes 11.33 per cent and 17.33 per cent in Koppal and Raichur districts, respectively. Only 3.33 per cent respondents in Koppal and 1.33 per cent in Raichur have monthly income above Rs. 10000. Thus, it is clear that most of the women respondents in rural areas in the present sample have an income less than Rs. 1000 and between Rs. 1001 to 2000. This shows that these respondents have a lower middle class income status which alone is sufficient to raise these women to a satisfactory position in their family. However, if their income is combined with the income of the husbands or of the parents, then these working women are contributing a lot to the economic stability of their family.

With regard to the results in urban areas of Hyderabad-Karnataka region, in Bidar district, 42.67 per cent women respondents possess less than Rs. 1000, 27.33 per cent women respondents have income between Rs.1001-2000, 10.00 per cent women respondents possess income between Rs. 2001-5000, 19.33 per cent women respondents have income between Rs. 5001-10000 and only 0.67 per cent have the monthly income above Rs. 10000. In case of Gulbarga district, 9.33 per cent women respondents have less than Rs. 1000, 26.67 per cent women respondents have income between Rs. 1001-2000, 38.67 per cent women respondents have income between Rs. 2001-5000, 16.67 per cent women respondents possess income between Rs. 5001-10000, and 8.66 per cent women respondents possess income above Rs. 10000. Further, Table 19 reveals that in Koppal and Raichur districts 14.67 per cent women respondents and 10.67 per cent women respondents possess income less than Rs. 1000, 23.33 per cent and 31.33 per cent women respondents have income between Rs.1001-2000, respectively. The income between 2001-5000 women respondents constitutes 42.67 per cent and 30.67 per cent in Koppal and Raichur districts, respectively; only 0.67 per cent women respondents in Koppal and 7.33 per cent women respondents in Raichur district possess income above Rs. 10000. This indicates that a comparatively women respondents in Urban areas have higher income higher income between Rs. 2001-5000 and Rs. 5001-10000 than rural areas.

MONTHLY INCOME BY EDUCATION

The distribution of income data on the basis of education, it suggests that there is a unsatisfactory correlation between the education level and income status of the women in Hyderabad-Karnataka region. For instance, according to Table 7.20, the women respondents who had primary education it is found that 57.89 per cent women respondents possess income less than Rs. 1000. 46.25 per cent and 40.00 per cent women respondents who had secondary education possess income upto Rs.1000 and Rs. 1001-2000, respectively. Further, 41.07 per cent and 33.94 per cent women

Table 7.20
Monthly Income of Women Respondents by Education in Hyderabad-Karnataka Region
(Comprising All Districts)

Education Level	Upto Rs. 1000		Rs. 1001-2000		Rs. 2001-5000		Rs. 5001-10000		Rs. 10001 and above		Total	
	Rural	Urban	Rural	Urban	Rural	Urban	Rural	Urban	Rural	Urban	Rural	Urban
Primary	132 (57.89)	40 (33.90)	78 (34.21)	41 (34.75)	04 (1.75)	35 (29.66)	13 (5.70)	02 (1.69)	01 (0.45)	00 (0.00)	228 (100.00)	118 (100.00)
Secondary	74 (46.25)	23 (21.50)	64 (40.00)	40 (37.38)	15 (9.37)	35 (32.71)	07 (4.38)	08 (7.48)	00 (0.00)	01 (0.93)	160 (100.00)	107 (100.00)
Pre-University	23 (41.07)	18 (21.45)	19 (33.94)	20 (23.81)	08 (14.28)	34 (40.48)	06 (10.71)	12 (14.28)	00 (0.00)	0 (0.00)	56 (100.00)	84 (100.00)
Graduation	11 (25.00)	20 (19.61)	17 (38.64)	21 (20.59)	06 (13.64)	29 (28.43)	09 (20.45)	29 (28.43)	01 (2.27)	03 (2.94)	44 (100.00)	102 (100.00)
Post-graduation	01 (6.67)	04 (7.69)	05 (33.33)	16 (30.77)	04 (26.67)	11 (21.15)	05 (33.33)	12 (23.08)	00 (0.00)	09 (17.31)	15 (100.00)	52 (100.00)
Professional	08 (8.25)	1: (8.03)	13 (13.40)	25 (18.25)	31 (31.96)	39 (28.47)	40 (41.24)	49 (35.76)	05 (5.15)	13 (9.49)	97 (100.00)	137 (100.00)
Total	249 (41.50)	116 (19.33)	196 (32.67)	163 (27.17)	68 (11.33)	183 (30.50)	80 (13.33)	112 (18.67)	07 (1.17)	26 (4.33)	600 (100.00)	600 (100.00)

Chi-square = 101.40323, p<0.05, S

Source: Field study.
Note: Figures in brackets denotes percentages.

respondents whose education level is PUC have income upto Rs. 1000 and Rs. 1001-2000, respectively. 25.00 per cent and 38.64 per cent Graduate women respondents earns income less than Rs. 1000 and 1001-2000, respectively. Only 05 (33.33 per cent) women respondent who had Post-Graduate degree earn income of Rs.5001-10000. Surprisingly, 31.96 per cent and 41.24 per cent women respondents who studied professional/vocational courses possess income of Rs. 2001-5000 and Rs. 5001-10000.

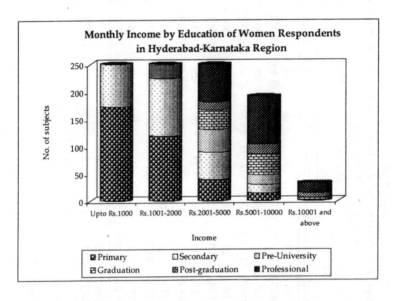

Further distribution of data in Table 7.20 for urban areas that the women respondents who had primary education it is found that 33.90 per cent, 34.75 per cent and 29.66 per cent have income upto Rs. 1000, Rs. 1001-2000 and Rs. 2001-5000, respectively. 37.38 per cent and 32.71 per cent women respondents who had secondary education possess income of Rs. 1001-2000 and Rs. 2001-5000, respectively. Further, 23.81 per cent 40.48 per cent women respondents whose education is Pre-university (PUC) have income between Rs. 1001-2000 and Rs. 2001-5000, respectively. Among graduate women respondents 28.43 per cent posses income Rs. 2001-5000 and Rs. 5001-10000. 30.77 per cent and 23.08 per cent women respondents who had post-graduation degree earn income of Rs. 1001-2000 and Rs. 5001-10000, respectively. Only 17.31 per cent Post-graduate women respondents earn income Rs. 10000 and above. Satisfactory point to note here is that 28.47 per cent and 35.76 per cent women respondents who completed 'Professional courses' have income of Rs. 2001-5000 and Rs. 5001-10000, respectively. The study shows that a majority of women in Hyderabad-Karnataka region work in low-earning and low-paying activities and earns low income. Further, it show that there is no correlation between education level and income of the women respondents except professional courses.

CONTROL OVER FAMILY BUDGET

The occupational status of the women has positively contributed to the enhancement of her prestige and power in the family. She has become an important agent in the decision making process in the family. Further, it has been found that the working women exerts more influence on family decision making than the non-working women. This part of the study has also elicited information on gender differentials in control over individual and household income.

The respondents in the present study have been asked to state whether person who has control over individual and household income in rural areas (Table 7.21). It has been found that in Hyderabad-Karnataka region 32.17 per cent women respondents reported that the income is spend by me, 39.83 per cent reported that income is handed over to the husband/parents and 28.00 per cent reported that some per cent of income is returned to husband/parents.

The distribution of data on district-wise of the women respondents reveals that the wife's maximum control on family budget has been found in Bidar district (45.33 per cent) followed by Koppal district (36.67 per cent), Raichur district (24.67 per cent) and Gulbarga district (22.00 per cent). The case of handed over the income to the husband/parents have been found more in the Gulbarga and Raichur districts (in both district 55.33 per cent) followed by Koppal district (38.00 per cent) and Bidar district (10.67 per cent). Similarly, some per centage of income returned to husband/parents has been found comparatively higher number of cases in Bidar district (44.00 per cent) followed by Koppal district (25.33 per cent), Gulbarga district (22.66 per cent) and Raichur district (20.00 per cent).

Table 7.21
Control over Women Respondent's Income in Hyderabad-Karnataka Region

District	Rural				Urban			
	Income is spend by me	Handed over to husband/parents	Some% returned to husband/parents	Total	Income is spend by me	Handed over to husband/parents	Some% returned to husband/parents	Total
Bidar	68 (45.33)	16 (10.67)	66 (44.00)	150 (100.00)	91 (60.67)	11 (7.33)	48 (32.00)	150 (100.00)
Gulbarga	33 (22.00)	83 (55.33)	34 (22.66)	150 (100.00)	55 (36.67)	50 (33.33)	45 (30.00)	150 (100.00)
Koppal	55 (36.67)	57 (38.00)	38 (25.33)	150 (100.00)	59 (36.67)	62 (41.34)	29 (30.00)	150 (100.00)
Raichur	37 (36.67)	83 (38.00)	30 (25.33)	150 (100.00)	56 (39.33)	55 (41.34)	39 (19.33)	150 (100.00)
H-K Region	193 (24.67)	239 (55.33)	168 (20.00)	600 (100.00)	261 (37.33)	178 (36.67)	161 (26.00)	600 (100.00)
	193 (32.17)	239 (39.83)	168 (28.00)	600 (100.00)	261 (43.50)	178 (29.67)	161 (26.83)	600 (100.00)

Chi-square = 85.7743, p<0.05, S   Chi-square = 54.1764, p<0.05, S

Source: Field study.
Note: Figures in brackets denotes percentages

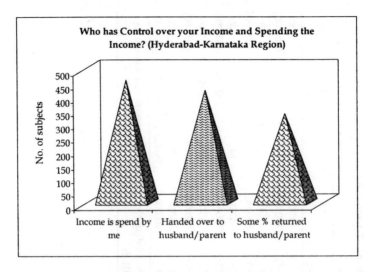

Further, it has been found in Urban areas of study region that 43.50 per cent women respondents handed over the income to husband/parents, 26.83 per cent respondents return some per centage of income to husband/parents. Data shows that working women themselves have maximum control over their income. Further, Table 7.21 shows that by this measure, 60.67 per cent of the earning women in our sample in Bidar district do not hand over their income to anybody after receiving them, followed by 39.33 per cent in Koppal district, 37.33 per cent in Raichur district and 36.67 per cent in Gulbarga district. 41.34 per cent of earning women in Koppal district hand over their income to their husband/ parents followed by 36.67 per cent in Raichur district, 33.33 per cent in Gulbarga district and 7.33 per cent in Bidar district. Remaining of the women earners, i.e. 32.00 per cent in Bidar district, 30.00 per cent in Gulbarga district, 26.00 per cent in Raichur district and 19.33 per cent in Koppal district returned some per centage of income to husband/parents. Thus, it is clear that working women's importance in family life is increasing. And family budget, the most crucial aspect of family life, is to be passing gradually under her direct control.

MONTHLY SAVINGS

Further, we examined savings patterns which are final and important source of income. It is found that those who are able to

Table 7.22
Monthly Savings of Women Respondents in Hyderabad-Karnataka Region

District	Rural			Urban			Total		
	Savings	No Savings	Total	Savings	No Savings	Total	Savings	No Savings	Total
Bidar	45 (30.00)	105 (70.00)	150 (100.00)	41 (27.33)	109 (72.67)	150 (100.00)	86 (28.67)	214 (71.33)	300 (100.00)
Gulbarga	31 (20.67)	119 (79.33)	150 (100.00)	97 (64.67)	53 (35.33)	150 (100.00)	128 (42.67)	172 (57.33)	300 (100.00)
Koppal	55 (36.67)	95 (63.33)	150 (100.00)	88 (58.67)	62 (41.33)	150 (100.00)	143 (47.67)	157 (52.33)	300 (100.00)
Raichur	29 (19.33)	121 (80.67)	150 (100.00)	87 (58.00)	63 (42.00)	150 (100.00)	116 (38.67)	184 (61.33)	300 (100.00)
H-K Region	160 (26.67)	440 (73.33)	600 (100.00)	313 (52.17)	287 (47.83)	600 (100.00)	473 (39.42)	727 (60.58)	1200 (100.00)
	Chi-square= 15.4090,df=3, $p<0.05$, S			Chi-square= 51.0490,df=3, $p<0.01$, S			Chi-square= 24.4660,df=3, $p<0.01$, S		

Source: Field study.
Note: Figures in brackets denotes percentages.

save money are exercising some degree of control over their personal and household income, and have greater economic security in their life.

The women respondents in our study area have been asked to state their monthly savings. About 160 (26.67 per cent) women respondents in rural areas and 313 (52.17 per cent) women respondents in urban areas of Hyderabad-Karnataka region reported that they have savings in some form or the other. Further, it has been found that in rural areas, 30.00 per cent of respondents in Bidar district, 20.67 per cent respondents in Gulbarga district, 36.67 per cent in Koppal district and 19.33 per cent in Raichur district are have the saving habits. The distribution of data for urban areas, reveals that 27.33 per cent in Bidar district, 64.67 per cent in Gulbarga district, 58.67 per cent in Koppal district and 58.00 per cent women respondents in Raichur district are in the saving habits (Table 7.22). The women who are working in low end/ income fields and increased expenditure were responsible for low level/no savings in Hyderabad-Karnataka region.

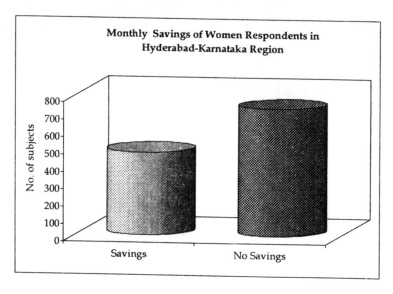

TAX DEDUCTED

In the present study the respondents have been asked to state whether they are tax payees or not. It has been found that 2.50 per

Table 7.23
Tax paid by Women Respondents in Hyderabad-Karnataka Region

Districts	Rural			Urban			Total		
	Yes	No	Total	Yes	No	Total	Yes	No	Total
Bidar	4 (2.67)	146 (97.33)	150 (100.00)	21 (14.00)	129 (86.00)	150 (100.00)	25 (8.33)	275 (91.67)	300 (100.00)
Gulbarga	7 (4.67)	143 (95.33)	150 (100.00)	16 (10.67)	134 (89.33)	150 (100.00)	23 (7.67)	277 (92.33)	300 (100.00)
Koppal	2 (1.33)	148 (98.67)	150 (100.00)	0 (0.00)	150 (100.00)	150 (100.00)	2 (0.67)	298 (99.33)	300 (100.00)
Raichur	2 (1.33)	148 (98.67)	150 (100.00)	11 (7.33)	139 (92.67)	150 (100.00)	13 (4.33)	287 (95.67)	300 (100.00)
H-K Region	15 (2.50)	585 (97.50)	600 (100.00)	48 (8.00)	552 (92.00)	600 (100.00)	63 (5.25)	1137 (94.75)	1200 (100.00)
	Chi-square= 4.5810,df=3, p>0.05, NS			Chi-square= 21.9200,df=3, p<0.01, S			Chi-square= 22.4320,df=3, p<0.01, S		

Source: Field study.
Note: Figures in brackets denotes percentages.

cent of women respondents are paying tax and 97.50 per cent of women respondents are not paying tax in rural areas of Hyderabad-Karnataka region. However, in urban areas, 8.00 per cent of women respondents are paying tax and 92.00 per cent women respondents are not paying tax. Further, it has been found that in rural areas, only 2.67 per cent women respondents in Bidar district, 4.67 per cent women respondents in Gulbarga district, 1.33 per cent women respondents in Koppal and Raichur districts are paying tax. Whereas, in urban areas, 14.00 per cent respondents in Bidar district, 10.67 per cent women respondents in Gulbarga district and 7.33 per cent women respondents in Raichur district are tax payers (Table 7.23). This indicates that in rural areas, as the income of the female respondents is low there is no question of tax paying. In urban areas, only those women respondents are paying tax whose income is high/above tax exemption limit, especially government employees. In general, however, income of the female workers in Hyderabad-Karnataka region is low, as the result, the tax papers are also few or limited.

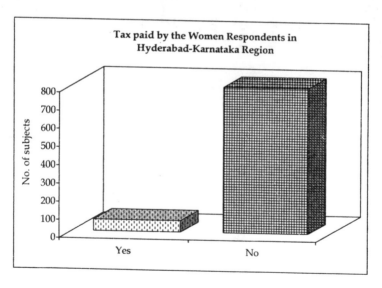

ARE YOU SATISFIED WITH THE WAGE RATE FIXED?

Discrimination refers to providing individuals with fewer rewards or facilities than are legitimately deserved. Sex-based

Table 7.24
Are you Satisfied with the wage Rate Fixed?

Districts	Rural			Urban			Total		
	Yes	No	Total	Yes	No	Total	Yes	No	Total
Bidar	30 (20.00)	120 (80.00)	150 (100.00)	42 (28.00)	108 (72.00)	150 (100.00)	72 (24.00)	228 (76.00)	300 (100.00)
Gulbarga	54 (36.00)	96 (64.00)	150 (100.00)	73 (48.67)	77 (51.33)	150 (100.00)	127 (42.33)	173 (57.67)	300 (100.00)
Koppal	40 (26.67)	110 (73.33)	150 (100.00)	66 (44.00)	84 (56.00)	150 (100.00)	106 (35.33)	194 (64.67)	300 (100.00)
Raichur	71 (47.33)	79 (52.67)	150 (100.00)	86 (57.33)	64 (42.67)	150 (100.00)	157 (52.33)	143 (47.67)	300 (100.00)
H-K Region	195 (32.50)	405 (67.50)	600 (100.00)	267 (44.50)	333 (55.50)	600 (100.00)	462 (38.50)	738 (61.50)	1200 (100.00)
	Chi-square= 28.8930,df=3, p<0.05, S			Chi-square= 27.6070,df=3, p<0.01, S			Chi-square= 54.0180,df=3, p<0.05, S		

Source: Field study.
Note: Figures in brackets denotes percentages.

discriminations against working women may be of two types. Access discrimination-discrimination that women may face in terms of the availability to them of particular job. Treatment discrimination-discrimination that women may confront once they have obtained jobs. Discrimination against women has not only been rampant in society at large but also in work organisation too where they have to ace some-time sex-based discrimination. Though in India there are no gross discriminatory roles in work organisation against women, yet in placement, promotion and in questions of transfer some times subtle and latent discriminatory practice are adopted and men are given precedence over women workers.

To enquire into this dimension, the respondents have been asked to state whether they are satisfied with wage rate fixed. The data from Table 7.24 reveals that in Hyderabad-Karnataka region as large as 67.50 per cent women respondents in rural areas and 55.50 per cent women respondents in urban areas were not satisfied with wage rate fixed. Only 32.50 per cent women respondents in rural areas and 44.50 per cent women respondents in urban areas were satisfied with wage rate fixed. These respondents who reported dis-satisfaction, say that in promotion, placement etc. have been neglected to give preference to male workers.

The district-wise distribution of data for rural areas reveals

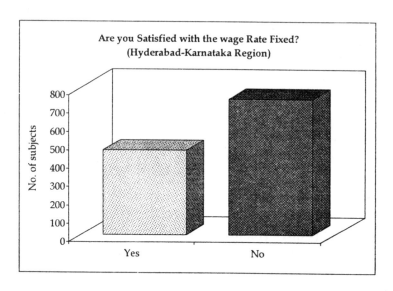

Are you Satisfied with the wage Rate Fixed?
(Hyderabad-Karnataka Region)

that dis-satisfaction with wage rate fixed has been reported by more respondents in Bidar district (80.00 per cent women respondents) followed by the Koppal district (73.33 per cent women respondents), Gulbarga district (64.00 per cent women respondents) and Raichur district (52.67 per cent women respondents). Whereas, in Urban areas, 72.00 per cent women respondents in Bidar district followed by Koppal district (56.00 per cent women respondents), Gulbarga district (51.33 per cent women respondents) and Raichur district (42.67 per cent women respondents).

DO YOU FEEL THAT YOUR HUSBAND OR OTHER MALE COLLEAGUES ARE MORE PAID THAN YOU?

Keeping all these in view, the respondents in the present study have been asked to state whether they are paid less than their husband or colleagues. It has been found from Table 7.25 in Hyderabad-Karnataka region that majority of the women respondents i.e. 83.17 per cent in rural areas and 79.67 per cent women respondents in urban areas have stated that they are paid less than their husband or colleagues. Only 16.83 per cent women respondents in rural areas and 20.33 per cent women respondents in urban areas state that they are paid equal to their husband or male colleagues. This shows the wage-discrimination in case of women respondents for same work in Hyderabad-Karnataka region.

District-wise distribution of data reveals that the proportion of women respondents who are paid less wages than their husband or male colleagues is high in Bidar district (89.33 per cent) followed by Raichur district (85.33 per cent), Koppal district (82.00 per cent) and Gulbarga district (76.00 per cent). As against this in Urban areas, 92.00 per cent women respondents in Bidar district and Koppal districts, 68.67 per cent women respondents in Raichur district and 66.00 per cent women respondents in Gulbarga district are paid less wages than their husband or male colleagues.

WAGE DIFFERENTIAL

Under competitive conditions, all worker would have to be homogenous; all jobs would have to display identical non-monetary advantages and dis-advantages; there would have to

Table 7.25
Do you feel that your Husband or other male Colleagues are more Paid than you?

Districts	Rural			Urban			Total		
	Yes	No	Total	Yes	No	Total	Yes	No	Total
Bidar	16 (10.67)	134 (89.33)	150 (100.00)	12 (8.00)	138 (92.00)	150 (100.00)	28 (9.33)	272 (90.67)	300 (100.00)
Gulbarga	36 (24.00)	114 (76.00)	150 (100.00)	51 (34.00)	99 (66.00)	150 (100.00)	87 (29.00)	213 (71.00)	300 (100.00)
Koppal	27 (18.00)	123 (82.00)	150 (100.00)	12 (8.00)	138 (92.00)	150 (100.00)	39 (13.00)	261 (87.00)	300 (100.00)
Raichur	22 (14.67)	128 (85.33)	150 (100.00)	47 (31.33)	103 (68.67)	150 (100.00)	69 (23.00)	231 (77.00)	300 (100.00)
H-K Region	101 (16.83)	499 (83.17)	600 (100.00)	122 (20.33)	478 (79.67)	600 (100.00)	223 (18.58)	977 (81.42)	1200 (100.00)
	Chi-square= 10.2263, $p < 0.05$,S			Chi-square= 56.6705, $p < 0.05$ S			Chi-square= 48.5296, $p < 0.05$,S		

Source: Field study.
Note: Figures in brackets denotes percentages.

be perfect knowledge and perfect have to be perfect knowledge and perfect mobility of labour. If these demanding conditions were fulfilled, wages in all occupations would be equalized, of course, with temporary fluctuations. But, unfortunately it should be recognized that the conditions necessary for the equalizations of wage rates are not fulfilled in practice (Savitri Arputhamurty, 1990). Women's earnings remain significantly below those of men inspite of the increase in the female labour force. Differences in rates of pay and conditions of service between men and women persist till today. At almost all occupational levels women do indeed earn substantially less than men.

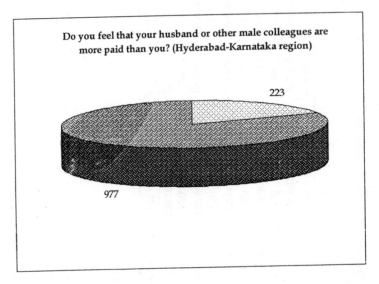

Now, the wage differential in case of women in each occupation is dealt. It is clear from Table 7.26 that in Agriculture the average less wage per day paid to the women respondents is Rs.29.75 in rural areas and Rs. 19.00 in urban areas of Hyderabad-Karnataka region. Further, the average (per day) less wage paid to the women respondents who are working in private sector accounts Rs. 24.50 in rural areas and Rs. 34.50 in urban areas. However, women are getting equal wages/salary in Government jobs and self-employed occupations in Hyderabad-Karnataka region.

Table 7.26

Less wages paid (Average per day) to Women Respondents in Hyderabad-Karnataka Region (In Rs.)

Occupation	Bidar		Gulbarga		Koppal		Raichur		H-K region	
	Rural	*Urban*	*Rural*	*Urban*	*Rural*	*Urban*	*Rural*	*Urban*	*Rural*	*Urban*
Government	-	-	-	-	-	-	-	-	-	-
Agriculture	30.00	25.00	28.00	12.00	35.00	24.00	22.00	15.00	29.75	19.00
Self-employed	-	-	-	-	-	-	-	-	-	-
Private	22.00	35.00	33.00	45.00	28.00	30.00	15.00	28.00	24.50	34.50

Source: Field study.

A cross tabulation of data on the basis of districts suggests that among those working rural women in agriculture are paid less than men (average per day) constitutes Rs. 30.00 in Bidar district followed by Gulbarga district (Rs. 28.00), Koppal district (Rs. 35.00) and Raichur district (Rs. 22.00). Whereas, in urban areas Rs. 25.00 in Bidar district, Rs. 12.00 in Gulbarga district, Rs. 24.00 in Koppal district and Rs. 15.00 in Raichur district women are paid less wage (average per day). This shows that the wage differential is more in rural areas than urban areas in agriculture sector.

Exploring the similar trend in private sector, it has been found that the average (per day) of Rs. 22.00 in Bidar district, Rs. 33.00 in Gulbarga district, Rs. 28.00 in Koppal district and Rs.15.00 in Raichur district less wage paid to the women. As against this, in urban areas the average(per day) of Rs. 35.00, Rs. 45.00, Rs. 30.00 and Rs. 28.00 less wage is paid to women respondents in Bidar district, Gulbarga district, Koppal district and Raichur district, respectively. This represents that wage differential in private sector in urban areas is greater than rural areas. It is noticed that wage differentials do exist in agriculture and private sectors of study area. Abject poverty, ignorance, pre-judice against women work are found the mains reasons for low wages in case of women. Further, the women who are working in private sector are unable to work in night, throughout the week/month, therefore women are paid less. Thus, women in study area face a more serious wage dis-advantage, especially in agriculture and private sectors.

BENEFITS FROM THE GOVERNMENT EMPLOYMENT PROGRAMMES

State and Central governments have been implementing target group oriented approach for creating employment opportunities in both rural and urban areas. The emphasis has also been laid on women because they are more vulnerable to the consequences of poverty as a marginalized section of the society. Keeping this in mind women respondents were asked to state whether they are benefited from any employment programmes of Government. It can be observed from Table 7.27 that only 11.83 per cent women respondents in rural areas and 11.00 per cent women respondents in urban areas of Hyderabad-Karnataka region stated that they are benefited from employment programmes of Government. An overwhelming women respondents (i.e., 88.17 per cent in rural areas and 89.00 per cent in urban areas) are unawares/not benefited from any kind of employment programmes of Government. District-wise data also present the similar trend. This reflects that how women are marginalized from the employment programmes in the region. This reflects that how women are marginalized from the employment progremmes in the region. Low-literacy of women, lack of awareness, lack of will by the bureaucrats and politicians, gender-discrimination were possible reasons for the non-utilisation of employment programmes.

Table 7.27
Have you benefited from any Employment Programmes of Government?

Districts	Rural			Urban		
	Yes	No	Total	Yes	No	Tota.
Bidar	26	124	150	12	138	150
	(17.33)	(82.67)	(100.00)	(8.00)	(92.00)	(100.00
Gulbarga	22	128	150	28	122	150
	(14.67)	(85.33)	(100.00)	(18.67)	(81.33)	(100.00
Koppal	08	142	150	16	134	150
	(5.33)	(94.67)	(100.00)	(10.67)	(89.33)	(100.00
Raichur	15	135	150	10	140	150
	(10.00)	(90.00)	(100.00)	(6.67)	(93.33)	(100.00)
H-K region	71	529	600	66	534	600
	(11.83)	(88.17)	(100.00)	(11.00)	(89.00)	(100.00)

Source: Field study.
Note: Figures in brackets denotes percentages.

MEMBERSHIP OF OCCUPATIONAL ORGANISATION

Organisational commitment refer to the nature of the association towards the functioning system as a whole. Two general factors which influence the strength of a persons' attachment to an organization are the rewards he has received from the organization and the experience he/she has had to undergo to receive them. Therefore, in order to attain their specific objectives, people will become members of formal organizations and fulfill their desires. The existence of occupational organization to protect the interest of its members as well as of the profession/occupation is a commonly accepted fact. Therefore, each profession/occupation will have such organization and the persons following will become its members.

In the present study the respondents have been asked to state whether they are members of any such organization. Data presented in Table 7.28 reveals that 254 (42.33 per cent) women respondents have stated that they are the members of some organizations and 346 (57.67 per cent) women respondents are not members of any such organization in rural areas of Hyderabad-Karnataka region. Whereas, in urban areas, only 86 (14.33 per cent) women respondents have registered as members of organizations and 514 (85.67 per cent) women respondents did not register their names in any organization. In rural areas, the members registered are more in number because of development of SHGs in Hyderabad-Karnataka region. Further, it has been found from the Table 7.28 that 32.00 per cent in Bidar district, 49.33 per cent in Gulbarga district, 38.00 per cent in Koppal district and 50.00 per cent in Raichur district are members of (one or other) occupational organizations in Rural areas. Other respondents are not members of any organization. Further, this table reveals that 22.67 per cent in Bidar district, 9.33 per cent in Gulbarga district, 19.33 per cent in Koppal district and 6.00 per cent in Raichur district are members of such organizations in urban areas. The proportion of respondents who are not member of any such organisation has been found comparatively higher in urban areas than rural areas.

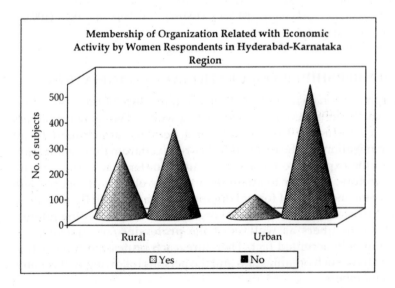

Table 7.28

Membership of Organization Related with Economic Activity by Women Respondents
in Hyderabad-Karnataka Region

Districts	Rural			Urban			Total		
	Yes	No	Total	Yes	No	Total	Yes	No	Total
Bidar	48	102	150	34	116	150	82	218	300
	(32.00)	(68.00)	(100.00)	(22.67)	(77.33)	(100.00)	(27.33)	(72.67)	(100.00)
Gulbarga	74	76	150	14	136	150	88	212	300
	(49.33)	(50.67)	(100.00)	(9.33)	(90.67)	(100.00)	(29.33)	(70.67)	(100.00)
Koppal	57	93	150	29	121	150	86	214	300
	(38.00)	(62.00)	(100.00)	(19.33)	(80.67)	(100.00)	(28.67)	(71.33)	(100.00)
Raichur	75	75	150	9	141	150	84	216	300
	(50.00)	(50.00)	(100.00)	(6.00)	(94.00)	(100.00)	(28.00)	(72.00)	(100.00)
H-K Region	254	346	600	86	514	600	340	860	1200
	(42.33)	(57.67)	(100.00)	(14.33)	(85.67)	(100.00)	(28.33)	(71.67)	(100.00)
	Chi-square = 14.3370, df=3, p < 0.01, S			Chi-squar e= 23.0750, df=3, p < 0.01, S			Chi-square = 0.3280, df=3, p > 0.05, NS		

Source: Field study.
Note: Figures in brackets denotes percentages.

8

Summary and Conclusions

The present study was conducted to find out the socio-economic factors responsible for the gender-discrimination in the field of education and employment in backward region like Hyderabad-Karnataka. The major findings of the study are as follows:

ECONOMIC PROFILE OF HYDERABAD-KARNATAKA REGION

Agriculture in the region largely depends on Rain and weather conditions. The rainfall in this area is scanty and erratic. A large part of the area therefore is officially recognized as drought prone area. Hyderabad-Karnataka region is situated in the semi-arid area. Therefore, agriculture is heavily dependent on the rain. In the post independence period the State government laid much stress on the development of irrigation facilities in the region. As on 1999-2000, the total area irrigated by major, medium and minor irrigation projects was 4,47,098 hectares, which accounts 18.80 per cent of net area sown in the region.

The population figures of Hyderabad-Karnataka region reveals that in 1991, the total population of the region was 6147852, by 2001 it has increased to 7467940. The density of population in Hyderabad-Karnataka region in 1991 was 171, by 2001 it increased to 219, which is lower than the State average of 275.

Sex ratio for Hyderabad-Karnataka region shows that in 1991 the sex ratio was 968 as against the State average of 960. In 2001 the sex ratio in Hyderabad-Karnataka region remains same i.e., 968 which is higher than the State average of 964.

Hyderabad-Karnataka region have 0.56 Human Development Index score when compared to the State average (0.63) in 1998. The Hyderabad-Karnataka region have improved composite index of development upto 1976-77 (76.34), however declined during 1998-99 (69.61).

LITERACY

Low literacy region like Hyderabad-Karnataka have registered impressive improvement during 2001 census, but yet continue to lag behind the State average literacy rate. Census data indicate that the total literacy rate in Hyderabad-Karnataka region has moved from 30.89 per cent in 1981 to 54.97 per cent in 2001. 2001 census figures show that although the male-female differential is narrowing, it is still high-literacy among males is 67.13 per cent while it is only 42.40 per cent among females (gender difference accounts 24.73 per cent).

The rural male literacy in Hyderabad-Karnataka region has moved forward by 15.22 per centage points from 1981-1991 (i.e. from 32.26 per cent to 47.48 per cent) and 13.31 per centage points from 1991-2001 (i.e. from 47.48 per cent to 60.79 per cent). Among females it has gone up by 9.64 per centage points during 1981-1991 (i.e. from 9.38 per cent to 19.02 per cent) and 15.62 per centage points during 1991-2001 (i.e. from 19.02 per cent to 34.64 per cent).

Literacy rate for urban males was 56.39 per cent during 1981, which increased to 75.70 per cent during 1991 and to 80.88 per cent during 2001. Among females, literacy rate was 32.45 per cent in 1981, which forwarded to 53.14 per cent in 1991 and to 62.65 per cent in 2001. The gap in male-female literacy rates of 23.94 per cent in 2001. This is definitely the largest number (per centage) of illiterate women existing in any region of the State.

WORK PARTICIPATION RATE

Work participation rates of total workers in Hyderabad-Karnataka region which had shown a slight decrease for male workers from 55.17 per cent to 51.23 per cent between 1981-1991 and further slightly to 50.76 per cent in 2001. Female work participation rates indicates a clear increase in both the decades; i.e., from 30.92 per cent in 1981 to 33.53 per cent in 1991 and 37.70 per cent in 2001.

Further, the work participation rate in rural areas of Hyderabad-Karnataka region was much higher among male than female. However, male work participation rate has decreased from 56.51 per cent in 1981 to 52.53 per cent in 2001, whereas the female work participation rate has increased from 37.64 per cent in 1981 to 39.03 per cent in 2001.

The male work participation rate in urban areas of Hyderabad-Karnataka region as a whole has come down from 49.13 per cent in 1981 to 44.2 per cent in 1991, however increased marginally to 45.63 per cent in 2001. Further, the female work participation rate in the urban areas of Hyderabad-Karnataka region has decreased from 18.10 in 1981 to 11.13 per cent in 1991, however, increased to 12.13 per cent in 2001.

MAIN WORKERS

The proportion of total main workers among males and females was 44.37 per cent and 18.3 per cent in 2001 respectively in the Hyderabad-Karnataka region showing wide gap in employment among males and females (gender-gap was 26.07 per cent). However, the number of women joining the labour force as main workers has declined during 1981-2001. The proportion of males as the main workers in Hyderabad-Karnataka region has declined from 54.47 per cent in 1981 to 44.37 per cent in 2001, and also proportion of female main workers has decreased from 24.27 per cent to 18.3 per cent during the same period.

In the case of rural male main workers proportion shows that there is decline in their share from 56.96 per cent in 1981 to 52.98 per cent in 1991, further decreased substantially to 45.23 per cent in 2001. Whereas, in case of female main workers, proportion of their share increased from 27.61 per cent in 1981 to 33.08 per cent in 1991, however declined substantially to 21.17 per cent in 2001. This simply indicates that between the 1991-2001 period, the scope of employment for a major part of a year, i.e. 183 days or more, becomes limited to the rural people in Hyderabad-Karnataka region.

Further, the proportion of urban males as the main workers in Hyderabad-Karnataka region has declined from 45.73 per cent in 1981 to 41.83 per cent in 2001, whereas the proportion of female main workers has increased from 7.67 per cent in 1981 to 10.38 per cent in 1991, however, declined marginally to 8.97 per cent in 2001.

MARGINAL WORKERS

Of the total male marginal workers who accounted for 0.52 per cent in 1981 declined to 0.16 per cent in 1991, whereas it increased to 10.33 per cent in 2001. Further, female marginal workers share also declined from 7.11 per cent in 1981 to 5.1 per cent in 1991, however, increased marginally to 6.4 per cent in 2001.

The share of rural male marginal workers was 0.59 per cent in 1981, which declined to 0.32 per cent in 1991, whereas it increased to 12.5 per cent in 2001. Among the female marginal workers, the share was 8.36 per cent in 1981, which declined to 6.24 per cent in 1991, however increased marginally to 7.3 per cent in 2001. The report on distribution of workers in the 2001 census shows a noticeable increase in the number of marginal workers in rural areas and also in the per centage of marginal workers to the total population. This may be due to the introduction of new technology in agriculture sector in recent period. The increase in male and female marginal workers indicates casualisation of the labour force as there is no employment of a stable nature for the major part of the year in rural areas of Hyderabad-Karnataka region.

The proportion of urban male marginal workers in the Hyderabad-Karnataka region has significantly increased from 0.14 per cent in 1991 to 3.77 per cent in 2001. The proportion of female marginal workers has declined from 1.52 per cent in 1981 to 0.78 per cent in 1991, however increased substantially to 3.13 per cent in Hyderabad-Karnataka region during 2001.

SECTORWISE DISTRIBUTION OF WORKERS

(a) Cultivators

The proportion of total male cultivators in the Hyderabad-Karnataka region declined from 40.65 per cent in 1981 to 37.81 per cent in 1991, further declined to 33.7 per cent in 2001. The share of female workers as cultivators moved up from 16.91 per cent in 1981 to 20.87 per cent in 1991, however it has come down to 17.47 per cent in 2001.

Among rural male cultivators, the share decreased from 46.95 per cent to 40.03 per cent during 1981-2001. However, the share of female cultivators increased from 17.90 per cent during 1981 to 19.53 per cent during 1991, but declined substantially to 18.53 per cent during 2001.

The proportion of urban male workers engaged as cultivators is quite low in Hyderabad-Karnataka region and it has declined from 9.77 per cent in 1981 to 7.86 per cent in 1991, further to 5.07 per cent in 2001. Like in case of urban male workers, the proportion of cultivators among the urban female workers constitutes a small proportion and declined from 6.48 per cent in 1991 to 3.97 per cent in 2001.

(b) Agricultural Labourers

The proportion of total male agricultural labourers in Hyderabad-Karnataka region has increased marginally from 28.97 per cent in 1981 to 30.6 per cent in 1991 and declined to 25.57 per cent in 2001. Among the female agricultural labourers in Hyderabad-Karnataka region, their share was increased marginally from 70.75 per cent in 1981 to 71.46 per cent in 1991, whereas, it declined to 64.03 per cent in 2001. Thus, the proportion of agricultural labourers was higher among female workers than among male workers in Hyderabad-Karnataka region.

The share of rural male agricultural labourers in Hyderabad-Karnataka region has increased marginally from 32.81 per cent in 1981 to 33.48 per cent in 1991, however, declined to 29.93 per cent in 2001. The share of female agricultural labourers has declined from 73.62 per cent in 1981 to 72.97 per cent in 1991, further to 64.4 per cent in 2001.

In case of urban male the proportion of agricultural labourers in Hyderabad-Karnataka region has registered a decline from 9.98 per cent in 1981 to 9.83 per cent in 1991, further to 5.57 per cent in 2001. However, there is sharp fall in the proportion of urban female agricultural labourers in Hyderabad-Karnataka region from 39.02 per cent in 1981 to 38.08 per cent in 1991 (0.94 per centage points), further to 24.67 per cent in 2001 (13.41 per centage points).

(c) Household Industry Workers

There is continuous decrease in total male household industry workers from 2.91 per cent in 1981 to 2.41 per cent in 1991, further to 2.30 per cent in 2001 in the Region. Further, there was fall in female household industry workers from 2.97 per cent in 1981 to 2.05 per cent in 1991, however, there was increase in female household industry workers to 2.73 per cent in 2001.

The share of household industry workers in Hyderabad-Karnataka region has declined between 1981-1991 from 2.62 per cent to 2.32 per cent and from 2.08 per cent to 1.60 per cent among rural male and female, respectively. During 1991-2001, there is marginal decline in the case of male from 2.31 to 2.27 per cent, whereas there is increase in the case of female workers from 1.60 per cent to 2.23 per cent during the same period.

The proportion of male household workers in urban areas of Hyderabad-Karnataka region has declined from 4.36 per cent in 1981 to 2.80 per cent in 1991, further to 2.50 per cent in 2001. The proportion of female urban workers in the category of household industry has gone down from 13.43 per cent in 1981 to 8.12 per cent in 1991, however it has gone up marginally to 8.80 per cent in 2001.

(d) Other Workers

Among total male 'other workers', there is continuous rise in proportion from 27.48 per cent in 1981 to 29.18 per cent in 1991, further substantially to 38.40 per cent in 2001. The proportion of female 'other workers' has gone down from 9.37 per cent in 1981 to 7.67 per cent in 1991, however it rose to 15.73 per cent in 2001.

The share of rural 'other workers' in the total working population of Hyderabad-Karnataka region increased from 17.65 per cent to 27.73 per cent in the case of male and from 4.47 per cent to 12.17 per cent in the case of female between 1991-2001.

The urban male 'other workers' in Hyderabad-Karnataka region has increased from 75.89 per cent in 1981 to 79.51 per cent in 1991 and further to 86.83 per cent in 2001. As in the case of males, other workers constitute a major portion of total urban female workers in Hyderabad-Karnataka region which increased from 41.48 per cent in 1981 to 47.98 per cent in 1991 and to 62.53 per cent in 2001.

WOMEN IN ORGANISED SECTOR

While the size of the organized sector has been growing steadily over the last few decades, the proportion of women employed in organize sector in Hyderabad-Karnataka region formed only 18.07 per cent in 1996, being 18.93 per cent in public sector and 15.37 per cent in private sector during the same period. The share of female employment in organized sector in 2000 constitutes 20.17

per cent (increased by only 2.10 per centage points); of this 22.08 per cent in public sector and 16.26 per cent in private sector. Thus, while the public sector offer more employment to women as compared to the private sector.

SOCIO-ECONOMIC PROFILE OF THE RESPONDENTS

Our exploration into socio-economic antecedents of the women in various occupations reveals that for the present and purposive study 150 women respondents were selected separately from urban and rural areas of each district comprising Bidar, Gulbarga, Koppal and Raichur of Hyderabad-Karnataka region.

In the study, the majority of working women who predominantly belong to the younger age group. Nearly half of the 1200 women respondents (i.e., 48.33 per cent) are concentrated in the 21-30 years age-group. 27.58 per cent of women respondents are between 31-40 years age-group. There are relatively fewer women in the 41-50 and 51 and above age-groups (7.50 per cent and 1.33 per cent, respectively).

Further examination of the study findings reveals that the mean-age of women respondents in rural areas is 28.89 years and in urban areas is 29.91 years. This signifies that the entrance of women into the job market and especially into the male-dominated occupational field is comparatively a recent phenomenon.

Our study with regard to the caste of respondents suggest some very significant facts that women belonging to different castes are successfully entering into different occupations. Further, intermediate groups are coming up. Women belonging to upper caste like Kshatriya, Lingayats, Vokkaliga caste groups are increasingly represented in modern occupations.

It is significant to note that majority of women had education upto primary and secondary level indicating less preference given to female education. The break up of educational levels shows that 28.83 per cent of the respondents had education up to primary level, 22.25 per cent up to secondary level, 12.25 per cent up to PUC (pre-university) level, 12.17 per cent respondents possess under-graduation, 5.50 per cent had post-graduation level and 19.00 per cent completed professional courses (i.e. TCH, B.Ed, ITI, Polytechnic etc.). Further, this shows that the women prefers to undergo professional courses to join as Teachers in either private or government schools.

Our exploration has also clearly indicates that women's participation in occupational life is becoming increasingly diversified and they are achieving top positions in male-dominated occupational fields as well. It has been found that 16.42 per cent respondents belong to the agriculture, and 36.83 per cent respondents belong to self-employed category. There are 31.83 per cent respondents who are in Government category. The last occupational group in the present study is related to the private employees who are employed in the various private business agencies or entrepreneurs (14.92 per cent).

Majority of the households are found to have 3-4 and 5-6 members (49.67 per cent and 33.33 per cent, respectively) in rural areas. Households with 1-2 members constitute 11.00 per cent and 7+ members constitute 6.00 per cent. The size of the household in urban areas of study region upto 2 and 3-4 members constitute 11.00 per cent and 49.17 per cent, respectively. Our exploration has underlined that the rural people generally have larger family members than urban people.

The mean size of the family is 4.29 for the sampled respondents in the rural area and 4.20 for the urban areas. Thus, the larger size of the households in rural areas indicate that the rural people generally prefer larger family members.

Among the 1200 respondents, a majority of 899 (74.92 per cent) women respondents are married, 301 (25.08 per cent) are unmarried. As regards the 461 married women respondents in rural areas 5.86 per cent got married between 10-15 years of age, 71.37 per cent between 16-20 years of age, 16.48 per cent between 21-25 years of age, 11.43 per cent between 26-30 years of age and 0.65 per cent above 31 years of age. Further, the study presents that among the women respondents in urban areas also child marriage is as prevalent as among the rural women respondents. Looking at the age of the marriage in the urban areas, it is found that 7.54 per cent of the females got married between 10-15 years of age. Those who married between the age of 16-20 years constitute 40.87 per cent, between the age of 21-25 years constitute 38.58 per cent and those between the age of 26-30 years constitute only 10.73 per cent and 2.28 per cent in the 31 and above years age group. This data further supports that the late marriage in urban areas (for example between 21-25 and 26-30 years age group) is practiced.

It has been found in study that mean age at marriage constitutes 19.73 years in rural areas and in urban areas data reveals that mean age at marriage accounts 21.60 years Thus, the mean age at marriage is higher in urban areas than rural areas.

FEMALE EDUCATION IN HYDERABAD-KARNATAKA REGION

The present study has shown that 90.17 per cent of sample women respondents completed/studied their primary education with Kannada medium (regional language) followed by the 87.63 per cent in secondary level. As against this, in urban areas, 80.67 per cent of female respondents in primary level and 80.71 per cent in secondary level studied with Kannada medium. This shows that the majority of respondents who studied in regional language.

As regards the type of education institution in which women respondents studied, it has been found that there are 24.33 per cent female respondents studied their primary education in girls independent school and 75.67 per cent studied in co-education schools in rural areas. Further, 37.63 per cent female respondents studied secondary education in independent schools and 62.37 per cent in co-education schools. In case of urban areas 19.50 per cent and 80.50 per cent female respondents in primary education level, 32.78 per cent and 67.01 per cent in secondary level completed in independent and co-education schools, respectively. This shows that number of independent/separate schools for girls are less.

At primary education level, most of the women respondents (79.50 per cent) studied in Government schools and 20.50 per cent in private school in rural areas. At secondary education level, 66.13 per cent women respondents have studied in Government schools and 33.87 per cent women respondents in private schools. Whereas, in urban areas, 72.83 per cent female respondents at primary education level followed by the 63.90 per cent at secondary level have studied in government schools. Further, 27.17 per cent at primary level, 45.64 per cent at secondary level have studied in private schools.

It is unsatisfactory to note that the overwhelming majority (67.00 per cent) women respondents stated that their family members did not encouraged them in their education in rural areas. However, in urban areas, 72.00 per cent of women respondents expressed that they received encouragement from their family members during their education period.

It has been found from the study that 71.83 per cent and 67.00 per cent women respondents stated that they had been encouraged by father followed by mother (21.33 per cent 22.00 per cent) in rural and urban areas respectively. Thus, it is clear that family members of the women respondents were main who encouraged their education.

Walking and availing of bus facility was a common practice in both the rural and urban areas, however, bicycles were also utilized by the women respondents in urban areas. It is found that 88.00 per cent in rural areas and 69.17 per cent in urban areas traveled/attended their schools/colleges by walk. Only 5.33 per cent and 5.83 per cent of women respondents in rural areas used bicycles and bus services, respectively. Whereas, in case of urban areas, 15.17 per cent and 13.17 per cent used bicycles and bus services respectively. This shows the less importance given to women education and facilities extended to complete their education.

In our study the majority of women respondents (83.00 per cent in rural areas and 84.83 per cent in urban areas) have not failed (at all) during their academic career. Only 17.00 per cent in rural areas and 15.17 per cent in urban areas have failed/repeated their grade.

Our study exploration indicate that the women's resentment of the lack of opportunity to study in their own childhood, as well as the impact of the growing awareness of women's equal right to education in urban areas. The data collected in this regard reveals that only 36.00 per cent women respondents in rural areas and 57.83 per cent women respondents in urban areas stated that their 'parents thought that girls must study as much as they want'. Since, in urban areas campaigning for literacy and school enrollment has been targeted at women, this could reflect parents perception that the girls should get education as much as they want.

In rural areas, of the 228 women respondents, 64 (28.07 per cent) dropped their education at lower primary level (between I-IV standard) and 170 (71.93 per cent) dropped their education at higher primary level(between V-VII standard). Whereas, in case of Urban areas of Hyderabad-Karnataka region, 48 (40.68 per cent) and 70 (59.32 per cent) women respondents dropped their education at lower primary level (between I-IV standard) and higher primary level (V-VII standard), respectively. Out of 228 women respondents in rural areas of Hyderabad-Karnataka region, 49 (21.49 per cent) reported the 'need to start earning' followed by 'need for household duties (18.86 per cent); 'got married(14.04 per cent)'; having to take care of younger siblings (13.60 per cent)'; 'no money to pay fee/purchase books (11.40 per cent) and 'school within village/areas was not available (14.04 per cent)'. When we observed the same in case of 118 women respondents who dropped their education at primary level in urban areas, it is found that they had to discontinue their education due to 'the need to start earning (37.29 per cent)' followed by 'having to take care of younger siblings (17.80 per cent)'; 'need for household duties (16.95 per cent); 'no money to pay fees/purchase books (11.02 per cent)' and 'got married (5.93 per cent)'. It seems that the poor economic condition of their parents and domination of traditional conditions compel them to discontinue their education.

EMPLOYMENT STATUS OF WOMEN

The exploration into the occupational status of the 600 women respondents in rural areas of Hyderabad-Karnataka reveals that 214 (35.67 per cent) women respondents belong to the self-employed occupation, 176 (29.33 per cent) women respondents belong to agriculture, 111 (18.50 per cent) women belong to Government employees and 99 (16.50 per cent) women respondents belong to private sector/business sector. Further, among the sample of 600 women respondents from urban areas, 189 (31.50 per cent) are self-employed, 60 (10.00 per cent) women respondents are agriculturist, 161 (26.83 per cent) women respondents are Government employees and 190 (31.67 per cent) women respondents are working in private sector/businesses. This clearly indicates that women's participation in the occupational life is becoming increasingly diversified and they are achieving top positions in male-dominated occupational fields as well.

Examining the mean age of women respondents when they entered in first work or job, it is found that the higher mean-ages are represented in urban areas than rural areas. The mean age of women respondents when they entered the work/job was 17.87 years in rural areas and 20.76 years in urban areas. Because poverty compel women to take work earlier in rural areas and higher education may be reason for late entry by women in urban areas.

371 (61.83 per cent) women respondents held regular jobs, 140 (23.33 per cent) women respondents held seasonal jobs and 89 (14.83 per cent) women respondents held irregular jobs in rural areas. In Urban areas, 470 (78.33 per cent) women respondents were permanent employed, 66(11.00 per cent) women respondents as temporary and 64 (10.67 per cent) women respondents employment was based on daily wages.

In the present study an attempt has been made to explore the most important factors which were influenced/forced the women to start working. It has been found from the study that of the 600 sample in rural areas, 45.50 per cent women respondents have started to work in order to have more money to support their families. Further, in rural areas, 23.67 per cent women respondents have stated that they have selected their jobs because of economic independence. There are 9.67 per cent and 10.50 per cent women respondents who have started the working outside due to laid off of work by their father/brothers/husband and break up of joint family, respectively. In urban areas an overwhelming majority of 41.50 per cent women started working because they needed economic independence and 39.00 per cent reported that they need money. Several other reasons cited by the respondents also emphasize the economic determinant of their participation, such as, male member laid off his work (3.67 per cent respondents), death of parents or husband (3.50 per cent) and desertion by husband (1.33 per cent).

Our exploration into the reasons to choose the present job reveals that in rural areas, 33.83 per cent respondents have selected the present job because it is 'very easy' and 27.17 per cent respondents stated that the 'supplementary job' is not available'. As against this, in urban areas, 41.33 per cent respondents stated that they have chosen the present job because it is 'very easy' and 16.17 per cent respondents stated that because of 'easy employment opportunity'. This indicates the lack of competitiveness to acquire the job among women respondents and lack of employment opportunities in both rural and urban areas.

As regard the constraints did women respondents face at the time of entering into workplace, it has been found that in rural areas 16.33 per cent women respondents stated 'lack of crèche facilities (care takers of children)' and 41.67 per cent women respondents stated 'lack of help in the household' were two important constraints they faced at the time of entry into workforce. Whereas, in urban areas, 24.00 per cent women respondents stated 'lack of help in the household', 24.50 per cent women respondents stated 'lack of crèche facilities (care taker)' and 13.83 per cent women respondents stated 'lack of education (desirable level)' were important constraints, that they faced at the time of entry into the workforce.

The study results shows that in rural areas 52.83 per cent of women respondents were in their occupations for 5 years or less. The period of stay of 23.33 per cent women respondents ranges from 6-10 years, 12.00 per cent women respondents between 11-15 years, 7.33 per cent women respondents have their stay period between 16-20 years, while 4.50 per cent respondents have been working since more than 20 years in their jobs or occupations. Further, it has been found that job in which most of the women respondents have spent is the shortest duration of time of 5 years or less (58.17 per cent). This is followed by 22.66 per cent (6-10 years), 9.17 per cent (11-15 years), 6.50 per cent (16-20 years) and 3.50 per cent women respondents (more than 20 years). Thus, women have recently started for getting formal education and most of them started their work/job recently, and therefore fall in the duration of 1-5 and 6-10 years.

It has also been evident from the study that only 15.83 per cent women respondents in rural areas and 20.50 per cent women respondents in urban areas had training after their involvement in economic activities. This shows that there is less encouragement for knowledge/skill improvement.

From the study it has been found that mean distance between the place of residence and working place in rural areas accounts 3.19 kms and 4.14 kms in Urban areas. Thus, most of the women respondents have to travel an average distance of 4 kms in both rural and urban areas.

To enquire into the dimension of effect of working outside on the upbringing of their children it has been found that 25.81per cent in rural areas and 31.05 per cent women respondents in urban areas feel adverse effect on the upbringing of their children due to their working outside.

An important problem with the married working woman is her strict time schedule which allocates less time to family obligations and particularly lesser time to spend with her husband. Inquiring into this aspect it has been found that 53.36 per cent in rural areas and 47.49 per cent women respondents in urban areas have complained that they did not find sufficient time to spend with their husbands. Thus, it is clear that the married working women because of their heavy work schedule, are not satisfied with the time they spend with their husbands.

It has been found from the study that 61.17 per cent married women in rural areas feel that their husbands are fully satisfied with their participation in work. There are 38.83 per cent women respondents who have reported that their husbands are not satisfied towards their work participation. Further, it has been found in urban areas that 56.62 per cent women respondents' husbands are satisfied with their work participation. Whereas, 43.38 per cent reported that their husbands are not satisfied about their working outside. It is clear from the study that though in majority of the cases working women have the support and approval of their husbands in work participation yet there are a significant number of cases where the husbands are against the work participation of their wives.

The findings in rural areas with regard to the overall satisfaction with their married life indicates that 55.10 per cent women respondents in the present study are fully satisfied with their marital life and 44.90 per cent women respondents are dissatisfied with it. In this regard, 56.62 per cent women respondents who are satisfied and 43.38 per cent women respondents are totally dissatisfied with their marital life in urban areas. Thus, a half of the women respondents in the present study are satisfied with their married life, yet there are many cases of marital disharmony and dissatisfaction in the present study.

Our explorations clearly suggest that the only 17.00 per cent women respondents have improved their education/professional qualifications and 83.00 per cent respondents reported that they have not improved their education/professional qualifications in rural areas. Even in urban areas, only 22.33 per cent women respondents in the sample have enhanced their academic professional qualification during their occupational career. Thus, it is clear that majority of the women respondents have not improved their education/professional qualifications after their entry into job in both rural and urban areas.

In the present study it has been found in rural areas that 74.67 per cent of women respondents have stated that their working outside has improved their family's living conditions and 25.33 per cent women respondents have stated that their working outside still has not improved their family's living conditions. In case of urban areas, 76.00 per cent of women respondents family's conditions have improved and 24.00 per cent respondents family's conditions have not been improved from their working outside. This shows that women in one or other way contributing to their family income which helps in improving their family conditions.

The data collected with regard to women respondents overall satisfaction with their present job presents that 54.50 per cent women respondents are fully satisfied with their present job and 45.50 per cent are totally dis-satisfied with their present job in rural areas. In urban areas 64.33 per cent of women respondents are satisfied and 36.67 per cent of women respondents are not satisfied with their present job. Thus, the women respondents who work in low-end jobs are not satisfied.

It has been found that in rural areas only 28.50 per cent women respondents have the leave facility and 71.50 per cent women respondents do not have leave facility. As against this, in urban areas, 50.17 per cent women respondents have leave facility and 49.83 per cent women respondents do not have leave facility.

As regards the income of women respondents considerable variation has been found in the income status of women respondents. In case of rural areas, 41.50 per cent women respondents possess a monthly income of upto Rs. 1000, 32.67 per cent of women respondents possess a monthly income Rs.1001-2000, 11.33 per cent women respondents possess income of Rs. 2001-5000, 13.33 per cent women respondents possess income of Rs. 5001-10000, and only 1.17 per cent of women respondents possess income of Rs. 10000 and above. Whereas, in case of urban areas, 19.33 per cent of women respondents belong to the income group of upto Rs. 1000, 27.17 per cent women respondents belong to income between Rs.1001-2000, 30.50 per cent women respondents belong to income between Rs. 2001-5000, 18.67 per cent women respondents belong to income between Rs.5001-10000 and only 4.33 per cent of women respondents belong to income group of Rs. 10000 and above. This indicates that a comparatively women respondents in Urban areas have higher income higher income between Rs. 2001-5000 and Rs. 5001-10000 than rural areas.

The distribution of income on the basis of education our study suggests that there is a unsatisfactory correlation between the education level and income status of the rural women. For instance, the women respondents who had primary education it is found that 57.89 per cent women respondents possess income less than Rs. 1000. 46.25 per cent and 40.00 per cent women respondents who had secondary education possess income upto Rs. 1000 and Rs. 1001-2000, respectively. Further, 41.07 per cent and 33.94 per cent women respondents whose education level is PUC have income upto Rs.1000 and Rs. 1001-2000, respectively. 25.00 per cent and 38.64 per cent Graduate women respondents earns income less than Rs. 1000 and 1001-2000, respectively. Only 05 (33.33 per cent) women respondent who had Post-Graduate degree earn income of Rs. 5001-10000. Surprisingly, 31.96 per cent and 41.24 per cent women respondents who studied professional/vocational courses possess income of Rs. 2001-5000 and Rs. 5001-10000. Further analysis of our study for urban areas reveals that the women respondents who had primary education it is found that 33.90 per cent, 34.75 per cent and 29.66 per cent have income upto Rs. 1000, Rs. 1001-2000 and Rs. 2001-5000, respectively. 37.38 per cent and 32.71 per cent women respondents who had secondary education possess income of Rs. 1001-2000 and Rs. 2001-5000, respectively. 23.81 per cent 40.49 per cent women respondents whose education is Pre-university (PUC) have income between Rs. 1001-2000 and Rs. 2001-5000, respectively. Among graduate women respondents 28.43 per cent posses income Rs. 2001-5000 and Rs. 5001-10000. 30.77 per cent and 23.08 per cent women respondents who had post-graduation degree earn income of Rs. 1001-2000 and Rs. 5001-10000, respectively. Only 17.31 per cent Post-graduate women respondents earn income Rs.10000 and above. Satisfactory point to note here is that the 28.47 per cent and 35.76 per cent women respondents who completed 'Professional courses' have income of Rs. 2001-5000 and Rs. 5001-10000, respectively.

It has been found from the study that 32.17 per cent women respondents reported that the income is spend by me, 39.83 per cent reported that income is handed over to the husband/parents and 28.00 per cent reported that some per cent of income is returned to husband/parents. Further, it has been found in urban areas of study region that 43.50 per cent women respondents handed over the income to husband/parents, 26.83 per cent respondents return some per centage of income to husband/parents. This indicates that working women themselves have maximum control over their income and further it is clear that working women's importance in family life is increasing.

About 160 (26.67 per cent) women respondents in rural areas and 313 (52.17 per cent) women respondents in urban areas reported that they have savings in some form or the other. The women who are working in low end/income fields and increased expenditure were responsible for low level/no savings. Further, it has been found that 2.50 per cent of women respondents are paying tax and 97.50 per cent of women respondents are not paying tax in rural areas. However, in urban areas, 8.00 per cent of women respondents are paying tax and 92.00 per cent women respondents are not paying tax. This indicates that in rural areas, as the income of the female respondents is low there is no question of tax paying. In urban areas, only those women respondents are paying tax whose income is high/above tax exemption limit, especially government employees.

The study reveals that as large as 67.50 per cent women respondents in rural areas and 55.50 per cent women respondents in urban areas were not satisfied with wage rate fixed. Only 32.50 per cent women respondents in rural areas and 44.50 per cent women respondents in urban areas were satisfied with wage rate fixed.

The study noticed that wage differentials do exist in agriculture and private sectors of study area. It is clear from study that in Agriculture the average less wage per day paid to the women respondents is Rs. 29.75 in rural areas and Rs. 19.00 in urban areas. Further, the average (per day) less wage paid to the women respondents who are working in private sector accounts Rs. 24.50 in rural areas and Rs. 34.50 in urban areas. However, women are getting equal wages/salary in Government jobs and self-employed occupations. Thus, women face a more serious wage dis-advantage, especially in agriculture and private sectors.

The study reflects that how women are marginalized from the employment programmes. It can be observed from study findings that only 11.83 per cent women respondents in rural areas and 11.00 per cent women respondents in urban areas stated that they are benefited from employment programmes of Government. An overwhelming women respondents (i.e., 88.17 per cent in rural areas and 89.00 per cent in urban areas) are unawares/not benefited from any kind of employment programmes of Government.

The study indicates that the proportion of respondents who are not member of any such organisation has been found comparatively higher in urban areas than rural areas. The findings that 254 (42.33 per cent) women respondents have stated that they are the members of some organizations and 346 (57.67 per cent) women respondents are not members of any such organization in rural areas. Whereas, in urban areas, only 86 (14.33 per cent) women respondents have registered as members of organizations and 514 (85.67 per cent) women respondents did not register their names in any organization. In rural areas, the members registered are more in number because of development of SHGs.

SUGGESTIONS

The present study has clearly revealed that there are discriminations with regard to women accessibility to education and work participation in Hyderabad-Karnatataka region. Therefore, the following suggestions are made to overcome these discriminations in the region. The suggestions are:

1. We should initiate educational programmes for girl children who are working in different fields, by involving them in these programmes it can be able to reduce children in labour and early marriages.

2. We should increase the number of government girls schools for the easy accessibility of basic education to girls.

3. To minimize the drop-outs among girls, the government programmes and other educational schemes must be implemented effectively.

4. Women must be facilitated to gain higher education, especially technical education, to obtain economic benefits from modern occupations.

5. To create awareness about the importance of women education and economic participation among parents, we should initiate programmes like adult education, mass media education and incentives to girl children while schooling and female

employment opportunities must also be provided.

6. By providing skilled and professional education/training, we can make their jobs fully secured and remunerative.

7. Number of agro-based, food-processing and small scale industries should be increased, so that women could get more employment and high wages.

8. By bringing change in the attitude of men-folk, women's economic participation can be increased. In order to change the mindset of men, the awareness programmes like adult education, mass media education and higher remunerative jobs to women should be given importance.

9. To avoid wage differences, the minimum wage rate programmes, self-employment programmes, skill improving programes must be introduced and implemented seriously. Further, necessary education must be provided to avail employment opportunities in service sector and information technology.

10. The women organizations and social movements should take up the cause with the Government for the restoration of the dignity of women and should fight for a constitutional guarantee to create an egalitarian society where women could enjoy equal status and opportunity.

11. To build-up organizational capacity among women, we should encourage formation of groups/professional organizations like SHGs, credit societies, employee's associations, etc.

Bibliography

BOOKS

Abhalakshmi et.al. (2005), 'Rural Women: Work and Health', The Women Press, Delhi.

Agnihotri Satish Balram (2000), 'Sex Ratio Patterns in the Indian Population: A Fresh Exploration', Sage Publications, New Delhi.

Amin Najma (2003), 'Participation of Muslim Families in the Education of Girl Child', Abhijeet Publications, Delhi.

Amin Nijma (2003), 'Participation of Muslim Families in the Education of Girl Child', Abhijeet Publications, Delhi.

Anitha B.K. (2000), 'Village, Caste and Education', Rawat Publication, New Delhi.

Arora K.K. (1963), 'Women and Career', Tata Institute of Social Sciences, Bombay.

Avasthi Abha and Srivastava A.K. (2001), 'Modernity, Feminism and Women Empowerment', Rawat Publications, Jaipur.

Bakshi S.R. (2002), 'Empowerment of Women and Politics of Reservation', Book Enclave, Jaipur.

Banerji Amita and Sen Raj Kumar (2000), 'Women and Economic Development', Deep and Deep Publications, New Delhi.

Batliwala Srilatha (1998), 'Status of Rural Women in Karnataka', National Institute of Advanced Studies, Bangalore.

Bhatia Anju (2000), 'Women's Development and NGO's' Rawat Publications, Jaipur.

Bhoite Anuradha (1987), 'Women Employees and Rural Development (problems of employed women in rural areas), Gain Publishing House, Delhi.

Bhuimali Anil (2004), 'Education, Employment and Empowering Women', Serials Publications, New Delhi.

Chanana Karuna (2001), 'Interrogating Women's Education Bonded Visions, Expanding Horizons', Rawat Publications, New Delhi.

Chandra Susmita (2001), 'Women and Economic Development: A Case Study of Uttar Pradesh', B.R. Publishing Corporation, Delhi.

Chandra Susmita (2001), 'Women and Economic Develoment : A Case study of Uttar Pradesh', B.R. Publishing Corporation, Delhi.

Chandramawli V. (1990), 'Labour Landscape : A Study of Industrial and Agrarian Relations in India', Sterling Publishers Pvt. Ltd., Delhi.

Chugh Sunita (2004), 'Why Children Drop out? Case Study of a Metropolitan Slum', Bookwell, New Delhi.

Dhameja S.K. (2004), 'Women Entrepreneurs Opportunities, Performance and Problems', Deep and Deep Publications Pvt. Ltd., Delhi.

Dubey Surendra Nath (2001), 'Education Scenario in India–2001', Authors Press, Delhi.

Dubin S.S. (1971), 'Professional Absolescence', The English Universities Press Ltd.

Gupta Krishna (2001), 'Women, Law Public Opinion', Rawat Publications, New Delhi.

Gupta Mukta (2000), 'Economic Participation of Women', Sarup and Sons, New Delhi.

Hans Asha and Patri Annie (2003), 'Women, Disability and Identity', Sage Publications, New Delhi.

Jayashree R. (1991), 'Women and Education in Kerala', B.R. Publishing Corporaton, Delhi.

Jena Sanjay Ketan (1993), 'Working Women and Modernization', Ashish Publishing House, New Delhi.

Jha Prem Kumar, (2005), 'Education for Rural Development', Vista International Publishing House, Delhi.

Kapadia K.M. (1958), 'Marriage and Family in India', Oxford University Press, Delhi.

Kapur P. (1974), 'The Changing Status of the WorkingWomen in India', Vikas Publishing House, Delhi.

Karkal Malini and Pandey Divya (1989), 'Studies on Women and Population : A Critique', Himalaya Publishing House, Bombay.

Kumar Maya Unnithan (2001), 'Identity, Gender and Poverty', New Perspectives on Caste and Tribe, Rawat Publications, Jaipur.

Kumari Indira Y. and Rao Samasiva B. (2005), 'Empowerment of Women and Rural Development', Serials Publications, New Delhi.

Lodha Neeta (2003), 'Status of Tribal Women: Work Participation and Decision-making Role in Tribal Society', Mangaldeep Publications, Jaipur.

Loutfi Martha Fertherolf (2002), 'Women, Gender and Work: what is equality and how do we get there?', Rawat Publications, Jaipur.

Mehta G.S., 'Education, Employment and Earnings', Deep and Deep Publications, New Delhi.

Murthy Ranjani K. (2001), 'Building Women's Capacities', Sage Publications, New Delhi.

Murthy S. and Gaur K.D. (2002), 'Women Work Participation and Empowerment: Problems and Prospects', R.B.S.A. Publishers, Jaipur.

Murthy Savitri Arputha, (1990), 'Women Work and Discrimination', Ashish Publishing House, New Delhi.

Murty S. and Gaur K.D. (2002), 'Women Work Participation and Empowerment: Problems and Prospects', RBSA Publishers, Jaipur.

Nahar U.R. et.al. (1996), 'Women's Place Options and Limits in Professional Career', Rawat Publications, Jaipur.

Narasimhan Sakuntala (1999), 'Empowering Women: An Alternative Strategy from Rural India', Sage Publications, New Delhi.

Nautiyal K.C. (1989), 'Education and Rural Poor', Common Wealth Publishers, New Delhi.

Nirmala J., Dhulasi Birundha and Varadarajan (2005), 'Empowerment of Women', Serials Publications, New Delhi.

Pant S.K. (2002), 'Gender Bias in Girl Child Education', Kanishka Publishers, New Delhi.

Papa Kondaveeti (1992), 'Women in Rural Areas', Chugh Publications, Allahabad.

Papola T.S. and Sharma Alakh N. (1999), 'Gender and Employment in India', Vikas Publishing House, New Delhi.

Ramana P.V.L. (2002), 'Women in Slums: A Study of Women in Muslim Slums of Visakhapatnam', Serials Publications, New Delhi.

Ramanamma A. and Bambawale Usha (1987),'Women in Indian Industry', Mittal Publications, Delhi.

Ramegowda A. (1997), 'Gender Inequality Power, Privilege and Poverty in Plantations', Rawat Publications, Jaipur.

Rani Thotajyothi (2005), 'Work, Income and Status of Rural Women', Serials Publications.

Ranjan Kumuda (1993), 'Women and Modern Occupation in India', Chugh Publications.

Rao R.K. (2000), 'Women in Eduation', Kalpaz Publications, Delhi.

Reddy Ranga A. (2002), 'Empowerment of Women and Ecological Development', Serials Publications, New Delhi.

Rehman M.M. and Biswal Kamalakanta (1993), Women, Work and Women, Commonwealth Publishers, New Delhi.

Saha Chandana (2003), 'Gender Equity and Equality Study of Girl Child in Rajasthan', Rawat Publications, New Delhi.

Saini J.S. and Gurjar B.R. (2001), 'Entrepreneurship and Education Changes and Strategies'. Rawat Publications, New Delhi.

Saksena Anu (2004), 'Gender and Human Rights Status of Women Workers in India', Shipra Publications, Delhi.

Seetaramu A.S. and Ushadevi M.D. (1985), 'Education in Rural Areas', Ashish Publishing House, New Delhi.

Sengupta P. (1960), 'Women Workers in India', Asia Publishing House, Bombay.

Seth Mira (2001),'Women and Development : The Indian Experience', Sage Publications, New Delhi.

Shailly Sahai (1996), 'Social Legislation and Status of Hindu Women', Rawat Publications, Jaipur.

Sharma K.L. (2001), 'Reconceptualising Caste, Class and Tribe', Rawat Publications, New Delhi.

Sharma Usha (2003), 'Women in South Asia: Employment, Empowerment and Human Development', Authors Press, Delhi.

Shukla Chaya (2003), 'Problems of Women Education and Employment in India', Mohit Publications, New Delhi.

Singh D.P. (2005), 'Women, Workers in Unorganized Sector', Deep and Deep Publications, New Delhi.

Singh Jyoti (2004), 'Education and Human Resource Development Emerging Issues, and Challenges in the 21st Century', Deep and Deep Publications, New Delhi.

Singh Reena (2001), 'Gender Composition Value, Preferences and Behavior', Rawat Publications, Jaipur.

Sisodia Yatindra Singh (2003), 'Girls Literacy in Rural India', Rawat Publications, New Delhi.

Sivaprakashan P. and Suriakala R. (2003), 'Women Employees Status and Satisfaction', Kanishka Publishers, New Delhi.

Srivastava N. (1978), 'Employment of Educated Married Women in India', National Publishing House, New Delhi.

Srivastava Nilima (2005), 'Women's March on the Path of Progress (A Study of Decadal Change in Role Conflict)', Serials Publications, New Delhi.

Srivastava Vinita (1978), 'Employment of Educated Married Women in India (its causes and consequences)', National Publishing House, New Delhi.

Sunny Dolly (2003), 'Women in leading Professions in Middle East', Serials Publications, New Delhi.

Tapam Neeta (2000), 'Need for Women Empowerment', Rawat Publications, New Delhi.

Tripathy S.N. and Pradhan Premananda (2003), 'Girl Child in India', Discovery Publishing House, New Delhi.

Vaidyanathan A. and Gopinathan Nair P.R. (2001), 'Elementary Education in Rural India', Sage Publications, New Delhi.

Verma S.B. (2005), 'Status of Women in Modern India', Deep and Deep Publications Pvt. Lt., New Delhi.

Wazir Rekha (2000), 'The Gender Gap in Basic Education NGOs as Change Agents', Sage Publications, New Delhi.

ARTICLES

Alam Anwar and Jhon A.Q. (2004), Education: An Index of Human Development', University News, November 15-21.

Balagurusamy E. (2004), 'Improving the Status of Women', University News, 42 (17): April 26–May 02.

Begum S. Mehartaj (2000), 'Women Rights and Rural Employment', Kurukshetra, April.

Chaturvedi Viba and Chaturvedi B.K. (1991), 'Women and Economic Growth: A Case Study', Yojana, March.

Dantwala M.L. (1979), 'Rural Employment: Facts and Issues', Economic and Political Weekly, January 23.

Dasu Bhagirathi (2000), 'Role of Women in Agriculture', Yojana, November.

Debi Sailabala (2004), 'Effect of Education of Women on their Earnings: Empirical Evidence from Orissa'. The Indian Journal of Labour Economics, Vol. 47, No. 4, October–November.

Dholkia J. (1981), 'Wage Determination in a Developing Economy', Indian Journal of Labour Economics, Vol. 23, XXIII, No. 4, January.

Dubey Amaresh, Veronica Pala and Engene D. Thomas (2004), 'Workforce Participation of Women in Rural India : The Role of Education. The

Women Education Employment and Gender-Discrimination

Indian Journal of Labour Economics, Vol. 47, No. 4, October–November.

Gill Kanwaljit Kaur (2001), 'Diversification of Agriculture and Women and Employment in Punjab', The Indian Journal of Labour Economics, Vol. 44, No. 2.

Gnanam A. (2004), 'Literacy and Education', University News, Vol. 42, No.28, July 12-18.

Gopalappa D.V. (1997), 'Diversified Agriculture and the Rural Women', Yojana, Vol. 14, No. 11, November.

Gurumurthy T.R. (1998), 'Women in Labor Force : Problems and Prospects', Kurukshetra, March.

Iqbal Ali Mohd and Reddy Ramesh M. (1996), 'Urbanisation Process in Andhra Pradesh: A Region-wise Analysis', Indian Journal of Regional Science, Vol. 28, No. 2.

Joshi Uma (1995), 'Rural Women in National Development', Kurukshetra, August.

Kalpana Baradhan (1997), 'Rural Employment Wages and Labour Market in India', Economic and Political Weekly, Vol. 12, No. 26, 27, 28, June – July.

Krishnaji N. (1971), 'Wages of Agricultural Labour', Economic an Political Weekly, Vol. 6, No. 39, September 25.

Krishnamurthy V. (1991), 'Trends in Industrial Diversification in Industrial Development of Andhra Pradesh', Indian Journal of Regional Science, Vol. XXV, No. 1.

Kumar Ajit (2001), 'Maharashtra-statehood for Vidharbha', Economic and Political Weekly, Vol. XXXVI, No. 50.

Laxmi Narayan H. (1977), 'Changing Conditions of Agricultural Labour', Economic and Political Weekly, Vol. 2, No. 43, Oct. 22.

Mahanty Ghanashama (1999), 'Regional Development in Andhra Pradesh-A District Level Analysis',Indian Journal of Regional Science, Vol. XXXI, No. 2.

Mahendradev S. (2004), 'Female Work Participation and Child Labour–Occupational Data from NFHS', Economic and Political Weekly, February 14.

Menon P.S.K. (1995), 'Development of Rural Women: A Challenging Task', Kurukshetra August.

Nakkeeran N. (2003), 'Women's Work, Status and Fertility: Land, Caste and Gender in a South Indian Villages', Economic and Political Weekly, September 13, Vol. XXXVIII, No. 37.

Nandini Manjrekar (2003),'Contemporary Challenges to Women's Education Towards an Elusive Goal?', Economic and Political Weekly, Vol. XXXVII, No. 43, October 25.

Padamanabhan B.S. (2001), 'Women Employment in Farm Sector', Yojana, Vol. 45, No. 1, January.

Parth Sarthy G. and Jayashree Anand (1995), 'Employment and Unemployment in Andhra Pradesh Trends and Dimensions', Economic and Political Weekly, April 15.

Prabhu Seeta K. and Sarkar P.C. (1992), 'Identification of Levels of Development- Case for Maharashtra', Economic and Political Weekly, Vol. XXVII, No. 36.

Rani Suverna G. (1995), 'Development and Rural Women of India', Kurukshetra, August.

Rao V.M. (1970), 'Agricultural Wages in India and Reliability Analysis', Indian Journal of Agricultural Economics, Vol. 38, No. 3, July-Sept.

Savant S.D. and Dawan Ritu, (1979), 'Rural Female Labour and Economic Development', Economic and Political Weekly, June.

Sha A.K. and Banerjee Kanchan (1999), 'Condition and Status of Rural Women–A Survey', Kurukshetra, August.

Shaban Abdul and Bhale L.M. (1999), 'Development and Disparities in Maharashtra: A Spatio-temporal Analysis', Indian Journal of Regional Science, Vol. XXXI, No. 1.

Sharma Poonam (1998), 'Women and Economic Empowerment', Yojana, Vol. 45, No. 1, April.

Singh V.K., Khatkar R.K. and B.S. Tomar (2001), 'Status of Diversification, Wage Rates and Employment in Agriculture in Hariyana', Indian Journal of Economics, Vol. 56, No. 3, July-September.

Sunanda Krishnamurthy (1988), 'Wage Differentials in Agriculture by Caste, Sex and Operations', Economic and Political Weekly, December 10.

Uniyal B.L. (1996), 'Women's Education: Harbinger of Rural Prosperity', Kurukshetra, August.

REPORTS

Abusaleh Shariff et.al. (2000), 'Household Expenditure on Elementary Education: Implications for Cost-Recovery Mechanisms', National Council of Applied Economic Research, New Delhi.

Census of India, 'Economic Tables and Socio-cultural Tables', Directorate of Census Operations, Karnataka State, 1981, 1991 and 2001.

David E. Sahn, 'Wage Determination and Gender Discrimination in a Transition Economy: The case of Romania', World Bank, Washington.

Degaonkar Chaya et.al. (2001), 'A Development Plan for Hyderabad-Karnataka region', Department of Economics, Gulbarga University, Gulbarga.

Devi Shamala (1980), 'Changing Status of Women in Independent India', Institute for Social and Economic Change, Bangalore.

Gayatri K.G. et.al. (1994), 'Formation of Women's Groups: The Karnataka Experience', ISEC, Bangalore.

Ghosh P.K. (1998), 'Disparity and Some Possible Determinants of Rural Literacy/education', National Council of Applied Economic, New Delhi.

Governmentof Karnataka (1995), 'District Socio-Economic Indicators 1994', Directorate of Economics and Statistics, Bangalore.

Governmentof Karnataka (2002), 'Statistical Abstract of Karnataka 1998-99', Directorate of Economics and Statistics, Bangalore.

Government of Karnataka, 'Karnataka at a Glance, 2001-02 2002-03', Directorate Economics and Statistics, Bangalore.

Government of Karnataka (2002), 'Women in Karnataka: A Regional Analysis of Socio-Economic Indicators', Manpower and Employment Division Planning Department, Bangalore.

Government of Karnataka, 'Women and Men in Karnataka: Directorate of Economics and Statistics, Bangalore, 1999-2000.

Governmentof Karnataka, 'Children and Women in Karnataka: A Situation Analysis 1990', Institute for Social and Economic Changes, Bangalore.

Governmentof Karnataka, 'Manpower Profile Karnataka 2000-2001', Manpower & Employment Division, Planning Department, Bangalore.

Governmentof Karnataka, 'Annual Plan', Vol. 1, 2004-2005, Planning and Statistics Department, Bangalore, September 2004.

Government of Karnataka, 'Report of the National Committee on Women's Education–May 1958 to January 1959', Ministry of Education, Govt. of India, New Delhi, 1959.

Governmentof Karnataka, 'Study on Trends in Employment and Unemployment in Karnataka', Directorate of Economics and Statistics', Bangalore 1995.

Governmentof Karnataka, Karnataka State Gazetteer Part I and II, Bangalore, 1982.

Government of Karnataka, 'Karnataka Socio-Economic Indicators 2001', Directorate of Economics and Statistics, Bangalore 2002.

Govinda R. 'Role of Head Teacher in School Management in India: Case Studies from Six States', Glof Links, New Delhi.

Gumber Anil (2002), 'Determinants of Unemployment in Rural India: An Exploration of NCAER, Household Survey Data of 1994', National Council of Applied Economic Research, New Delhi.

Gupta Mukta (2000), 'Economic Participation of Women', Institute of Environment Development Studies, Lucknow.

Hanumantha Rayappa P. and Deepak Grover (1979), 'Labour Force Participation Among Weaker Sections in India: Scheduled Caste and Schedule tribes', Institute for Social and Economic Change, Bangalore.

N.S.S.O., 'Participation of Indian Women in Household Work and Specified Activities 1999-2000', N.S.S.O, Ministry of Statistics and Programme Implementation, Government of India, September 2001.

Nanjundappa D.M. (2002), High Power Committee for Redressal of Regional Imbalances.

National Family Health Survey of India-1998-99 'Background Characteristics of Respondents', International Institute for Population Sciences, Mumbai, 2001.

Ranade S.N. and Ramachandan P. (1970), 'Women Employment', Tata Institute of Social Sciences, Series No. 20, Bombay.

Sarita Date, 'Technical Education of Women: An Assessment', Vidthaldas Vidyavihar SNDT, Women's University, Bombay.

Satakopan Usha, (1983), 'Male-Female Differences in Educated Unemployment', ISEC, Bangalore.

Shantha N. (1996), 'A Study of the Profile of Employed Women in the Public Sector in Bangalore City', Institute for Social and Economic Change, Bangalore.

Shirly Samuel (1983), 'Enrolment of Women in Higher Education: A Trend Analysis', Institute for Social and Economic Change, Bangalore.

UNDP (2005), 'Human Development Report –2005', Oxford University Press, New Delhi.

Unni Jeemol (2001), 'Earnings and Education Among Ethnic Groups in Rural India', Gujarat Institute of Development Research, Gota, Ahmedabad

Visaria Pravin et.al. (1992), 'School Enrolment Attendance, Drop-outs and Literacy in Western India: Some Data on levels and Determinants', Gota, Ahmedabad.

World Bank, 'India, Karnataka; Financing Education in the Context of Economic Restructuring', Human Development Sector Unit, South Asia, June 13, 2002.

World Bank, 'Reshaping the Future: Education and post-conflict reconstruction', World Bank, Washington, D.C., 2005.

World Bank 'World Development Report 2005 : A Better Investment Climate for Everyone', Oxford University Press, New York, 2004.